WORLD HISTORY
FOR A
GLOBAL AGE

ANCIENT HISTORY to the INDUSTRIAL REVOLUTION

JACK ABRAMOWITZ

◆

GLOBE FEARON
Pearson Learning Group

Jack Abramowitz, Ph.D.

Dr. Abramowitz has had a distinguished career as a teacher of social studies. His work includes over twenty years of classroom experience at a variety of levels, and curriculum development and consulting for school districts in Oregon, Ohio, New York, Texas, California, Indiana, Georgia, and New Hampshire. Dr. Abramowitz is the author of numerous texts and journal articles in the social sciences, and speaks frequently to teacher and other professional groups. He was Visiting Professor at the University of London's Goldsmith's College.

Consultants:

Donald Schwartz, Ph.D.

Dr. Schwartz is Assistant Principal of Social Studies,
Sheepshead Bay High School, Brooklyn, New York.

Sara Moore, M.A.

Ms. Moore is a teacher of History and English,
Palo Duro High School, Amarillo, Texas.

Acknowledgments begin on page 282.

Maps by: General Cartography, Mel Erikson

ISBN: 1-556-75683-6
Printed in the United States of America
12 13 14 15 16   05 04 03 02 01

1-800-321-3106
www.pearsonlearning.com

Contents

Unit 4 Democracy and Nationalism Grow in Europe   *186*

Unit 5 The Industrial Revolution Has Global Impact   *236*

Maps, Charts, and Graphs

Maps, Charts, and Graphs

Enrichments

Unit 1

What Factors Influence the Development of Civilization?

This book is about living in a global community. It will tell you about the people and places of the past and the present. It will also help prepare you to deal with the events of the future. As you read this unit, and the ones that follow, you will discover that several main ideas are woven into the study of global history. First, you will begin to explore how nations are bound to one another by many ties. These ties influence a nation's economy, its government, and its way of life.

Second, nations are influenced by their environment. You will read how some people have adjusted to their environment while others have tried to change it. Third, you will see that different cultures and societies have many of the same characteristics. For example, you will discover that providing for individual and group needs is a common goal of all people and cultures.

As you try to understand these and other ideas, you will learn how the past has shaped the present world. You will learn how historians have pieced together the story of civilization. This story begins with the early humans and their achievements. The picture opposite shows an early human drawing a picture on a rock. Such drawings were an early form of written communication.

Finally, you will learn what it means to live and work in a global community—a community that includes not only your family and friends, but people from all over the world.

Each chapter in Unit 1 begins with a list of important ideas. These ideas are about living in a global community. They will help you better understand the global view of world history that is the subject of this textbook.

In Unit 1, you will read the following chapters:

1 Living in a Global Community
2 The Environment and the Global Community
3 Using the Social Sciences to Study People and Places

4 The Common Traits of Cultures and Societies
5 People and Nations as Seen in Global History

1

Living in a Global Community

Understanding Global History

As you read this chapter, think about the following statements.
1 Our view of the world changes as we grow older.
2 Events in one part of the world affect other parts of the world.
3 The nations of the world are dependent upon each other economically.
4 Problems in the environment affect people who live miles apart.

The global community is made up of many people and many nations.
They share many of the same interests. These people are attending the
Olympic games.

Learning New Words and Terms

The following words are used in this chapter. Think about the meaning of each one.

dependent: needing something or someone
interdependent: in global terms, the idea that nations are bound to one another
famine: a time when people do not have enough to eat
economy, or economic system: a nation's system of producing, distributing, and consuming goods
physical environment: our surroundings, such as rivers, lakes, trees, air, and soil

Think As You Read

1. What is the global community?
2. How does the United States get the products it needs?
3. What are some causes of pollution?

1 Our view of the world changes as we grow older.

When we are small children our world is made up of our home, our school, and our friends. But as we grow older, our world also grows. As young adults, our world includes not just our family and friends. It also includes the city, the state, and the nation in which we live. In fact, it includes every nation around the globe. With this in mind, try to start thinking of our world as a global community.

The global community is made up of millions of families, thousands of neighborhoods and cities, and more than 166 different nations. More than 5 billion (5,333,000,000) people live and work in our global community. That seems like a great deal of people. But the number is always growing. By the year 2000, there will be more than 6 billion people living in our global community.

There is nothing new about the growth of the world's population. It has been growing for many hundreds of years. However, the rate of growth has increased greatly in recent times. In 1650, there were about 500 million people living on the earth. It took 200 years for that number to double to 1 billion people. But in the next 130 years the world population more than tripled! Experts say that this rapid increase in population is likely to continue in the years ahead.

Providing for the health, safety, and welfare of these billions of people requires much planning and work. Along with concern for our families, cities, and nation, we must also be concerned for the world as a whole. We are **dependent** upon other people for many things. And they are dependent upon us. These ties make the countries of the world **interdependent.**

If our world is to prosper, we must try to understand the people and places that make up the global community.

2 Events in one part of the world affect other parts of the world.

As you know, the world is made up of many nations. Because we live in a global community what happens in one nation often affects people in many other nations. Think about the following example.

TIME: 1840s   PLACE: Ireland

When the potato crop failed in Ireland, in the 1840s, a **famine** occurred in that country. Hundreds of thousands of Irish people went hungry. Faced with death from lack of food many Irish left their homes to seek a new life in other lands. In time, their decision to leave Ireland affected life in the United States. Look at the chart that follows.

| People from Ireland Moving to the United States ||
Year	Number
1846	51,000
1847	105,000
1848	112,000
1849	159,000
1850	164,000
1851	221,000

Ireland is about 3,000 miles (4,800 kilometers) from the United States. But the Irish famine had a lasting effect upon American life. The chart shows that thousands of Irish people emigrated, or left their country, to come to the United States during the 1840s. The emigration of the Irish to the United States continues to this day. However, the desire for a better life has taken the place of the famine as the main reason for Irish emigration. In the years since 1846, the Irish people who have come to the United States have added to the cultural, religious, political, and economic life of all Americans.

3 The nations of the world are dependent upon each other economically.

Consider the following example.

TIME: 1990s
PLACE: The United States

The United States is the richest and most powerful nation in the world. Its **economy** is the most complex of any nation. Nevertheless, the United States depends upon other nations for certain products that it needs. Look at the following chart. It shows many of the products that the United States imported, or bought from other nations, in one year. It also shows the amount of money spent on each import during that year.

United States Imports	
Products Imported	Value of Imports
Machinery	$113 billion
Crude oil (petroleum)	$75 billion
Autos and parts	$74 billion
Metals and manufactures	$26.6 billion
Wood pulp	$3.6 billion
Natural gas	$3.5 billion
Coffee beans	$2.3 billion
Cocoa beans	$.4 billion

In the same year, the United States exported, or sold various products to other nations. Look at the chart opposite. It shows some of the products the United States sold and the money earned from each export.

United States Exports	
Products Exported	Value of Exports
Machinery	$88.4 billion
Chemicals	$32.3 billion
Manufactured goods	$22.8 billion
Grain	$12.3 billion

As you can see, the United States does billions of dollars worth of business with nations around the globe. At the same time that it is buying crude oil, autos, and coffee beans, it is selling machinery, chemicals, and grain. Our trade touches areas all around the world.

4 Problems in the environment affect people who live miles apart.

People of the global community share the earth's air and water. It is not surprising that ashes and soot given off by factories in one nation are carried by the wind to other nations. Or that harmful chemical wastes dumped off the shores of Europe or the United States are often carried by ocean currents to all parts of the world. The pollution in the ocean harms fish, birds, and animals living thousands of miles away.

The nations of the world are all affected by what happens to the **physical environment.** As members of the global community, we must work together to control pollution and keep our air, water, and soil safe.

The United States is a major wheat producer. This farmer is harvesting his crop of wheat.

Exercises

A. Finding the Main Ideas:

Put a check next to the sentences that give the main ideas of what you have just read.

_____ **1.** Events in one part of the world can affect people in many other places.

_____ **2.** Ireland suffered a famine in the 1840s.

_____ **3.** Nations are dependent upon each other economically.

_____ **4.** Problems in the environment have mainly a local effect.

_____ **5.** Problems in the environment can affect people who live miles apart.

_____ **6.** Air pollution is a serious problem.

B. Checking for Details:

Read each statement. Put a T in the space next to each statement if it is true. Put an F in that space if it is false. If the statement is false, rewrite it to make it true.

_____ **1.** The world population is continuing to grow.

_____

_____ **2.** Ireland is located about 6,000 miles (9,600 kilometers) from the United States.

_____

_____ **3.** In 1981, the United States exported $21 billion of chemicals.

_____

4. The United States is the richest and most powerful nation in the world.

_____

_____ **5.** The population of the world doubled in the 100 years after 1650.

_____

C. Remembering What You Have Read:

Use the following words to complete each sentence below.

global   dependent   physical environment   famine

1. We are in many ways _____ upon others.

2. A potato crop failure produced a _____ in Ireland in the 1840s.

3. Damage to the _____ can affect people all over the world.

4. The _____ community is made up of millions of families.

D. Word Meanings:

Match each word in Column A with the correct meaning in Column B. Write the letter of each answer in the space provided.

Column A

_____ 1. export
_____ 2. physical environment
_____ 3. dependent
_____ 4. import
_____ 5. polluted
_____ 6. famine

Column B

a. to purchase goods from another nation
b. a time when people do not have enough to eat
c. dirty air, water, or soil
d. our surroundings
e. to sell goods to another nation
f. needing something or someone very much

E. Understanding Graphs:

A pictograph uses a drawing like ⍢ to show certain facts. The drawing can stand for a number or amount. Prepare a pictograph showing Irish immigration into the United States. You can find the figures given in the chart on page 3. The first one has been done for you.

Year	People from Ireland Moving to the United States
	Number of People ⍢ = 20,000 people
1846	⍢ ⍢ ⍩
1848	
1850	
1851	

F. Thinking it Over:

Answer the following questions in one or two sentences.

1. What is happening to the world population?

_____

_____

_____

2. We are dependent upon other nations for many things. What are some of these things?

_____

_____

_____

Enrichment:

Using Globes and Maps

A GLOBE

As you begin reading about our global community, you will need an accurate, or correct, picture of the earth. You can use various tools to get this correct picture. A globe is one tool to help you look at the entire earth. Globes show the true shape of the earth, which is shaped almost round like a sphere. Because globes have the same shape as the earth, they are very accurate.

trái đất

quả cầu

Globes are accurate, but they are not as useful as maps. These show the world, or some part of it, as it would look if a globe were flattened out. Maps are useful tools because they show the entire world at a glance. They are also easier to carry than globes. Maps are used most often, even though they are not as accurate as globes.

Globes and maps show the location of places on the earth. They can also show distances. A map often has a distance key, or scale. A distance key shows what distance on a map stands for what distance on the earth. For example, one inch on a map might stand for 100 miles (160 kilometers) on the earth. On another map, one inch might stand for 500 miles (800 kilometers).

A distance key can make use of centimeters instead of inches. One centimeter on a distance key might stand for 160 kilometers. Or one centimeter on the distance key might stand for 800 kilometers.

The distance key makes it possible to tell the distance between places. This helps maps give a more accurate picture of the earth.

A MAP

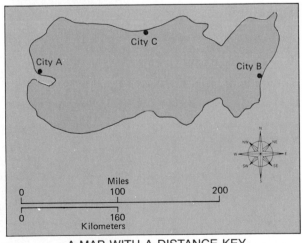

A MAP WITH A DISTANCE KEY

Chapter 2

The Environment and the Global Community

全
球，中，quả đất

Understanding Global History

As you read this chapter, think about the following statements.
1 Our community, natural surroundings, and culture make up the total environment.
2 Basic human needs are influenced by our environment and our culture.
3 The physical environment can affect contact among people.
4 People use the environment to achieve economic goals.

Bedouins live in a desert environment. This man's headdress protects him from the heat of the sun and the dust of the desert.

khăn trùm 头

Learning New Words and Terms

The following words are used in this chapter. Think about the meaning of each one.

natural resources: useful materials supplied by nature

traditions: beliefs and customs handed down from earlier times *nay dây mai đó . du*

nomadic: moving from place to place in *a* search of food and water

landforms: features on the surface of the earth, such as mountains, hills, and plains *hình dạng bề mặt trái đất*

Think As You Read

1. What is the difference between rural and urban environments?
2. Who are the Bedouins? Where do they live?
3. Why did city-states develop in ancient Greece?
4. What are some examples of natural resources? Why are they important?
5. What are some characteristics of Mexico's environment?

1 Our community, natural surroundings, and culture make up the total environment.

Many different things influence how people live and work. One of the most important influences is the environment. As you recall, the environment refers to the world around us. It is the air, water, and soil upon which we depend. It is also the climate, **natural resources,** and vegetation of an area. Yet, the environment is something more than our physical surroundings. It is the community in which we live and work. It is our art, literature, language, music, and **traditions.** It is our culture.

The global community is made up of many different kinds of environments. Some environments are rural. They have few people and are not built up. People living in rural areas might work on farms or on ranches. Urban areas, on the other hand, have many people and are very built up. City dwellers might work in factories, in offices, or in stores.

2 Basic human needs are influenced by our environment and our culture.

Food, clothing, and shelter are basic human needs. They influence the way in which we live. In turn, the food we eat, the clothing we wear, and the houses we live in are shaped by our physical environment and by our culture.

The following examples should help you understand the role of the environment in shaping our way of life.

TIME: 1990s
PLACE: Saudi Arabia

The Bedouins are a group of people who live in the deserts of Saudi Arabia and the Sahara region of Africa. Their basic human needs are strongly influenced by their desert environment.

Lack of good soil and a shortage of water force the Bedouins to live a **nomadic** life. They use camels to move from one oasis, or water hole, to another. The Bedouins use water for washing and drinking and for feeding their camels, sheep, and goats. These animals provide wool for clothing and milk and meat for food. Some of the wool, meat, and animal skins are traded for flour, cooking oil, and other products sold at markets in the oasis towns.

Clothing of the Bedouins consists of loose fitting cotton or wool shirts, trousers, and robes. These garments protect the Bedouins from the harsh sun. Their homes are tents which are carried from place to place. Carpets are used to cover the walls and the floor of the tent. Everything about Bedouin life shows how they have learned to live in the desert environment.

In recent years, many Bedouin families have given up their nomadic desert life. They have moved to the cities in order to find work. This change in environment has also changed their way of life. They are no longer nomads living in tents. They no longer need camels, goats, and sheep. Many former Bedouins now wear western-style clothing and shop for food in super-markets. There is even some loosening of old customs and traditions. Without the environment of the desert, these Bedouins have become a changed people.

3 The physical environment can affect contact among people.

You have read that the environment influences how people live. Yet, it also affects where they can go. Suppose someone built a wall through the middle of your city or town. Most likely you would spend more time with the people who lived on the same side as you do. In fact, you might never see the people on the other side. In a similar way, **landforms** sometimes separate nations or the people of a nation. Think about the following example from an earlier time.

TIME: 600 B.C.
PLACE: Ancient Greece *gõ thũ ι thổ kịch*

In ancient Greece, rugged mountains covered about three-fourths of the land. And thick forests covered most of the mountain slopes. As a result, the people living in different parts of Greece had little contact with each other. Even though they shared a common language and culture, their land was divided into many small parts, called city-states. The various city-states quarreled with one another instead of joining together. Each one collected its own taxes and had its own money and calendar. Imagine how Greece might have developed if it were covered with flat, grassy plains instead of rugged mountains.

4 People use the environment to achieve economic goals.

As you know, the environment plays an important role in shaping the way in which people live and work. Consider the following example.

TIME: 1990s
PLACE: United States and Mexico

Think of the United States and its neighbor Mexico. You have read that the United States is one of the richest nations in the world. Mexico, on the other hand, is one of the poorest. What accounts for this difference? One reason is the environment. The United States has large areas of fertile soil. It has plenty of water, large forests, and great numbers of animals. In addition, it has great mineral supplies. These natural resources, combined with a moderate climate, have helped make the United States a rich country.

Mexico, on the other hand, is mostly mountainous. It receives little rainfall. As a result, large areas are not suitable for growing crops. Despite this fact, about 26 percent of Mexicans work as farmers. They are able to grow only a few crops and they make little money.

In recent years, Mexico has begun to make more use of the huge oil reserves that lay beneath its surface. The people of Mexico have begun to make wider use of their particular environment.

The early Greeks built this temple in a mountainous and rocky part of Greece.

Exercises

A. Finding the Main Ideas:

Put a check next to the sentences that give the main ideas of what you have just read.

_____ **1.** Food, clothing, and shelter are basic human needs.

_____ **2.** Bedouins live a nomadic life.

_____ **3.** The physical environment can affect contact among people.

_____ **4.** People use the environment to achieve economic goals.

_____ **5.** Ancient Greece was never a united country.

B. Checking for Details:

Read each statement. Put an F in the space next to each statement if it is a fact. Put an O in that space if it is an opinion. Remember that facts can be proved, but opinions cannot.

_____ **1.** Climate is part of the environment.

_____ **2.** Life in Mexico will soon become easier than life in the United States.

_____ **3.** Many people in Mexico work as farmers.

_____ **4.** Bedouins are influenced by a desert environment.

_____ **5.** Bedouins are happier in the desert than they are in the city.

_____ **6.** Mexican food is tastier than American food.

_____ **7.** Bedouins herd camels, sheep, and goats.

_____ **8.** The people of ancient Greece shared a common culture.

_____ **9.** The hills in Mexico are the most beautiful in the world.

_____ **10.** A plentiful water supply is a natural resource.

_____ **11.** Rural life is better than life in the city.

_____ **12.** Moving from one oasis to another is part of the nomadic life of the Bedouins.

C. What Does it Mean?

Select the best meaning for each of the words in capital letters.

_____ **1.** URBAN
      a. rich area
      b. city area
      c. farm area

_____ **2.** CULTURE
      a. the arts, language, and traditions of an area
      b. climate
      c. the people of an area

_____ **3.** NOMADIC
      a. religious
      b. moving from place to place
      c. poor

_____ **4.** LANDFORMS
      a. related to the surface of the earth
      b. far apart
      c. not enough of something

D. Understanding Graphs:

The following graph is called a bar graph. Bar graphs make it easy to compare amounts or numbers. Here, slanted lines stand for rural areas. Straight up and down lines stand for urban areas. Use the facts about people living in rural and urban areas to complete the bar graph. The first pair of bars has already been done for you.

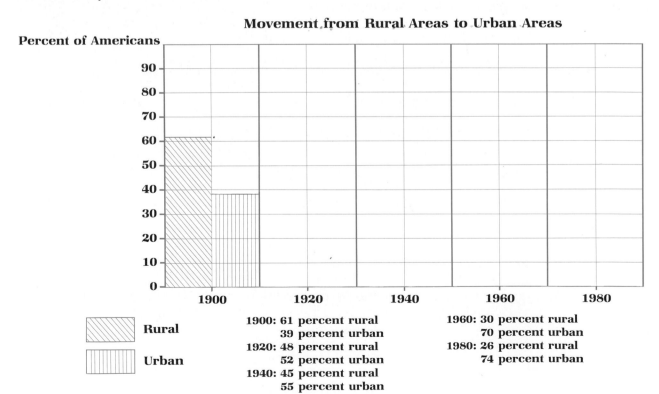

Movement from Rural Areas to Urban Areas

Rural

Urban

1900: 61 percent rural
39 percent urban
1920: 48 percent rural
52 percent urban
1940: 45 percent rural
55 percent urban

1960: 30 percent rural
70 percent urban
1980: 26 percent rural
74 percent urban

Enrichment
Hemispheres, Continents, and Oceans

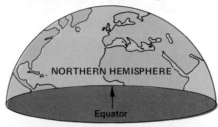

The earth was once thought to be round and shaped like a sphere. We now know that the earth's shape is not perfectly round. However, we still speak of the earth as shaped like a sphere. Half of the earth is called a hemisphere because "hemi" means half.

The equator is an imaginary east–west line that divides the earth in half. The two halves are the Northern Hemisphere and the Southern Hemisphere. Another imaginary line, the prime meridian, divides the earth on a north–south line. The Western Hemisphere lies west of the prime meridian. The Eastern Hemisphere lies east of the prime meridian.

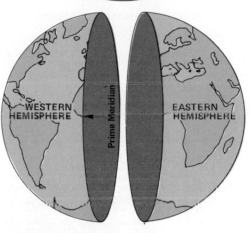

The earth is made up of land and water. The seven major land masses are called continents. The continents are North America, South America, Europe, Africa, Asia, Australia, and Antarctica.

The major bodies of water are called oceans. The oceans are the Atlantic Ocean, Pacific Ocean, Indian Ocean, and Arctic Ocean.

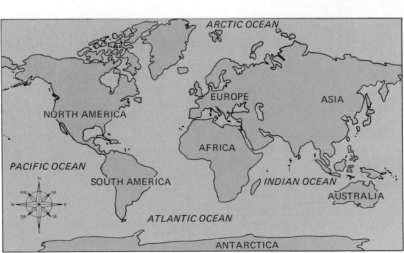

Chapter 3

Using the Social Sciences to Study People and Places

Understanding Global History

As you read this chapter, think about the following statements.
1 The social sciences study people and societies.
2 The tools of the social scientist are as varied as the branches of knowledge that make up the social sciences.
3 Each of the social sciences focuses on different parts of the total environment.

The early Egyptians buried their rulers in elaborate tombs. These tombs were discovered by archaeologists.

Learning New Words and Terms

The following words are used in this chapter. Think about the meaning of each one.

disciplines: areas of knowledge or learning
institutions: organizations with a special purpose such as schools
primary source: original documents, articles, and eyewitness accounts of an event written by people who took part in the event
secondary source: anything written by people who did not take part in the event they are writing about
artifacts: objects made by human work, such as tools or weapons
deciphered: made understandable

Think As You Read

1. Why do we need to know what happened in earlier times?
2. How did social scientists find out about life in ancient Egypt?

Learning about our global community requires the use of many tools. These tools help us understand the different people and environments that exist in the world. As you read further, you will see that our studies include the past, the present, and the future. It has been said that "there can be no future where there has been no past." We need to know what happened in earlier times to understand our own world and the world of the future. This is where the social sciences come in.

1 The social sciences study people and societies.

Each of the following **disciplines** is part of the social sciences:

- Geography is the study of the earth, its continents and oceans, climates, and resources. It also deals with the plants, animals, and people of the earth.
- History is the study of people, their **institutions,** and their activities. It provides a written and spoken record of the past.
- Sociology is the study of people and their relationships to one another. In other words, it is the study of society.
- Economics is the study of the production, distribution, and use of goods and services. It deals with a group's economic development.
- Archaeology is the study of very old things. Archaeologists (ar-kee-AHL-uh-jists) uncover old bones, weapons, and tools in order to learn more about the life of early peoples.
- Anthropology is the study of people's cultures. By careful observation and by gathering facts and information, anthropologists learn how different groups of people live and work.
- Political Science is the study of politics, law, and government. It is one of the oldest social sciences.
- Psychology is the study of the human mind—how it works and how it influences people's behavior.

As you can see, the social sciences deal with a large range of subjects. Some may be familiar to you while others may seem new. How do you think each of these disciplines is studied?

2 The tools of the social scientist are as varied as the branches of knowledge that make up the social sciences.

These tools include **primary** and **secondary sources, artifacts,** oral interviews, maps, charts, and graphs. Consider the following example.

TIME: 5,000 years ago to the present
PLACE: Egypt

The civilizations of the Egyptians existed in Africa more than 5,000 years ago. It was then conquered by many outsiders. Some of these included the Assyrians, Persians, Macedonians, Romans, Arabs, and Ottoman Turks. By the late 1700s A.D., only the ruins of the once mighty Egyptian civilization in Africa remained. The huge pyramids and the gigantic Sphinx stood for all to see and puzzle over. Everywhere on the buried walls, statues, and ruins of ancient buildings were elaborate pictures whose meanings had long been forgotten.

Hieroglyphics are the picture writing of the early Egyptians.

The life of the early Egyptians was a mystery until about 200 years ago. The work done by social scientists helped change this. First, students of archaeology discovered primary written sources about Egypt. Primary sources are documents, articles, and eyewitness accounts of people who lived at that time. They were the work of Egyptians living 5,000 years ago. These primary written sources were the hieroglyphics (hie-roe-GLIF-iks), or picture writing, uncovered in the ruins of Egyptian villages and cities. For many hundreds of years no one understood the meaning of the hieroglyphics. But when they were **deciphered** in the 1800s, the story of ancient Egypt could finally be told. *l di sai √ l giải (mã)*

In addition to the hieroglyphics, thousands of weapons, tools, and other artifacts were found buried in the ruins. Social scientists began to write about these findings. Their accounts are called secondary sources. They were written by people who did not take part in the life of ancient Egypt. Today we know what life was like in Egypt over 5,000 years ago because of the work of social scientists. *l hairoglifik l chữ tượng #/. chữ khổ toc*

3 Each of the social sciences focuses on different parts of the total environment.

Think about the following example.

TIME: 5,000 years ago
PLACE: Egypt

Let us return to ancient Egypt. Geography has established the physical setting of the Egyptian civilization. Look at the map of Egypt on this page. Most of the land in the center of the country is dry and barren. Geography also teaches us about the

influences of climate. Later on you will read how the yearly flooding of the Nile River affected the growth of civilization in Egypt.

You have read about the discoveries in the field of archaeology. Not only did archaeologists uncover the writing of the ancient Egyptians, they also found their bodily remains. They studied the bones of the early Egyptians. With this information, archaeologists could figure out the height and weight of the people, the food they ate, and the diseases they suffered from. They also learned much about the burial customs of the ancient Egyptians.

Political scientists also made use of the Egyptian hieroglyphics. These ancient writings included descriptions of how Egyptians governed themselves and about the different classes of people in society. They also told about different Egyptian rulers.

Finally, historians gathered the results of archaeology, anthropology, political science, and other branches of the social sciences. By collecting, assembling, and interpreting these findings, they pieced together the story of Egypt 5,000 years ago. You will read about this story in Unit 2.

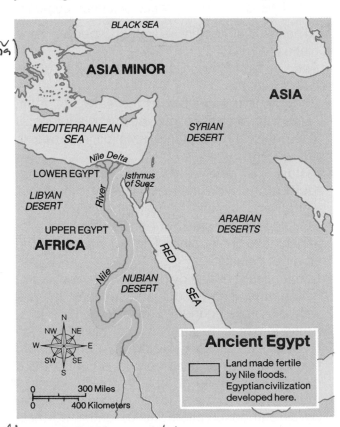

Ancient Egypt

Land made fertile by Nile floods. Egyptian civilization developed here.

X barēn l cằn cỗi . o có 표果 . o 生 đẻ . khô khan (文)

16

fertile l fətəl l mầu mỡ (肥沃)

Exercises

A. Finding the Main Ideas:

Put a check next to the sentences that give the main ideas of what you have just read.

_____ **1.** Each of the social sciences focuses on a different part of the total environment.

_____ **2.** The past is very important.

_____ **3.** The social sciences include many branches of study.

_____ **4.** The Egyptian past is fairly well-known today.

_____ **5.** The tools of the social scientist include many sources of information.

_____ **6.** The social sciences are studied in schools.

B. Checking for Details:

Read each statement. Put a T in the space next to each statement if it is true. Put an F in that space if it is false. If the statement is false, rewrite it to make it true.

____ **1.** The picture writing of ancient Egypt is called hieroglyphics.

_____

_____ **2.** Political science deals with wars of the past.

_____

____ **3.** Global history requires few tools for studying the past.

_____

_____ **4.** The social scientist uses only primary sources.

_____

_____ **5.** The Egyptian civilization existed more than 5,000 years ago.

_____

_____ **6.** Psychology is one of the social sciences.

_____

_____ **7.** Hieroglyphics serve as primary source material about Egyptian life.

_____

_____ **8.** Artifacts add to our understanding of a civilization.

C. Word Meanings:

Match each word in Column A with the correct meaning in Column B. Write the letter of each answer in the space provided.

Column A   Column B

_____ **1.** disciplines   **a.** something written by people who did not take part in the event they are writing about

_____ **2.** artifacts   **b.** to make understandable
_____ **3.** secondary source   **c.** eyewitness accounts of people
_____ **4.** primary source   **d.** objects made by human work
_____ **5.** decipher   **e.** areas of knowledge

D. Matching:

Match each description in Column B with the correct term listed in Column A. Write the letter of each answer in the space provided.

Column A   Column B

_____ **1.** geography   **a.** study of the culture of people
_____ **2.** history   **b.** study of people and their relationships to one another
_____ **3.** economics   **c.** study of the production, distribution, and use of goods and services

_____ **4.** archaeology   **d.** study of politics and government
_____ **5.** sociology   **e.** study of human and animal behavior
_____ **6.** anthropology   **f.** study of the earth—its continents and oceans, climates, plants and animals, natural resources, and people

_____ **7.** political science **g.** study of old things
_____ **8.** psychology   **h.** study of people, their institutions, and their activities from the past to the present

E. Thinking it Over:

Answer each of the following questions in two sentences.

1. Why is the story of ancient Egypt available to scholars today?

_____

_____

_____

2. Describe how *one* of the social sciences might be used to increase our knowledge of a civilization.

_____

_____

_____

Enrichment
Directions on Earth

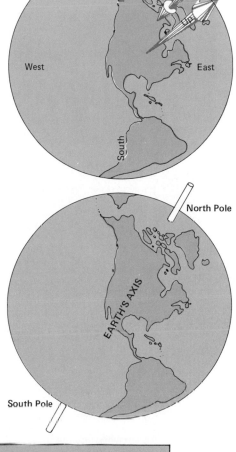

The four main directions on earth are north, south, east, and west. The north direction is the key to finding the other directions. North must never be thought of in terms of "up" or "down." A map often shows north "up," or at the top of the map, but this is only done to make a map easier to read. "Up" is the direction away from the center of the earth. "Down" is the direction toward the center of the earth. Neither "up" nor "down" has anything in common with the north direction.

North is the direction toward the North Pole. South is the direction toward the South Pole. When we face north, the east direction is to our right. The west direction is to our left. The south direction is behind us as we face north.

North, south, east, and west are the main directions. There are also in-between directions. They are northeast (NE) and northwest (NW) and southeast (SE) and southwest (SW). These are the intermediate directions.

The compass rose, or direction guide, on a map will show the main directions and intermediate directions.

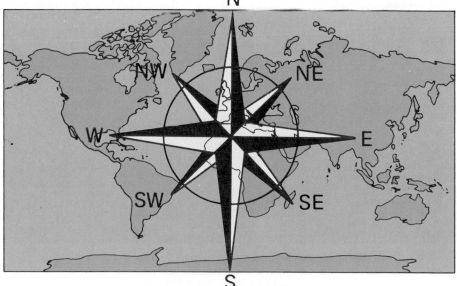

The Common Traits of Cultures and Societies

As you read this chapter, think about the following statements.
1. The culture in which we live influences our view of other people.
2. People should learn to understand cultures different from their own.
3. Providing for individual and group needs is a common goal of all peoples and cultures.
4. Present culture is shaped by the past.
5. Interaction, or contact, among people can lead to cultural change.
6. Location, topography, and resources affect interaction.

Getting food and water is a basic human goal. In many Indian villages, farmers use animal power to draw water from wells. The water is then used to irrigate the fields.

Learning New Words and Terms

The following words are used in this chapter. Think about the meaning of each one.

ethnic: usually having to do with the various races within a country

Anglo-Saxon: a white person of English nationality or descent

Hispanic: a person of Spanish-speaking origin

topography: the word used by geographers when they talk about features on the surface of the earth

Think As You Read

1. Which group of settlers began the original thirteen colonies that became the United States?
2. During what time did Spain rule Mexico?
3. Which groups invaded England from about 700 B.C. to A.D. 1066?

The more than 5 billion (5,333,000,000) people who make up the global community live in many different places. They speak hundreds of different languages. They also follow many different religions, customs, and traditions. As a result, our global community might seem to be divided into many separate parts. However, if you look closer, you will find that these different cultures and societies have many common traits, or features. The following examples will help you better understand what makes cultures similar and what keeps them apart.

1 The culture in which we live influences our view of other people.

Consider the following example.

TIME: Present
PLACE: United States and Mexico

You have read that the United States and Mexico are neighbors. They share a common geographical border. Yet, in spite of this closeness, there are important differences between the two nations. These differences often affect how the people of the United States and the people of Mexico view one another. / Sãc sinh /

The United States contains many **ethnic** groups. But its outlook is based largely upon a North European, **Anglo-Saxon,** Protestant culture. Remember from your study of American history that the original thirteen colonies were begun by English settlers. Not surprisingly, British law is the basis for much American law. And English is the national language of the United States. In addition, the great majority of people in the United States follow the Protestant religion.

The cultural outlook of most Americans influences their view of the Mexican people. The Mexican population is mainly **Hispanic.** Thirty percent of the people are Native Americans, or Indians. The Spanish language and culture were introduced in Mexico from 1521 to 1810. Those were the years Spain ruled Mexico. During this time the Spanish tried to convert the Mexican people to Catholicism. As a result, most Mexicans today belong to the Roman Catholic church.

The differences in language, religion, and culture have sometimes hurt Mexican-American relations. The people of both nations often fail to understand each other. And they frequently get into conflicts over minor differences. However, if Americans and Mexicans try to develop better relations, this situation is likely to improve in the years ahead.

2 People should learn to understand cultures different from their own.

Perhaps you have heard a lecture or seen a film about the people of another land. Or maybe you once had a pen pal who lived on the other side of the world. Did these activities give you a view of life in another country?

If the people of our global community are to live in peace, it is important that they understand and appreciate each other. Cultural exchange programs are one way of helping people learn about societies that differ from their own. Films made in other lands also help teach us about different ways of life.

You might never meet someone from the nation of India. But if you read about its people and see movies about its villages and towns, you will have a better chance of understanding a group of people who make up part of our global community.

Do you think that Americans have any common characteristics with the people of other lands? The people of India wear different styles of clothes and eat different kinds of food than the people of the United States. Still, they share certain common goals. Can you name some of these goals?

3 Providing for individual and group needs is a common goal of all peoples and cultures.

All societies try to provide enough food and water to meet the needs of their people. They also try to look after the health, welfare, and safety of various groups and individuals. In some countries special help is given to those in need. In the United States, for example, towns and cities often have agencies that help the poor and sick. In addition, special attention is given to senior citizens and the handicapped. This goal of helping people ties together all the nations of our global community.

4 Present culture is shaped by the past.

The way a nation is today depends a great deal on the story of its past. For example,

TIME: 700 B.C. to the present
PLACE: England

During the early years of English history, Britain was invaded by many different groups. Among the earliest were the Celts (SELTZ) after 700 B.C. These people brought their languages, including Gaelic (GAY-lik). A new language, Latin, was brought to England by Roman invaders in A.D. 43. Over the next 400 years Latin developed along with the Celtic languages.

During the 400s A.D., Rome withdrew its soldiers from England. This led to invasions by other groups of people. The Jutes, Angles, and Saxons invaded England from German lands. Other invaders came from Denmark. Each time, they added their languages to the existing Celtic and Latin languages. From this mixture came the language generally referred to as Anglo-Saxon.

Another addition to the language of England came after A.D. 1066. In that year the Saxon rulers were defeated by invaders from Normandy and northern France. The Normans soon introduced elements of their language. The English language that emerged was a rich mixture of many languages and many cultures. About half of

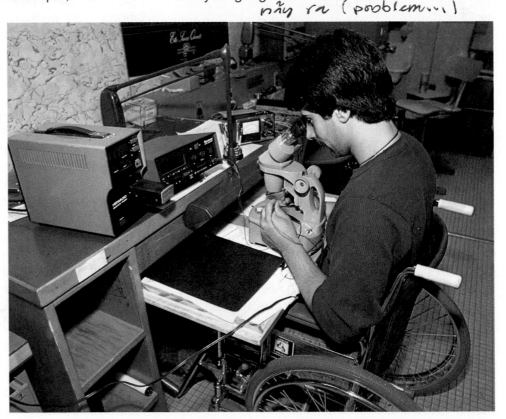

In many societies, handicapped workers hold important jobs.

This picture shows one of the highest peaks in the Himalaya Mountain range. The Himalayas are found in Pakistan, northern India, Tibet, China, and Nepal.

the words in the English language are of Germanic origin. These words come from the Anglo-Saxons. Thirty to forty percent are of Latin origin. This is the influence of the Romans and the Norman-French. The rest comes from Greek, Arabic, and other sources. As you can see, the English language of today reflects the story of the English people.

5 Interaction, or contact, among people can lead to cultural change.

You have read that a nation's past has an important effect on its culture. Part of this past includes learning from and adopting the ways of other people. For example,

TIME: 1930s to the present
PLACE: Middle East

/di ˈpazət/

In the past fifty years, rich oil deposits have been found in many parts of the Middle East. Islamic people of the region and non-Islamic workers from Europe, the United States, and Asia have come together to work there. (Islam is the religion of most people in the Middle East. Muslims are followers of Islam.) As a result of this contact, Muslim peoples have begun to adopt some foreign ways. For example, they drive cars and wear western-style clothing. They also have food and drinks not allowed by Islam.

Many Muslims are concerned that their customs and traditions are being worn away as a result of this contact. In fact, Muslims in many countries are divided over the need and value of these cultural changes. *ta palod ši Indja 形势*

6 Location, **topography,** and resources affect interaction.

In this chapter, you have read about how cultures are similar and about what makes them different. You have also seen how groups are influenced by the people they meet. Sometimes, this exchange of ideas and traditions is a friendly one. At other times, cultures are blended together because one group takes over another. Finally, there are times when nations develop on their own. For example, /bju ˈtan/ 1 工 quốc ở Hy mã

Today, Tibet (also known as Xizang) is part of 拉 L China. It also shares borders with India, Bhutan, 不丹 and Nepal. However, the high, cold mountains 尼泊尔 and plateaus of Tibet cut it off from contacts with 在 the outside. Much of Tibet remains unchanged India and untouched by contact with other cultures.

/nə ˈpɔːl/ 1 水 ở Đông北 india
capital katmandu

23

Exercises

A. Finding the Main Ideas:

Put a check next to the sentences that give the main ideas of what you have just read.

_____ **1.** Providing for the needs of the people is a common goal of all cultures.

_____ **2.** The culture in which we live influences our opinions of the outside world.

_____ **3.** The needs of the people are not always met.

_____ **4.** People should learn to understand cultures different from their own.

_____ **5.** Cultures of today are like the cultures of the past.

_____ **6.** Present cultures are shaped by the past.

B. What Did You Read?

Choose the answer that best completes each sentence. Write the letter of your answer in the space provided.

_____ **1.** The original thirteen colonies were settled by

    a. the English.

    b. the Spanish.

    c. Mexicans.

_____ **2.** The United States contains

    a. no ethnic groups.

    b. few ethnic groups.

    c. many ethnic groups.

_____ **3.** The Saxon rulers of England were defeated by the

    a. Romans.

    b. Celts.

    c. Normans.

_____ **4.** High, cold mountains and plateaus are found in

    a. England.

    b. Tibet.

    c. the Middle East.

_____ **5.** The Mexicans learned all of the following from the Spanish _except:_

    a. Hispanic culture.

    b. Roman Catholicism.

    c. Anglo-Saxon law.

C. Remembering What You Have Read:

Use the following words to complete the sentences below.

Catholic	English	Latin
Celts	Anglo-Saxon	India
Islamic	Hispanic	

1. The United States outlook is based largely upon a _____ _____ culture.

2. _____ is the national language of the United States.

3. Mexico's _____ _____ religion is evidence that the nation was once ruled by Spain.

4. The Mexican population is mainly _____ .

5. Gaelic was one of the languages brought to England by the invading _____ .

6. _____ was the language of the Roman invaders of England.

7. The Middle East oil fields have brought interaction between the _____ people of the region and others.

8. Tibet shares borders with Nepal and _____ .

D. Word Meanings:

Look up the following words in the glossary. Write the meaning next to each word.

Topography

_____

_____

Ethnic

_____

_____

_____

E. Who Are They?

Name the people or group described in each sentence. Write in the answer in the space provided.

_____ **1.** This nation ruled Mexico for nearly 300 years.

_____ **2.** The system of law in this nation serves as a basis for law in the United States.

_____ **3.** This group makes up 30 percent of the population of Mexico.

_____ **4.** They were the first invaders of England.

_____ **5.** This is the religion of the Middle East.

F. Cultural Differences in the News

Read the newspaper item below and answer the questions on page 27.

Japanese Bosses Confused about U.S. Workers

When the workers at the Sanyo Manufacturing Corporation in Forrest City, Arkansas, went on strike, Tanemichi Sohma, the vice-president for administration, found himself in a cross-cultural bind.

His bosses back in Japan were not used to strikes. The few they had seen lasted only a day or two....So when the Arkansas strike entered its third week, Sanyo management in Japan thought something was terribly wrong. Mr. Sohma must have offended [hurt the feelings of] his workers, headquarters reasoned. They told Mr. Sohma to humble himself before union leaders. Mr. Sohma advised against this and was rebuked [scolded].

"They thought I was too Americanized," Mr. Sohma said of his superiors. "They didn't trust me anymore. They sent experts to see the strike." What the Japanese businessmen found, he said, was "America is a different country."

Source: *The New York Times*, November 7, 1982.

1. Why was the Japanese manager of the American-based branch of the company caught in a "cross-cultural" bind?

_____

_____

_____

2. What advice did officials in Japan offer to the Japanese manager of the American plant? Why do you think he felt it was bad advice?

_____

_____

_____

3. How does this story point out the cultural differences between Japan and the United States?

_____

_____

_____

4. How might events of this type help people to understand cultures different from their own? How might interaction, or contact serve to influence cultural changes?

_____

_____

_____

Enrichment:
Latitude and Longitude

Imaginary lines help us locate places on maps. East-west lines on a map are called lines of latitude. Numbering the lines makes it easier to locate places on maps. The numbers are referred to as "degrees" and marked with a ° sign.

The equator is the zero degree (0°) east-west line on the map. All the other east-west lines are numbered from 0° to 90° north of the equator and from 0° to 90° south of the equator. Lines of latitude show how far north or south of the equator a place is located.

The north-south lines on the map are called lines of longitude. The prime meridian is shown as the zero degree (0°) line of longitude.

North-south lines are numbered from 0° to 180° east from the prime meridian. North-south lines are also numbered from 0° to 180° west from the prime meridian. Lines of longitude show how far east or west of the prime meridian a place is located.

Maps often show lines of latitude and longitude as a grid. The grid, or crossed lines, makes it easier to locate places.

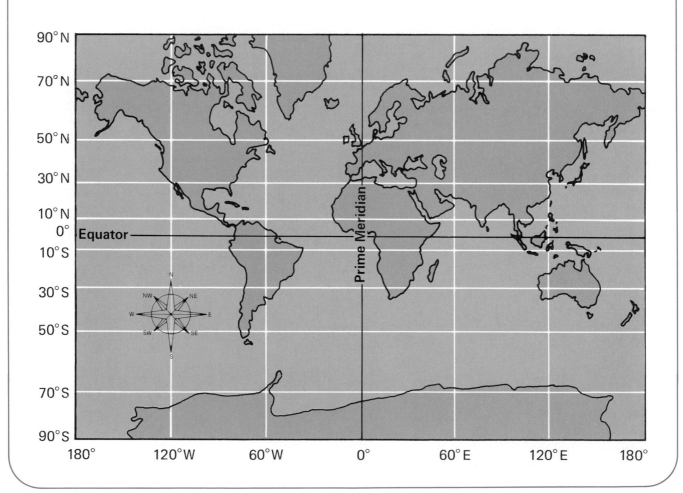

28

Enrichment:
Chronology and Time Lines

Chronology helps us put events and dates in the proper order. This can be useful when we are measuring time in terms of the past.

People in different parts of the world have many ways of measuring time in history. Usually, time is measured in relation to some great event in history. This event forms the basis for a system that measures time from the past to the present.

Our system of measuring time makes use of dates accompanied by the letters B.C. or A.D. These letters are related to an event, the birth of Jesus Christ. The letters B.C. and A.D. help us understand when things happened and the order in which they happened.

The longest period of time is listed under B.C. (before Christ). Events that took place before the birth of Christ are counted back from that date. For example, 500 B.C. means 500 years before the birth of Christ. The years since the birth of Christ are referred to as A.D. (Anno Domini), which in Latin stands for "in the year of the Lord."

Dividing time into B.C. and A.D. can help us measure time in terms of history. The letters are especially useful when used in a time line. A time line helps to show when events took place, and the order in which they took place. It is a visual form of chronology. A simple time line might look like this:

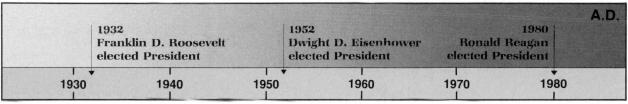

If we go further back in time, the time line can show the years in the B.C. period as well as in the A.D. period. For example,

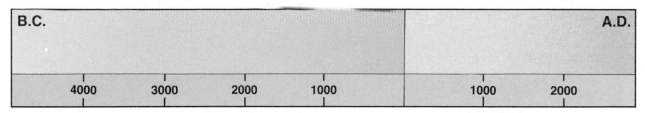

In time lines the dates become lower as they move from B.C. toward the start of A.D. They then become higher in the A.D. period. Events and general periods can be shown on the time line for the dates indicated. For example,

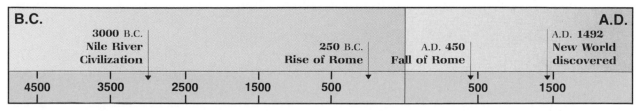

Chapter 5

People and Nations as Seen in Global History

Understanding Global History

As you read this chapter, think about the following statements.
1 Contact among people can lead to the spreading of cultures.
2 Nations borrow and adapt ideas and institutions developed in other nations.
3 Nations choose what they borrow and adapt from other nations.
4 Events occurring in one part of the world have influenced developments in other parts of the world.
5 Nations are sometimes dependent upon other nations for economic and political survival.

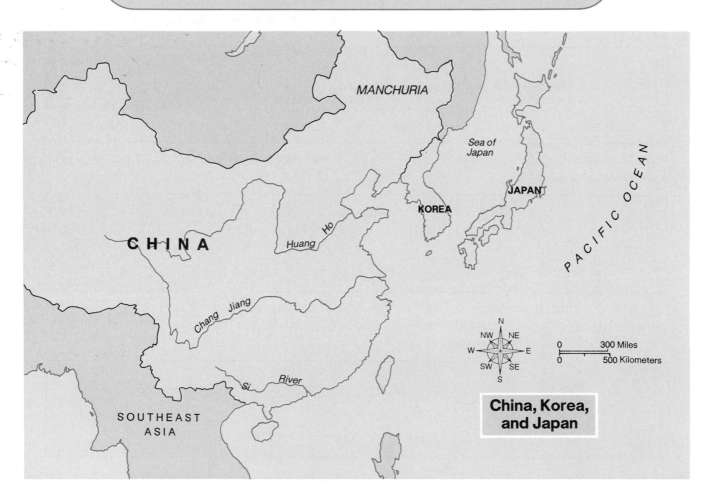

China, Korea, and Japan

Learning New Words and Terms

The following words are used in this chapter. Think about the meaning of each one.

cultural diffusion: the spreading of ideas and customs from one culture to other cultures

adapt: to change something to fit your own needs

Parliament: a political body that makes laws for the nation

majority: more than half of any number

prime minister: the head of government in Parliament

Think As You Read

1. How did geography influence the early history of Japan?
2. How does a parliamentary system of government work?
3. What is meant by "quality control"?
4. What happened to oil-importing nations when the price of oil rose between 1970 and 1980? What happened to the oil-producing nations when the price of oil fell in the early 1980s?
5. How was Europe able to rebuild after World War II?

Global history offers a chance to see different people and nations within the framework of the world community. As a result, history becomes more than just the study of continents, regions, and countries.

Global history looks at the world in a special way. It shows how people and places are connected to one another. For that reason, it is concerned with the art, music, and literature of all parts of the world. You will read, for example, that there are similarities in the painting and sculpture of China and Japan. Global history also takes account of languages, ideas, religions, foods, and customs throughout the entire world. In short, global history involves all the people of the past, the present, and the future.

Your study of global history will differ from other history courses you have taken. The following examples will help you understand the global approach to studying history and the development of nations throughout the world.

1 Contact among people can lead to the spreading of cultures.

The following example of China and Japan will help explain **cultural diffusion.** This is another way to describe the spreading of cultures.

TIME: Before 1100 B.C. to the present
PLACE: China and Japan

The historian Edwin O. Reischauer has said that, "Culturally, Japan is a daughter of Chinese civilization...." By this he means that Japanese culture owes much to its contact with the Chinese.

China and Japan are separated by 500 miles (800 kilometers) of open sea. This fact caused the people of Japan to live in isolation for thousands of years. During this time they had little contact with the Asian mainland. It was only after about 1000 B.C. that Japan was touched by other people and by other cultures.

Invaders from China, Manchuria, Malaysia, Indonesia, and Korea were the first outsiders to influence Japan. They forced the original Ainu people to move to distant parts of the country. In fact, it was these invading groups who eventually became the people we now call the Japanese.

In the years from about 1028 B.C. to about A.D. 250, Japan was in close contact with the people of China and Korea. Like Japan, Korea was strongly influenced by Chinese culture. As a result, both nations began to follow many of the practices of the Chinese people. Consider the example of rice growing. Planting and growing rice probably began thousands of years ago in Southeast Asia (see map, p. 30). Contacts between that region and China brought rice growing to China and Korea. It was later introduced into Japan by Chinese merchants and traders.

Other aspects of Chinese culture also spread to Japan. Chinese writing came to Japan from Korea about A.D. 405. It became the Japanese way of writing. Another influence was the religion of Buddhism. The Chinese had learned about Buddhism from the people of India. Then, in about A.D. 550, a Buddhist monk carried Buddhism to Japan.

The Ainu were the first people to live in Japan. Today, most Ainu live in Hokkaido, the northernmost island of Japan.

Although the first statue of Buddha sent to Japan was viewed as worthless, the religion gradually became part of Japanese life.

2 Nations borrow and adapt ideas and institutions developed in other nations.

The history of Japan is just one example of a group learning from the people it meets. As you continue your study of global history, you will come across many other examples. For instance, many nations have borrowed or **adapted** the British system of government. In England, the main body of government is called the **Parliament.** Parliament is divided into two houses, or branches. Each house is made up of members of several political parties. From the party that has a **majority** of members a **prime minister** is chosen. The prime minister becomes the head of government. He or she, in turn, chooses a cabinet. This group of men and women helps the prime minister lead Parliament.

Former British colonies, including Canada, Australia, India, and Jamaica have borrowed Britain's system of government. Other former British colonies have borrowed the system but have adapted, or changed it to fit their own needs.

Among these changes is the replacement of the multi-party political system with a single-party system. This change has often brought about the end of the democratic basis of parliamentary rule.

3 Nations choose what they borrow and adapt from other nations.

This is true in religion and government as well as in business and the economy. For example, let us return to Japan. In the early 1900s, the Japanese borrowed many ideas about mass production from other industrial nations. Mass production is the system of manufacturing large numbers of items that are exactly alike. Industrial nations such as the United States used mass production to build a strong and varied economy. Japanese business leaders were very interested in the American idea of quality control of production. Quality control means that the mass-produced items (clothing, automobiles, television sets and radios, for example) are tested for quality before they are sold. The Japanese not only borrowed the idea of quality control, they improved it. The result was that Japanese industries became leaders in the world markets. They became known for producing good products at low cost.

Today, many industrial nations are studying Japanese production methods. The United States and others are borrowing and adapting methods that the Japanese borrowed and adapted from someone else.

4 Events occurring in one part of the world have influenced developments in other parts of the world.

By now, you are probably beginning to understand the many ties that connect one nation to another. These ties are even stronger today than they were hundreds of years ago. Because of modern methods of communication, nations influence not only countries that are located close by. They also affect people who live on the other side of the world. For example,

TIME: 1970s and 1980s
PLACE: Middle East

Think about recent events in the Middle East. Events in that region influenced developments in all other parts of the world. Moreover, decisions made in other parts of the world influenced developments in the Middle East. How did this happen?

Between 1970 and 1980, the oil-producing nations of the Middle East and their allies or friends raised the price of oil. It rose from less than $4 a barrel to about $40 a barrel! The oil-importing nations, including the United States, suffered as the price of oil shot up. Gasoline shortages in the United States became common. Americans realized that the economy of the United States was closely tied to decisions that were made on the other side of the world.

Several years later, events in the United States and other lands had an effect on the oil-producing nations. Rich oil fields were discovered in Canada and the North Sea. At the same time, Americans began saving energy in any way they could. Some industries just stopped using oil. They used coal and other fuels instead. A decline in the world's economy further reduced the demand for oil. These world events caused oil prices to fall. The oil-producing nations began to lose money. Even the very oil-rich nations of the Middle East suffered a loss of income.

5 Nations are sometimes dependent upon other nations for economic and political survival.

Japan is one of the world's leading producers of electronics. These workers are putting together tape recorders.

Think about how nations help each other. Aid, in whatever form it takes, creates a bond among people of the world. For example,

TIME: Years after World War II
PLACE: Western Europe

At the end of World War II (1939–1945), Europe was badly damaged. People had no food. Whole cities lay in ruins. As a result, the United States worked out a plan to help the nations of Europe. Billions of dollars worth of food and other goods were sent across the Atlantic. This aid helped save the nearly-ruined economies of Europe. In a few years after the war, Europe's factories were able to start production. The aid also helped governments in Europe. People began to trust their political leaders once more as life improved.

33

Exercises

A. Finding the Main Ideas:

Put a check next to the sentences that give the main ideas of what you have just read.

_____ 1. Events occurring in one part of the world have influenced developments in other parts of the world.

_____ 2. Wars have greatly damaged many nations.

_____ 3. Contact among people can lead to a diffusion, or spreading of cultures.

_____ 4. Nations borrow and adapt ideas and institutions developed in other nations.

_____ 5. The parliamentary form of government is used by many nations.

_____ 6. Nations are sometimes dependent upon other nations for economic and political survival.

_____ 7. Nations choose what they borrow and adapt from other nations.

B. Checking for Details:

Read each statement. Put a T in the space next to each statement if it is true. Put an F in that space if it is false. Put an N in the space if you cannot tell from the reading if the statement is true or false.

_____ 1. Global history shows how people and places are connected to one another.

_____ 2. Japan always had close ties with the Asian mainland.

_____ 3. Korea was strongly influenced by the Japanese culture in ancient times.

_____ 4. Rice growing probably began in Southeast Asia.

_____ 5. Buddhism came to China from Japan.

_____ 6. The British system of parliamentary government is more democratic than the system of government in the United States.

_____ 7. A prime minister is chosen from the majority party in Parliament.

_____ 8. An increase in the price of oil from the Middle East had no effect on the United States.

_____ 9. American aid to Europe after 1945 helped bring about the economic and political survival of Western Europe.

_____ 10. The British people strongly favor a monarchy for their nation.

C. What Does it Mean?

Select the best meaning for each of the words below.

_____ **1.** MAJORITY

    a. half of all the people
    b. the most important people
    c. more than half of a total

_____ **2.** ADAPT

    a. to take over for personal use
    b. to change or adjust to special needs
    c. to fix something that is broken

_____ **3.** PARLIAMENT

    a. a political body
    b. the leader of a political party
    c. the ruler of a nation

D. Behind the Headlines:

Each headline has a story behind it. Write two sentences that support or tell about each headline.

GAS PRICES RISE IN THE UNITED STATES

_____

_____

_____

_____

NEW RELIGION COMES TO JAPAN FROM CHINA

_____

_____

_____

_____

UNITED STATES PLEDGES AID TO SAVE EUROPE

_____

_____

_____

_____

E. Understanding Global History:

On page 30 you read about five factors in global history. Which of these factors applies to each statement listed below? Write in the correct statement on page 30 in the space provided.

1. American industrial managers study Japanese use of robots in production.

_____

_____

_____

2. The Soviet Union sets up a chain of supermarkets, but forbids private ownership.

_____

_____

_____

3. Discovery of new oil fields in Canada forces Middle East oil producers to reduce their prices.

_____

_____

_____

4. Business opportunities with the nations of the Middle East lead to an increase in Arabic studies in American colleges.

_____

_____

_____

5. Mexico, Poland, and other borrowing nations face ruin if they do not receive loans from richer nations.

_____

_____

_____

Enrichment:
Immigration and the Merging of Cultures

Each of us is born into a culture that influences our ideas and our attitudes. It even affects us when we move to other areas or countries. This can provide a severe "culture shock" to those who move from one country to another. Sometimes immigrants try to hold on to the way of life they grew up with. At the same time, they are eager to accept the customs, traditions, and language of their adopted country. In a sense, they live in two worlds with two cultures.

The two people shown in this photograph offer an example of the merging of two cultures. The immigrant couple came to the United States from a small town in Russia in the early 1900s. The photo was taken shortly after their marriage in the United States. In Russia, the young man and woman had grown up in a Jewish area that existed within the larger non-Jewish culture. There, they had a limited, lower status. Limits were placed upon their education, employment, and civil and religious rights. In spite of these limits, they absorbed parts of the Russian culture. They blended Russian culture with the customs, religion, and language of the Jewish community.

Then the couple moved to the United States. They became American citizens, voted in elections, and became involved in local affairs. In short, they adopted at least part of the American culture. Still, the man and woman remembered their past life in Russia. And they continued to practice some of their old traditions.

Years later, the children and grandchildren of the couple were able to get some sense of their cultural ties. Parents and immigrant relatives described their way of life in Russia.

Old photographs, letters, and cards also helped provide an understanding of the past. In addition, novels, biographies, and history books—many written by the children of immigrants—helped bring to life what it was like to live in Russia. In this way, the foreign culture of the immigrants blended with the American culture of their children and grandchildren. That American culture is itself a product of the blending of the many different culture groups who had come to the United States from all parts of the world.

Unit 2

nền 文明、sự 开化

Early Civilizations Around the World

Stonehenge built in England /stanɛhɛndʒ/
trụ đá to lớn ở vùng đồng bằng Salu Salbury vào thời tiền sử.

Civilization is the product of human beings and the environment in which they live. The earliest humans lived under the most difficult conditions. They struggled to get food and find shelter. Their lives were short. However, early men and women learned ways to change their lives. They farmed the land. They built larger structures. One of these is Stonehenge, shown opposite. It is a circle of standing stones built by the early people of England. Stonehenge was built about 1800 B.C. Historians still wonder about the purpose of Stonehenge.

As the struggle for survival became less difficult, people turned their minds to other kinds of work. They continued to farm the land. They also built towns and cities. People began to use written languages. They also formed religious beliefs. They had ideas about government. These developments marked the beginning of civilization.

The first civilizations were located in river valleys. You will read about these river valley civilizations and other cultures in this unit.

In Unit 2, you will read the following chapters:

Chapter 1

The Early World and Its People

Understanding Global History

In Unit One, you read about many factors that shape the course of history. As you read the following chapter, try to discover how the factors listed below worked together to create the early world and its people.

1 Basic human needs—food, clothing, and shelter—are influenced by our environment and our culture.

2 Contact among peoples and nations can lead to cultural changes.

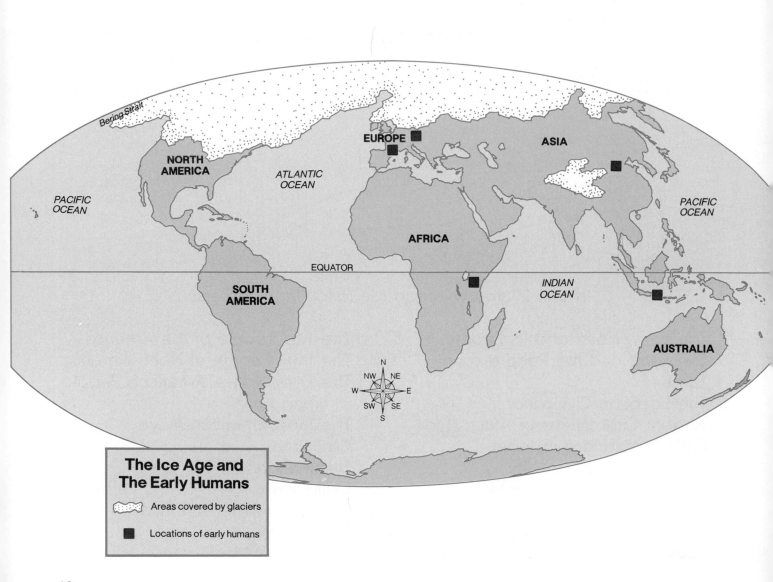

The Ice Age and The Early Humans

Areas covered by glaciers

Locations of early humans

Learning New Words and Terms

The following words are used in this chapter. Think about the meaning of each one.

/ˈgleɪsəl sɔːŋ bʌŋ/

glaciers: slow moving sheets of ice

domesticated animal: an animal tamed by humans

/dəˈmestɪkət/ thuần hóa (animal)

Think As You Read

1. What is meant by the Ice Age?
2. How did the New Stone Age differ from the Old Stone Age?
3. How did tools influence the way people lived?

B.C.

← 1,500,000 years ago
Beginning of Ice Age

10,000 years ago
Beginning of Middle Stone Age

| 158,000 | 128,000 | 98,000 | 68,000 | 38,000 | 8,000 |

150,000 years ago
Old Stone Age

25,000 years ago
End of Ice Age

8,000 years ago
Beginning of New Stone Age

The Ice Age

About a million and a half years ago the surface of the earth began to change. Up to that time the northern part of the world had been covered by **glaciers,** or large, slowly moving masses of ice and snow. As a result, large areas of the earth's surface were buried under sheets of ice. This period of cold weather is known as the Ice Age.

It took tens of thousands of years for the glaciers to move south. Then they melted slowly, until ice remained only in the far north. These glaciers formed, spread out, and melted away several times. All this started to take place about 1,500,000 years ago. The Ice Age ended about 25,000 years ago.

The Early Humans

The first humans lived on earth more than three million years ago. Human life probably began in what is today eastern Africa. It took hundreds of thousands of years for humans to move across Africa to Europe and Asia.

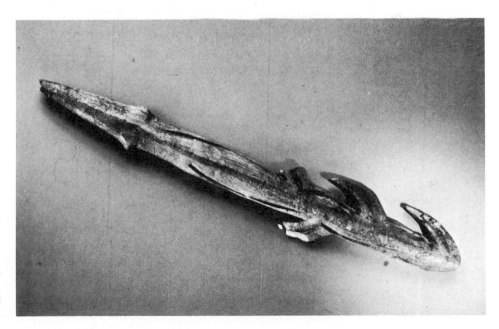

Humans who lived during the Ice Age used this tool. It is a harpoon head made from bone.

Life was very difficult for the early humans. They spent most of their days gathering food from the ground, shrubs, and trees. Slowly, over a period of many years, the early humans learned to make and use tools and weapons. They passed these skills on to family members and to people whom they met.

The Ice Age glaciers forced the early humans to move southward. They finally settled in the warmer areas of the earth. These early humans looked something like us. But they differed from us in some ways too. Their ability to think and talk was not as highly developed as ours. As time went on, however, they increased their knowledge. The early humans learned to improve their crude, or simple, tools and weapons.

The Old Stone Age

About 150,000 years ago, people lived in what is now called the Old Stone Age. During the Old Stone Age, people made weapons and tools out of wood and stone. These weapons and tools included crude chisels, saws, hatchets, spears, and bows and arrows.

During the Old Stone Age, people fished and hunted for food. Later, they sewed the skins of the animals they killed to make clothing. The people of the Old Stone Age lived mostly in caves, and they used fire for warmth and cooking. They drew pictures of the animals they hunted on the walls of their caves. Most likely, they believed the drawings would bring them luck in hunting. The Old Stone Age way of life ended about 10,000 years ago.

Next came the Middle Stone Age. This was the period from about 10,000 to 8,000 years ago. During this time, certain animals, such as dogs and goats, were **domesticated,** or tamed.

The New Stone Age

During the next 4,000 years, people lived in

This Old Stone Age painting was found on the walls of a cave in Spain. It shows a bison.

what is known as the New Stone Age. The people of the New Stone Age made many advances over the men and women who lived before them. They learned to farm, raise animals, and weave baskets. They made clothing from plant fibers and wool. They also made clay jars and pots to use for storing food. One of the greatest New Stone Age advances was the invention of the wheel. As time passed, the use of the wheel spread to many parts of the world. How do you think this spreading of culture came about?

Early humans continued to make many advances in living and working. About 6,000 years ago, people began making tools and weapons out of copper and bronze. About 2,500 years later, they began using iron for weapons and tools. In the years since then, iron and the products made from iron have been used to make everything from coat hangers to spaceships.

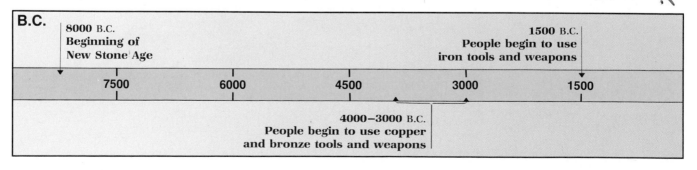

B.C.	8000 B.C.\nBeginning of\nNew Stone Age				1500 B.C.\nPeople begin to use\niron tools and weapons	
	7500	6000	4500	3000	1500	
			4000–3000 B.C.\nPeople begin to use copper\nand bronze tools and weapons			

Exercises

A. Finding the Main Idea:

Put a check next to the sentence that gives the main idea of what you have just read.

_____ **1.** The invention of the wheel helped transportation.

_____ **2.** People in early times made advances over the people who lived before them.

_____ **3.** The use of iron tools is a recent event.

_____ **4.** The Ice Age began many years ago.

B. What Did You Read?

Choose the answer that best completes each sentence. Write the letter of your answer in the space provided.

_____ **1.** The Old Stone Age began about
   a. 150,000 years ago.
   b. 10,000 years ago.
   c. 4,000 years ago.
   d. 1,000 years ago.

_____ **2.** During the New Stone Age, people
   a. invented tools and weapons.
   b. invented iron weapons.
   c. discovered fire.
   d. invented the wheel.

_____ **3.** The world we live in is
   a. very young.
   b. very old.
   c. the same as it has always been.
   d. full of glaciers.

_____ **4.** Most likely, people of the Old Stone Age drew pictures of animals
   a. to frighten their enemies.
   b. to decorate their homes.
   c. to increase their success in hunting.
   d. to decorate their burial places.

C. Organization of Ideas:

List the following ideas in the order in which they appeared in the reading selection. If necessary, you may look at the text for help.

_____ Old Stone Age people made tools and weapons out of wood and stone.

_____ Most early humans settled in the warmer places on the earth.

_____ The Ice Age glaciers took tens of thousands of years to move south.

_____ About 1500 B.C. people learned to make tools and weapons out of iron.

D. Checking for Details:

Read each statement. Put an F in the space next to each statement if it is a fact. Put an O in that space if it is an opinion. Remember that facts can be proved, but opinions cannot.

_____ **1.** Human life began in eastern Africa.

_____ **2.** People were happier during the Stone Ages than they are today.

_____ **3.** The glaciers moved slowly during the Ice Age.

_____ **4.** Spears and bows and arrows were used during the Old Stone Age.

_____ **5.** Pots and jars were useful for storing food.

_____ **6.** Cave paintings brought luck to hunters.

_____ **7.** The wheel changed transportation.

_____ **8.** The Ice Age changed the surface of the earth.

E. Time Skills:

Listed below are five historical items. Number each one in the order in which it took place on earth.

_____ **A.** End of the Ice Age

_____ **B.** The wheel is invented

_____ **C.** Use of crude wood and stone tools

_____ **D.** Use of iron weapons and tools

_____ **E.** Humans begin to tame certain animals

F. Understanding Global History:

On page 40, you read about two factors in understanding global history. Which of these factors applies to each statement listed below? Fill in the number of the correct statement on page 40 in the space provided.

_____ **1.** This early human walked five miles each day in search of drinking water and berries and insects for food.

_____ **2.** This early human found a new type of spear that a stranger had lost. He used the spear, liked it, and copied its design in making his own spear.

_____ **3.** These early humans were fearful of large animals. They moved to a higher, colder area and made their homes in caves. They used leaves and twigs from nearby bushes to make fires to heat the caves.

Enrichment:
The Early Civilizations

The lives of the early humans were short and filled with danger. This did not change until about 6,000 years ago. It was then that the first civilizations began to appear in the world.

Most of the early civilizations shared these features:

- the development of farming and the use of domestic animals
- the formation of villages, towns, and cities
- the use of written and spoken languages for communication
- the development of religious beliefs and a class of religious leaders.

The first civilizations began in or near river valleys. These places had rich soil and large amounts of water. They included four great regions: (1) the Nile River Valley in Egypt, (2) the valley between the Tigris and Euphrates (yoo-FRAY-teez) rivers in southwestern Asia, (3) the Indus River Valley in northwestern India, and (4) the Huang Ho Valley of China. (see map on this page)

These early civilizations were similar in a number of ways. For example,

(1) Most people remained farmers. As time passed, towns and cities arose. The cities became centers of trade, government, and religion.

(2) As people began working together, governments were formed. If a group of farmers wanted to stop a river from flooding, they needed to combine their efforts. It became necessary for governments to decide who should do what work, and when they should do it.

(3) As life became more complicated, people needed better ways of communicating with each other. At first, spoken languages were greatly improved. Then, in many areas, a written language was developed.

(4) Finally, advances in thinking, such as the invention of the calendar, allowed people to get along better with the growing complexity of life in the early civilizations.

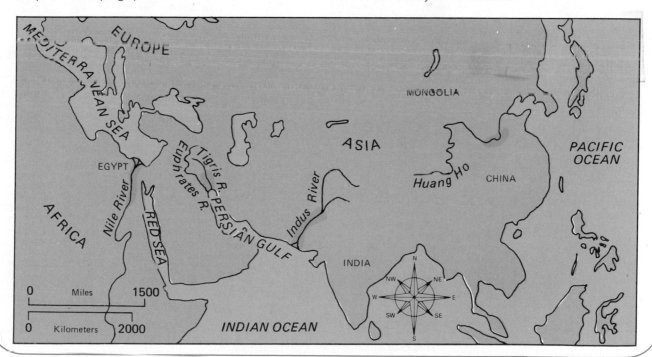

Chapter 2

The Land and the People of Sumer

sumerian 1 sumerian1 L sumer

Understanding Global History

Think about the following statements as you read about the land and the people of Sumer.
1 People use the environment to achieve economic goals.
2 The tools of the social scientist can help unlock secrets of the past.
3 Contact among peoples and nations can lead to cultural changes.

This clay tablet shows a Sumerian family.

Learning New Words and Terms

The following words are used in this chapter. Think about the meaning of each one.

fertile: able to produce much plant growth
crescent: shaped like a quarter moon
irrigation: system of supplying land with water from ditches or pipes
cuneiform: wedge-shaped writing used in ancient Sumer
arch: curved structure made to bear weight from above

Think As You Read

1. Why did people settle in the Tigris-Euphrates area?
2. What was the importance of cuneiform?
3. What were the contributions of the Sumerian civilization?
4. How have the social sciences helped us to better understand the civilization of Sumer?
5. What empires were formed in the Fertile Crescent?

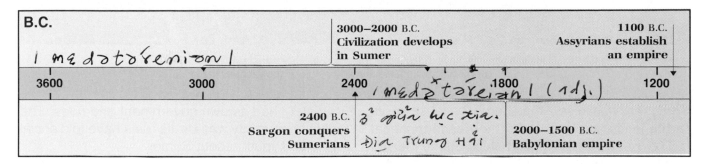

B.C.			
		3000–2000 B.C. Civilization develops in Sumer	1100 B.C. Assyrians establish an empire
3600	3000	2400 1800	1200
	2400 B.C. Sargon conquers Sumerians		2000–1500 B.C. Babylonian empire

The Land Between the Rivers

Between 3000–2000 B.C., civilization developed in the land of Sumer. Like all other early civilizations, Sumer was located in a river valley. This valley was between the Tigris and Euphrates rivers (see map below). The river valley is part of a larger area sometimes called the Fertile Crescent. The Fertile Crescent begins in the valley of the Tigris and Euphrates rivers and runs along the coast of the Mediterranean Sea as far as Egypt.

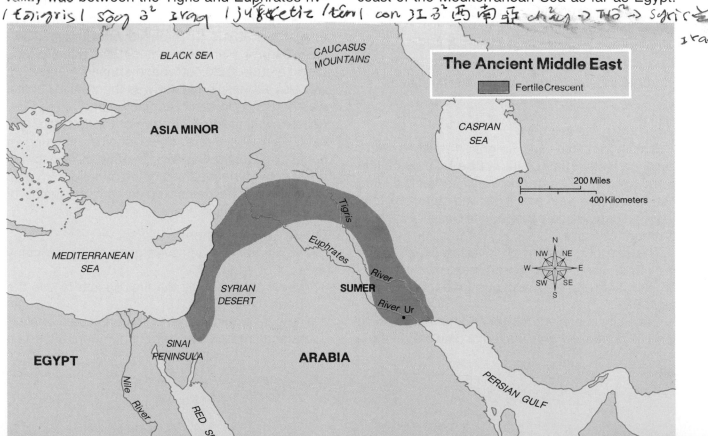

The Ancient Middle East

Fertile Crescent

BLACK SEA

CAUCASUS MOUNTAINS

ASIA MINOR

CASPIAN SEA

MEDITERRANEAN SEA

0   200 Miles
0   400 Kilometers

SYRIAN DESERT

Tigris

Euphrates

River

SUMER

River Ur

N NW NE W E SW SE S

EGYPT

SINAI PENINSULA

ARABIA

Nile River

RED SEA

PERSIAN GULF

Archaeologists have uncovered the ruins of Ur in ancient Sumer. The ruins of the ziggurat are at the top of the picture.

The area was given that name because of its **fertile** lands and because of its **crescent** shape.

The people who moved into Sumer settled mostly in the southern part of the valley. This was a flat, dry, lowland region. The Tigris River flooded the valley area nearly every year. As the river overflowed, it carried with it rich soil that helped make the surrounding land fertile. Unfortunately, the flooding also caused much damage.

In order to farm, the people of Sumer had to find a way to control the flow of water. Their solution was to build a flood control system based on canals and **irrigation** ditches. This system turned the dry lands of Sumer into fertile farmlands.

City-State Government

Building canals and irrigation ditches were large projects. They could not be built by people working alone. Teamwork was needed. Leaders had to plan the work and direct the many projects. In time, these leaders formed the basis of the government of Sumer.

The rise of a system of government led to the growth of cities. Here, government officials, merchants, soldiers, and religious leaders lived and worked.

Each city in ancient Sumer and the surrounding land it controlled was called a city-state. Each city-state had its own government and rules. The most famous city was Ur. Its ruins have told social scientists much about Sumer.

A New Way of Writing

In Sumer, many of the dealings of government officials and merchants were complex. Laws and treaties had to be written down. Merchants had to keep records of business deals. What was needed was some sort of written record. The people of Sumer developed a new style of writing to meet their needs. It is called **cuneiform** (kew-NEE-a-form). Sumerian writers used a sharp tool, called a cuneus, to cut wedge-shaped marks on a wet clay tablet. The tablet was then baked until it was hard. Traders and armies helped spread cuneiform writing to other parts of the Fertile Crescent. Over the years, however, the meaning of cuneiform writing was lost. In 1846, a British scientist solved the meaning of the cuneiform marks. By doing so, he helped unlock the mysteries of the Sumerian past.

Other Contributions

The Sumerians achieved great things in many areas. For example,

• They were probably the first people to use the wheel.

• They developed some of the principles of algebra and created a system of numbers based on

60. This led to such measurements as the 60-second minute and the 60-minute hour.

- In building their homes and temples, the Sumerians used sun-dried clay bricks. They were probably the first people to use the **arch**—a curved structure made to bear weight from above. By combining several arches, builders were able to create curved roofs.
- The Sumerians had a religion based on many gods.
- To honor their gods, the Sumerians built great temples, or ziggurats (ZIG-uh-ratz). The ziggurat was a building with many stories. Each story was a little narrower than the one below it.

The Decline of Sumer

As you have read, the Sumerians developed cities early in their history. The Sumerian city-states were rarely united under a single government. They frequently fought with one another. As a result, Sumer became weak.

About 2400 B.C., Sargon of Akkad conquered the Sumerians. Akkad was a city to the north of Sumer. For 61 years Sargon ruled over an empire that spread all the way to the Mediterranean Sea. About 90 years after the death of Sargon, the empire fell apart. Later, other empires were formed in the Fertile Crescent. They included the empires of Babylonia and Assyria (uh-SIHR-ee-uh). Some of the nearby peoples and civilizations included the Phoenicians (fuh-NEESH-uhnz) and the Hebrews. These groups borrowed many of the ideas and inventions of the Sumerians.

The Assyrians set up an empire in the Fertile Crescent. They were fierce warriors. This picture shows them in battle. Notice their chariots and other weapons.

Exercises

A. Finding the Main Idea:

Put a check next to the sentence that gives the main idea of what you have just read.

_____ **1.** The Fertile Crescent was located in Africa.

_____ **2.** The Tigris River overflowed nearly every year.

_____ **3.** The Ice Age did not affect the Fertile Crescent area.

_____ **4.** The Sumerian civilization developed in the Tigris-Euphrates River Valley.

B. What Did You Read?

Choose the answer that best completes each sentence. Write the letter of your answer in the space provided.

_____ **1.** Sumer was located in a
   a. desert area.
   b. river valley.
   c. mountain region.
   d. damp, wet land.

_____ **2.** Cuneiform was a form of
   a. farming.
   b. government.
   c. speech.
   d. writing.

_____ **3.** Sumer's neighbors included the
   a. Hebrews.
   b. Phoenicians.
   c. Babylonians.
   d. all of the above.

_____ **4.** The contributions of Sumer include all of the following *except*:
   a. creating a system of numbers.
   b. using the wheel.
   c. uniting under one central government.
   d. building urban centers.

C. Checking for Details:

Read each statement. Put a T in the space next to each statement if it is true. Put an F in that space if it is false. Put an N if you cannot tell from the reading if it is true or false.

_____ **1.** The Tigris-Euphrates Valley area is sometimes called the Fertile Crescent.

50

_____ **2.** Flood control and irrigation were part of the Sumerian civilization.

_____ **3.** Sargon of Akkad was not a good ruler.

_____ **4.** Cuneiform was the spoken language of Sumer.

_____ **5.** The government of Sumer was located in urban centers.

_____ **6.** The ziggurat had a religious purpose.

_____ **7.** Sumer was the greatest of the ancient civilizations.

_____ **8.** The Sumerian city-states were rarely united under a single government.

_____ **9.** The ruins of Ur tell us much about ancient Sumer.

D. Word Meanings:

Match each word in Column A with the correct meaning in Column B. Write the letter of each answer in the space provided.

Column A

_____ **1.** fertile
_____ **2.** ziggurat
_____ **3.** crescent
_____ **4.** arch

Column B

a. far away
b. shaped like a quarter moon
c. able to produce rich crops
d. curved structure made to bear weight from above
e. a building with many stories

E. Reviewing Your Reading:

Fill in the word or term that best completes each statement below.

1. The early Sumerian civilization developed mainly in a flat, dry _____ region.

2. Flood waters and rich soil made the Sumer region _____.

3. The _____ was used to cut marks on a wet clay tablet.

4. Sumerian flood control was based on canals and _____ ditches.

5. Sumerian religion was based upon many _____.

6. The _____ was developed in Sumer to hold weight from above.

7. About 2400 B.C., Sargon of Akkad conquered the _____.

8. After the fall of Sumer, other _____ were formed in the Fertile Crescent.

F. Behind the Headlines:

Each headline has a story behind it. Write two sentences that support or tell about each of the following headlines.

1. SCIENTIST SAYS HE CAN READ SUMER TABLETS

_____

_____

2. THE TIGRIS RIVER FLOODS AGAIN

_____

_____

3. RUINS OF UR TELL A STORY OF THE PAST

_____

_____

G. Understanding Global History:

On page 46, you read about three factors in global history. Which of these factors applies to each statement listed below? Fill in the number of the correct statement on page 46 in the space provided. If no factor applies, write in the word NONE.

_____ **1.** The Sumerian use of cuneiform writing was copied by other, nearby civilizations.

_____ **2.** The wheel was developed in Sumer, but its use spread to other lands.

_____ **3.** The Sumerians learned to control the flood waters to enrich their soil.

_____ **4.** Social scientists have unlocked many of the mysteries of the Sumerian past.

_____ **5.** Many Sumerian ideas were borrowed and adapted by later civilizations.

H. On Your Own:

Why do you think the Tigris-Euphrates area has been called the "cradle of civilization"? On a separate piece of paper, give your answer in at least five sentences.

Enrichment:
People of the Fertile Crescent

The Sumerians were only one of many groups of people who settled in the Fertile Crescent. Some time after 2000 B.C., the Sumerians were attacked and conquered by a new people. These were the Babylonians.

The Babylonians are best known for the collection of laws they followed. About 1700 B.C. a Babylonian king named Hammurabi (hah-mu-RAH-bee) established an early system of laws. He borrowed many of his ideas from the Sumerians and other neighboring cultures. The Hammurabi Code, or system of laws, touched nearly every aspect of Babylonian life. There were laws dealing with property, marriage, and divorce, as well as a variety of different crimes.

Hammurabi's Code was an important step forward for civilization. It set down the punishments for any violation, or breaking, of the law. Without such a system of laws, each person has to depend upon personal revenge rather than law for justice.

Another group of people lived farther north in the Tigris-Euphrates Valley. They were the Assyrians. Their most famous city was Nineveh (NIHN-uh-vuh). The Assyrians were a powerful, warlike people. In time, they conquered the Babylonians just as the Babylonians had earlier conquered the Sumerians. Each conquest helped spread ideas and inventions.

West of the Tigris-Euphrates Valley were the Hebrews. They lived near the eastern shore of the Mediterranean Sea. Once ruled by a single king, the Hebrews later divided into the kingdoms of Israel and Judah. Like the Babylonians, the Hebrews had their own code of laws. These laws as well as the writings of the Hebrews are collected in the Hebrew Bible. The Hebrews were the first people to practice monotheism, or belief in one God. The Hebrew God was called Yahweh or Jehovah. Their religion, called Judaism, was unlike any other religion of the time. It demanded righteous, or moral, conduct of its followers. The Hebrews' code of laws, their work of literature, and their religion, have greatly influenced the rest of the world.

Other people who lived in the Fertile Crescent and Mediterranean area developed their own cultures. They included the Hittites in Asia Minor (present-day Turkey), the Phoenicians who lived in present-day Syria, and the Persians who lived in present-day Iran. The Phoenicians were important in carrying ideas to other areas. They traded across the Mediterranean Sea and came into contact with many groups of people. All the peoples of the Fertile Crescent built their cultures upon the ideas of others. In turn, they made important contributions to future civilizations, including our own.

Hammurabi, king of Babylon.

Chapter 3

The Egyptian Civilization

Understanding Global History

Think about the following statements as you read about the civilization of Egypt.
1 People use the environment to achieve economic goals.
2 The tools of the social scientist can help unlock secrets of the past.
3 Contact among peoples and nations can lead to cultural changes.
4 Present culture is shaped by the past.

This picture shows the fertile banks of the Nile River. The civilization of Egypt grew up along the banks of the Nile.

Learning New Words and Terms

The following words are used in this chapter. Think about the meaning of each one.

isthmus: a narrow strip of land, bordered on both sides by water; an isthmus connects two larger bodies of land

delta: deposit of earth and sand at the mouth of a river

civil wars: wars between groups of people of the same nation

artisan: a person skilled in a craft

scribes: people who keep records and do other kinds of writing

Think As You Read

1. Why was Egypt said to be the "gift of the Nile"?
2. What were the main classes of people in Egypt?
3. What were the contributions of ancient Egypt?

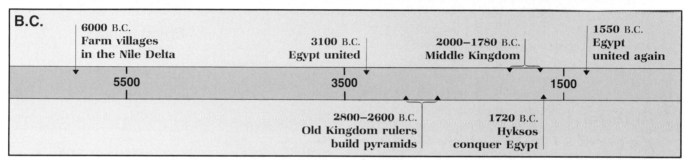

B.C.				
6000 B.C. Farm villages in the Nile Delta	3100 B.C. Egypt united	2000–1780 B.C. Middle Kingdom		1550 B.C. Egypt united again
5500	3500		1500	
	2800–2600 B.C. Old Kingdom rulers build pyramids	1720 B.C. Hyksos conquer Egypt		

The Gift of the Nile

Ancient Egypt was one of the earliest river civilizations. The land called Egypt extended along the Nile River for about 600 miles (960 kilometers). Most Egyptians lived along the banks of the Nile. Every spring the river overflowed and enriched the land with fertile soil and water. For this reason, Egypt has been called "the gift of the Nile."

Look at the map on page 56. Notice that Egypt is located in Africa. For hundreds of years the **isthmus** of Suez served as a gateway into Egypt and Africa. It provided a link between Asia and Africa and was a route for many different peoples and ideas from Asia. From Egypt, these Asians then moved into southern and western Africa.

The Egyptian Civilization

The civilization of Egypt began as a group of villages in the Nile **delta** about 6000 B.C. It is called a delta because it is shaped like the Greek letter Δ, delta. By about 3100 B.C., Egypt was united under a ruler, called a pharaoh (FAIR-oh). This period, called the Old Kingdom, was probably the greatest time in Egyptian history. Egypt was wealthy and powerful. And people were called upon to build and create many things. The

Egyptian pharaohs were often shown wearing beards. This was a symbol of their royal power. The other figure shown here is of the god Isis. She was one of the main gods worshipped by the early Egyptians.

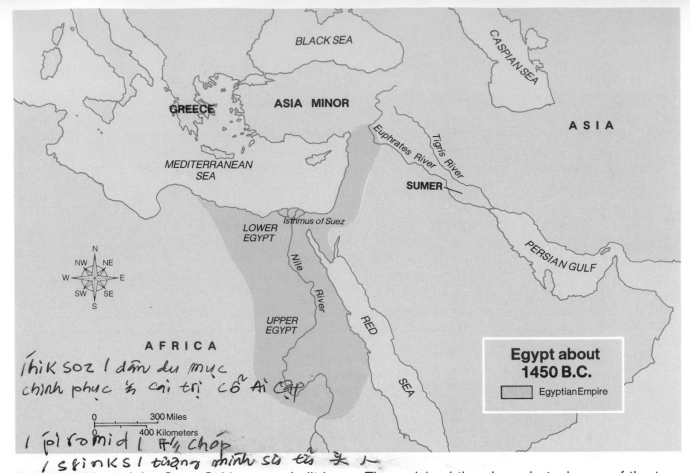

Egypt about 1450 B.C.
☐ Egyptian Empire

[handwritten notes]
Thik soz / dân du mục
chinh phục & cai trị cổ Ai Cập

1 piromid / tháp chóp
1 sfinks/ tượng mình sử tử 头人

first pyramids and the Great Sphinx were built in Egypt during the Old Kingdom.

Civil wars between the pharaohs and a group of nobles eventually led to the end of the Old Kingdom. In about 2000 B.C., another line of pharaohs reunited Egypt. This period, known as the Middle Kingdom, ended in disorder in 1780 B.C. Again, the country was left weak by civil wars. Then, in about 1720, Egypt was conquered by a warlike people known as the Hyksos (HIHK-sohs). The Hyksos warriors were better equipped than the Egyptians. They had horses and chariots. As a result, the Hyksos were able to rule parts of Egypt for about 170 years. *[handwritten] từ đánh trận*

[handwritten margin] quân & chiến sĩ

In 1550 B.C., the Egyptians united. They had learned to use horses and chariots from the Hyksos. The Egyptians were able to drive out the Hyksos. These factors gave Egypt the power to create a new empire. This was the New Kingdom. It lasted until about 1085 B.C.

Egyptian Society

The Egyptian pharaoh was an absolute ruler. That is, he had complete and unlimited power over the people he ruled. The pharaohs were religious leaders as well as political leaders. That was one reason they became so powerful.

Next in power to the pharaohs were the priests.

They advised the pharaoh, took care of the temples, and ran the schools.

Egyptian nobles shared power with the pharaoh and the priests. The nobles owned land given to them by the pharaoh. In return, they collected taxes for the pharaoh and served in his armies.

The pharaohs, nobles, and priests were few in number. Most Egyptians were either free people, peasants, or slaves. Free people worked as merchants, **artisans,** or **scribes.** The peasants worked for the nobles in the fields or on the farms. Slaves did the heavy work. They dug the ditches for irrigation systems and hauled the huge stones used for building pyramids.

Most Egyptian women, like most Egyptian men, had few rights. However, in the noble class women had many of the same privileges as men. For example, they could buy and sell goods, own property, and inherit property.

Contributions to Civilization

The people of ancient Egypt contributed much to civilization. They developed
* the kingdom—one of the first systems of organized government. This was different from the city-state government of Sumer. The Egyptians had a central government. The pharaoh divided the kingdom into provinces.

[handwritten] faravons/ tỉnh ly

Thai
Thaioggaglifl
chữ viết tượng hình

- a system of picture writing, called hieroglyphics (HY-ruh-GLIF-iks). This writing was carved on walls and stone tablets. It was also written on papyrus (puh-PY-rus), a kind of paper made from reeds. Hieroglyphics were used mostly by priests for religious inscriptions or for other formal documents. They tell much of the story of ancient Egypt. *câu ghi viết để tặng*
- a new kind of structure called the pyramid. The pyramids required skillful engineering to build.
- beautiful sculpture and vivid paintings.
- a number system based on 10—similar to our decimal system.
- a calendar based upon 365 days.

Egyptian Religion

The Egyptians believed in a life after death. The pharaohs prepared for the afterlife while they were still alive. They had great tombs built in which they would be buried when they died.

Isekrad / thiêng

These tombs are known as pyramids because of their shape. A dead pharaoh was buried in his pyramid together with all the things he might need in the next life. Thus, food, clothing, jewels, and weapons were placed alongside the dead ruler. When the tombs of the pharaohs were uncovered thousands of years later, they provided valuable information about art and life in ancient Egypt.

The Egyptians worshipped many gods. Each god had an animal as its symbol. Sacred animals included the cat, the bull, and the crocodile. The Egyptians also worshipped such natural forces as the sun and the moon. Of the various gods, the sun god was the most important.

Around 1375 B.C., a pharaoh named Akhenaton (ahk-uh-NAH-tun) tried to establish a religion based on one god—Aton, the sun god. But the priests opposed Akhenaton's religion. After his death, they were able to regain power and bring back their religion of many gods.

These Egyptian peasants are shown harvesting crops. Notice the hieroglyphics that are part of the wall painting.

Exercises

A. Finding the Main Idea:

Put a check next to the sentence that gives the main idea of what you have just read.

_____ **1.** Pyramids were important to the Egyptians.

_____ **2.** Most Egyptian farmers depended upon irrigation.

_____ **3.** One of the earliest civilizations developed in Egypt.

_____ **4.** Egyptians were fearful of death.

B. What Did You Read?

Choose the answer that best completes each sentence. Write the letter of your answer in the space provided.

_____ **1.** In Egypt the priests
    a. served in the armies.
    b. took care of the fields.
    c. took care of the temples.
    d. did all of the above.

_____ **2.** The pharaohs built the pyramids
    a. as tombs.
    b. as forts.
    c. as religious temples.
    d. to show how rich they were.

_____ **3.** Most Egyptians were
    a. nobles or priests.
    b. peasants, slaves, or free people.
    c. forced to serve as soldiers.
    d. buried in the pyramids.

_____ **4.** All the following were contributions of ancient Egypt _except:_
    a. new kinds of buildings.
    b. advances in science.
    c. an alphabet.
    d. a religion based on many gods.

C. Checking for Details:

Read each statement. Put a T in the space next to each statement if it is true. Put an F in that space if it is false. Put an N if you cannot tell from the reading if it is true or false.

_____ **1.** The Egyptian civilization lasted for less than 1,000 years.

_____ **2.** Most Egyptians lived in the area of the Nile River.

_____ **3.** The Old Kingdom of Egypt was ended by civil wars.

_____ **4.** The Hyksos ruled over Egypt for about 170 years.

_____ **5.** Upper Egypt is the area in northern Egypt.

_____ **6.** The pharaoh had little real power.

_____ **7.** Nobles helped the pharaoh collect taxes.

_____ **8.** The majority of Egyptians were nobles or priests.

_____ **9.** Egyptians believed in life after death.

_____ **10.** Papyrus was a kind of Egyptian building.

D. Behind the Headlines:

Each headline has a story behind it. Write two or three sentences that support or tell about each headline below.

1. PHARAOH CALLS UPON NOBLES TO FIGHT HIS ENEMIES

_____

_____

_____

2. HYKSOS DRIVEN FROM EGYPT

_____

_____

_____

3. WORK STARTS ON NEW PYRAMID

_____

_____

_____

E. Capital Letters:

A capital letter is used as the first letter of the name of a person, nation, continent, and city, and as the first letter in a title used with a name. Do the words below need to be written with capitals? If so, rewrite them correctly in the space provided.

1. delta _____

2. akhenaton _____

3. nile _____

4. hyksos _____

5. aton _____

6. scribe _____

7. pyramid _____   **9.** africa _____

8. egyptian _____   **10.** isthmus _____

F. On Your Own:

It has been said that Egypt lost power because its rulers were more concerned with death than with life. What is meant by this? On a separate piece of paper, explain your answer in about two or three sentences.

G. Map Skills:

Write the letter of each place in the correct box on the map.

A. Egypt

B. Black Sea

C. Sumer

D. Tigris River

E. Mediterranean Sea

F. Euphrates River

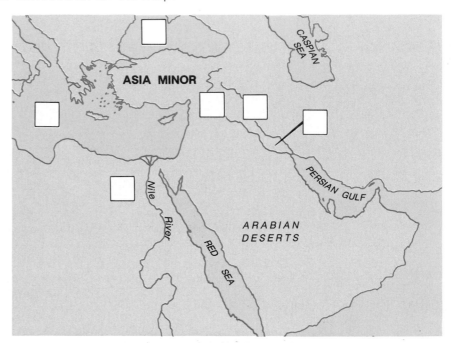

H. Understanding Global History:

On page 54, you read about four factors in global history. Which of these factors applies to each statement listed below? Fill in the number of the correct statement on page 54 in the space provided.

_____ **1.** Egyptians learned the use of horses and war chariots from the Hyksos.

_____ **2.** Different peoples and cultures moved from Asia into Egypt; then from Egypt, they moved into southern and western Africa.

_____ **3.** Every year the Nile River overflowed and enriched the soil of Egypt.

_____ **4.** The contents of the tombs of the pharaohs told social scientists much about ancient Egypt.

_____ **5.** Ancient Egypt contributed to our present knowledge of mathematics, measuring time, and art.

Enrichment:
Progress Through The Rise and Fall of Civilizations

The path from the past to the present seems to be a continuous one. However, progress often comes from discontinuity. That is, it comes from the rise and fall of civilizations, nations, and individuals.

The great civilizations of ancient times are all gone. But their contributions still influence the present. Ancient Egypt and Sumer no longer exist. However, their ideas and inventions are an important part of civilization today.

The British poet, Percy Bysshe Shelley, understood how the greatness of the past can vanish. In a poem written in the early 1800s, he showed how time and events can blot out our memory of the past. The poem tells of the broken remains of a giant statue in a land where an ancient empire once stood.

And on the pedestal these words appear:
'My name is Ozymandias, king of kings:
Look on my works, ye Mighty and despair!'
Nothing beside remains. Round the decay
of that colossal wreck, boundless and bare
The lone and level sands stretch far away.

The study of early civilization often deals more with kings and empires than with ordinary people. But there were millions of men, women, and children living in ancient times. There are no statues or monuments for these people. Yet, what would ancient civilizations have been without them? A modern poet, Bertolt Brecht, put the matter well when he wrote in the early 1900s:

Who built the seven towers of Thebes?
The books are filled with the names of kings.

Statue of an Egyptian pharaoh

Was it kings who hauled the craggy blocks of stone?...
In the evening when the Chinese wall was finished
Where did the masons go?

The history of our world does not follow a smooth, unbroken path. Nor is it only a story of kings, queens, and empires. It is also the story of those who carry the heavy stones or dig the ditches and canals. A global view of history helps us keep these things in mind.

Other Civilizations of Africa

Understanding Global History

Think about the following statements as you read about the ancient civilizations of Africa.

1 Environmental problems can affect people who live miles apart.
2 The physical environment can encourage or limit contact among people.
3 Contact among peoples and nations can lead to cultural changes.
4 People use the environment to achieve economic goals.

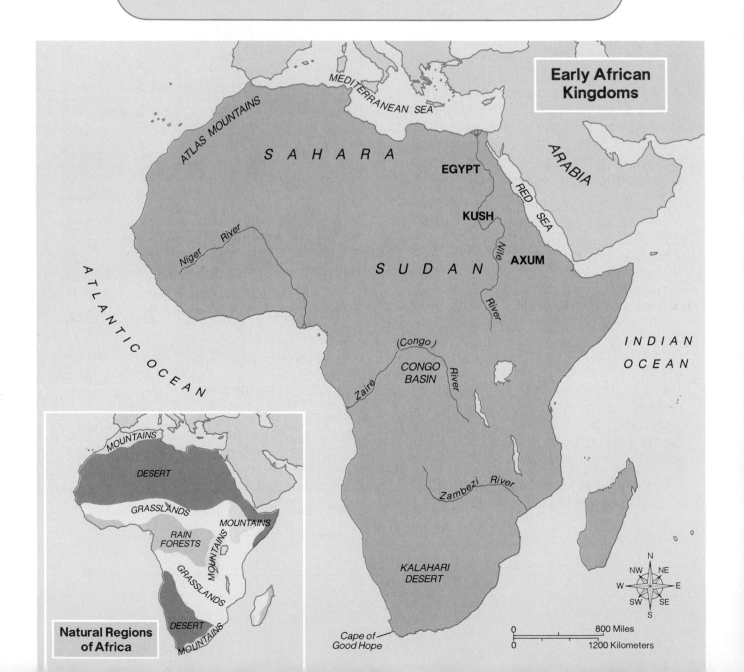

Early African Kingdoms

MEDITERRANEAN SEA

ATLAS MOUNTAINS

S A H A R A

EGYPT

ARABIA

RED SEA

KUSH

Niger River

Nile River

AXUM

S U D A N

ATLANTIC OCEAN

(Congo)

CONGO BASIN

Zaire

Congo River

INDIAN OCEAN

Zambezi River

KALAHARI DESERT

N NE NW E W SE SW S

Cape of Good Hope

0 800 Miles
0 1200 Kilometers

Natural Regions of Africa

MOUNTAINS

DESERT

GRASSLANDS

MOUNTAINS

RAIN FORESTS

MOUNTAINS

GRASSLANDS

DESERT

MOUNTAINS

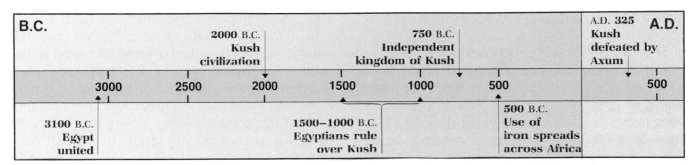

Learning New Words and Terms

The following words are used in this chapter. Think about the meaning of each one.

climate: the kind of weather in a place over a long period of time
desert: very dry land
flourish: to grow and prosper
iron ore: raw material from which iron can be produced *quặng*

Think As You Read

1. How was life in Africa affected by changes in climate?
2. Who were the different types of people who lived in Africa?
3. What is the importance of the kingdom of Kush?

B.C.										A.D. **325** Kush defeated by Axum	**A.D.**
			2000 B.C. Kush civilization			750 B.C. Independent kingdom of Kush					
	3000	2500	2000	1500	1000	500					500
3100 B.C. Egypt united				1500–1000 B.C. Egyptians rule over Kush			500 B.C. Use of iron spreads across Africa				

The Climate of Africa Changes

The Stone Age people of Africa lived by hunting, fishing, and gathering food. About 10,000 years ago the **climate** in the Sahara area changed (see map, p. 62). Greater rainfall caused the **desert** to bloom with grasses and plants. Many Africans from the north and south of the Sahara moved into the area. The change in environment caused the people to adopt a new way of life. Instead of hunting and fishing, they turned to farming. They also learned many of the skills and ideas brought by people from Asia to Egypt. These new skills and ideas spread from Egypt to the Sahara and to other parts of Africa.

Farming slowly took the place of food gathering and hunting in many parts of Africa. This situation changed, however, about 5,000 years ago. A decrease, or decline, in the amount of rainfall slowly turned the Sahara back into a desert. In fact, the word *Sahara* means "desert" in Arabic. *nghĩa là*

As the environment became hot and dry, people were forced to move either north or south of the Sahara. The desert cut off contacts between people in northern Africa with people to the south. Today, the area north of the Sahara is called North Africa. The area at the southern edge of the Sahara is known as the Sahel. South of the Sahel

/ sə'harə /

lies the sub-Saharan lands. Life in North Africa and life in sub-Saharan Africa differ greatly. Climate, languages, customs, religions, and resources have produced distinct cultures within the continent of Africa.

These early Africans are shown praying. Note their different hairstyles.

Peoples of Ancient Africa

Many different types of people lived in ancient Africa. The San (Bushmen) were short with light yellow or light brown skin. They lived in sub-Saharan Africa. The Mbuti (Pygmies) lived in the same area. They had light brown skin and were shorter than the San.

An Asian group also lived in Africa. Malaysians came from Asia thousands of years ago. They settled on or near the island of Madagascar off the west coast of Africa (see map, p. 62). Other groups came from western Asia. They lived mainly in northern Africa. Each of these groups brought its own customs and traditions to the African continent.

The Bantu-speaking peoples were another group who lived in Africa. Like the San and Mbuti, the Bantu peoples had been in Africa for thousands of years. Most of them lived in central Africa. However, they moved north when the Sahara area was able to support farming. Later, when the region again became a desert, the Bantu peoples moved southward. They slowly began taking over areas once held by the San and Mbuti.

These African villagers use traps to catch fish.

The Kingdoms of Kush and Axum

Two early African civilizations developed in eastern Africa. One was the kingdom of Kush, which arose after 2000 B.C. in the Sudan region south of Egypt (see map, p. 62). Like Egypt, the Kush civilization grew up along the banks of the Nile River. It was located near the sub-Saharan areas of eastern Africa.

Egypt ruled Kush from about 1500 B.C. to about 1000 B.C. During this period, close cultural ties bound the two civilizations together. The decline of Egypt after 1000 B.C. allowed Kush to gain independence from Egyptian rule. Kush grew powerful and eventually conquered and ruled Egypt.

In 671 B.C., Kush was defeated by the Assyrians. After this, Kush moved its capital to the south. The move allowed Kush to grow and **flourish** for nearly another one thousand years. Kush was the first of the great African merchant, or trading, empires. After spreading south, it gained control of grazing lands, mines rich with **iron ore,** and a fine seaport. As a result, the people of Kush traded with Egypt for many years. They also had contacts with India and other Asian lands.

During the 300s A.D., the people of the nearby kingdom of Axum made war on Kush and completely destroyed it. The people of Axum remained a power in eastern Africa until about A.D. 700.

Iron Weapons and Tools

Most of the people who lived south of the Sahara were black Africans. Over the years the importance of the black African peoples grew steadily. In Kush, for example, most of the leaders were black.

Archaeologists have found evidence that Africans began to use iron about 500 B.C. Tools and weapons of iron and bronze helped make the black African tribes the most powerful groups in southern Africa. Food production among the black African tribes grew as a result of the use of iron plows. Tribes who had iron weapons could easily defeat those who did not.

The San and Mbuti peoples were gradually pushed out of most parts of Africa. The civilizations that later arose in the sub-Saharan region were developed by black Africans.

64

Exercises

A. Finding the Main Ideas:

Put a check next to the three sentences that give the main ideas of what you have just read.

_____ **1.** The kingdom of Kush greatly influenced African history in ancient times.

_____ **2.** Changes in climate have greatly influenced the people of Africa.

_____ **3.** The kingdom of Kush existed for many years.

_____ **4.** People of different skin colors and places of origin lived in Africa in ancient times.

_____ **5.** Ironworking developed in parts of sub-Saharan Africa.

B. Checking for Details:

Read each statement. Put an F in the space next to each statement if it is a fact. Put an O in that space if it is an opinion. Remember that facts can be proved, but opinions cannot.

_____ **1.** The climate in the Sahara has changed a number of times.

_____ **2.** The San lived in the same part of Africa as the Mbuti.

_____ **3.** The people of southern Africa were better farmers than the people of northern Africa.

_____ **4.** The desert made it difficult for people of northern and southern Africa to remain in contact.

_____ **5.** The people of Kush were more advanced than the Assyrians who conquered them.

_____ **6.** The San have lived in Africa longer than any other people.

_____ **7.** Lack of rainfall turned the Sahara back into a desert.

_____ **8.** Egypt and Kush had close cultural ties.

C. What Did You Read?

Choose the answer that best completes each sentence. Write the letter of your answer in the space provided.

_____ **1.** Kush had cultural ties and contacts with Egypt and
     a. Europe.
     b. India.
     c. China.
     d. none of the above.

_____ **2.** The civilization of Kush was located in
     a. North Africa.
     b. northern Egypt.
     c. the Sudan region, south of Egypt.
     d. Madagascar.

_____ **3.** Kush was an African kingdom ruled by the
     a. San.
     b. black Africans.
     c. Mbuti.
     d. Asians.

_____ **4.** The Malaysians in Africa
     a. originally came from Europe and western Asia.
     b. settled on the island of Madagascar.
     c. lived mainly in southern Africa.
     d. developed the use of iron weapons.

D. Who Were They?

In one or two sentences, tell something about the following groups of people.

San _____

_____

Bantu peoples _____

_____

Mbuti _____

_____

E. Reviewing Your Reading:

Fill in the word or term that best completes each statement below.

1. About 10,000 years ago there was a change in the _____ in the Sahara area.

2. Sub-Saharan Africa lies _____ of the Sahara.

3. Many ideas and skills were brought from _____ to Egypt.

4. The _____ were shorter than the San.

5. When the Sahara area again became a desert, the _____ people moved southward.

6. Kush gained its freedom after the decline of _____.

7. Black African warriors gained greatness by using _____ weapons.

8. The early African kingdom of _____ had blacks as its leaders.

F. What Does It Mean?

Choose the best meaning for each of the words in capital letters.

_____ **1.** FLOURISH
    a. to stay in the same place
    b. to grow richer or larger
    c. to die out

_____ **2.** IRON ORE
    a. a weapon
    b. a raw material
    c. a mine

_____ **3.** CLIMATE
    a. history of an area
    b. size of an area
    c. the weather of an area over a long period of time

_____ **4.** DESERT
    a. region without mountains
    b. region without water, trees, or grasses
    c. region that is cool and damp

G. Understanding Global History:

On page 62 you read about four factors in global history. Which of these factors applies to each statement listed below? Fill in the number of the correct statement on page 62 in the space provided. If no factor applies, fill in the word NONE.

_____ **1.** New skills and ideas spread from Egypt to the Sahara and other parts of Africa.

_____ **2.** Kush's location gave it control over grazing land and iron ore.

_____ **3.** The Sahara was a barrier between northern and southern Africa.

Chapter 5

Early Civilizations of India

Understanding Global History

Think about the following statements as you read about the early civilizations of India.
1 The tools of the social scientist can help unlock secrets of the past.
2 Present culture is shaped by the past.
3 Contact among peoples and nations can lead to cultural changes.
4 Nations borrow and adapt ideas and institutions from other nations.

The Indus River begins in the Himalaya Mountains and flows through northern India and Pakistan into the Arabian Sea.

Learning New Words and Terms

/radʒə/ 王 公 (ấn độ)

The following words are used in this chapter. Think about the meaning of each one.

rajah: Indian tribal chief or ruler hôn l khác race

intermarriage: marriage between people from different groups

caste: a social group into which a person is born

Think As You Read

1. Who were the Indo-Aryan people?
2. How did the caste system begin in India?
3. Why is Hinduism important in the history of India?
4. What is the importance of the Maurya Empire?

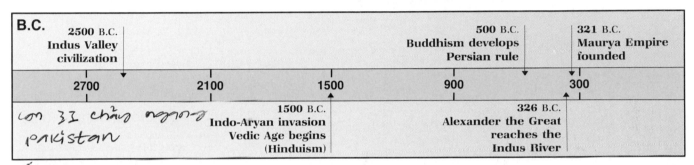

B.C.

2500 B.C. Indus Valley civilization			500 B.C. Buddhism develops Persian rule	321 B.C. Maurya Empire founded
2700	2100	1500	900	300
con 31 chảng người pakistan		1500 B.C. Indo-Aryan invasion Vedic Age begins (Hinduism)	326 B.C. Alexander the Great reaches the Indus River	

/ɪndəs/

Indus Valley Civilization

By about 3000 B.C., there were civilizations in many parts of the world. You have already read about two of these, Sumer and Egypt. One of the early civilizations was located in the Indus River Valley (see map, p. 70). The Indus River, near the western border of present-day India, overflows each year. This flooding enriches the soil along the river bank.

Sometime around 2500 B.C., the first Indus Valley civilization came into being. It was called the Harappa (hah-RAHP-uh) civilization. The people were farmers who grew wheat and raised livestock. They used metal tools and weapons and had a written language. The cities were large and well-planned. Merchants traded with cities in the Fertile Crescent far to the west.

In about 1500 B.C., the Indus Valley civilization was destroyed. We know of its existence from the ruins that were discovered by archaeologists in the early 1920s. The most important ruins are those of two cities, Mohenjo-Daro (moh-HEN-joh-DAH-roh) and Harappa. The reasons why the Indus Valley civilization collapsed are not yet known. Perhaps invaders destroyed it. Or it may have been wiped out in an earthquake. What is known is that the civilization was almost gone

when invaders came to the Indus Valley after 1500 B.C.

The Aryans /ˈɛəriən/ l ˈɑːrjən

The invaders of the Indus River Valley were probably from central Asia. They are known as the Indo-Aryans, or Aryans (AIR-ee-UNZ). As a group, the Aryans were extremely warlike. They

This seal was used by the people of the Indus Valley civilization.

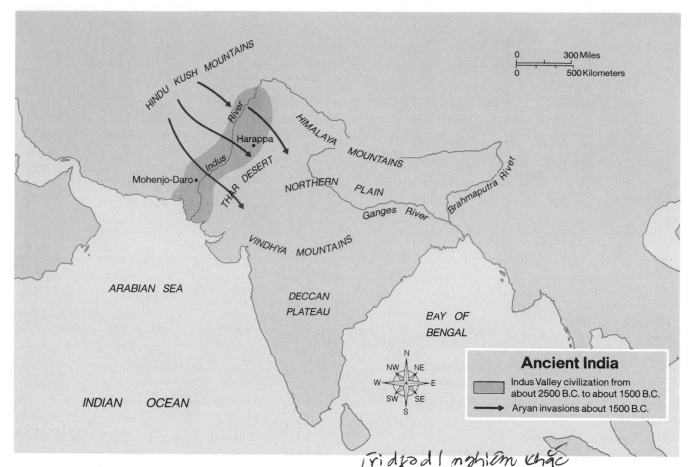

Ancient India

Indus Valley civilization from about 2500 B.C. to about 1500 B.C.

→ Aryan invasions about 1500 B.C.

were loosely organized into tribes. Tribes are groups of people who have a common ancestor, speak the same language, and share the same traditions and beliefs. Each Aryan tribe had its own **rajah,** or chief.

The Aryans swept south, past the Indus River Valley and came upon a group of people called the Dravidians (druh-VIHD-ee-uhnz). The Dravidians had a more advanced civilization than the Aryans. But the Dravidians were defeated and forced to move to southern India.

Despite their lower level of culture, the victorious Aryans looked down on the people they had conquered. Skin color had much to do with this attitude. The light-skinned Aryans viewed the dark-skinned Dravidians as inferiors, or people of lower rank. The Aryans feared being outnumbered by the Dravidians. To prevent this, they did not allow **intermarriage** between the Aryans and the Dravidians. This policy helped lay the basis for the **caste** system in India. The caste system is a way of dividing society into social groups.

Aryan Society

At first, there were four major classes in Aryan society. These were as follows: 1) warriors, 2) priests, 3) landowners, merchants, and herders, and 4) servants and peasants. In time, the priests replaced the warriors as the highest class in Aryan society.

Over the centuries the four main classes divided into castes, or social groups based on birth. The caste system became rigid. It became impossible to move from one caste to another. Birth alone decided what caste a person belonged to. And as the caste system developed, strict rules were set down. These rules governed marriage and what kinds of work people in a caste could do.

More than 3,000 castes developed in India. But there were also people who lived outside the caste system. These people were considered impure. They were called "untouchables." The Untouchables have the lowest position in society.

In recent years, Indian leaders have tried to wipe out the caste system. But it continues to exist. Some Untouchables have risen to high positions in political and business life. On the other hand, Untouchables have also suffered violence at the hands of other Indians.

Aryan Beliefs

After the Aryans settled in India, they formed a number of city-states. During the years that followed they developed their own religious beliefs. These were first handed down to the people in spoken form. Later, they were written down in Sanskrit, an Indo-Aryan language. The religion and history of the Indo-Aryans are contained in sacred books called the Vedas (VAY-duz). These books include poems and prayers. They tell us much about early Indian civilization. Because of the importance of the Vedas, the period from about 1500 B.C. to 1000 B.C. is called the Vedic Age.

Two Religions

The Vedic Age was a period of great advances in language, literature, and art. It was during this period that the Hindu religion developed in India (see p. 75). Hinduism arose out of earlier religions that were based on the sacred writings of the Vedic Age.

Hinduism was only one of the religions that developed in India. Around 500 B.C., it was followed by Buddhism (see p. 75). This religion is based on the teachings of Siddhartha Gautama (GOWT-uh-muh). After finding the knowledge he sought, Gautama became known as the Buddha, or "the Enlightened One." The term refers to a person who sees and understands the meaning of life. Though Buddhism started in India, it later spread to China, Korea, and Japan. Today, most Buddhists live in mainland Southeast Asia and Japan.

The First Indian Empire

The Aryans were the first of many groups of people to invade India. Parts of India were ruled by Persia by the early 500s B.C. Later, in 326 B.C., the Greek and Macedonian armies of Alexander the Great reached the Indus River Valley. But Alexander died before he could take over India. You will read more about Alexander in Unit 3.

The first empire that was ruled by Indian kings was founded in 321 B.C. This was the Maurya (MAWR-yah) Empire. It extended over about two-thirds of India. The Maurya Empire lasted until about 184 B.C.

Hindus made pilgrimages, or religious trips, to Hurdwar, shown here.

Exercises

A. Finding the Main Ideas:

Put a check next to the sentences that give the main ideas of what you have just read.

_____ **1.** Alexander the Great reached the Indus River Valley.

_____ **2.** The establishment of the Hindu and Buddhist religions greatly influenced life in India.

_____ **3.** The fall of the Indus Valley civilization occurred about 1500 B.C.

_____ **4.** Many different people brought their beliefs and customs to India.

_____ **5.** At the height of its rule, the Maurya Empire covered two-thirds of India.

B. What Did You Read?

Choose the answer that best completes each sentence. Write the letter of your answer in the space provided.

_____ **1.** The Indus River Valley is located
- **a.** in northern India.
- **b.** on the eastern border of India.
- **c.** in central India.
- **d.** on the western border of India.

_____ **2.** Sanskrit was the
- **a.** name of a Dravidian tribe.
- **b.** religion of India.
- **c.** written language of the Aryans.
- **d.** capital of the Indus Valley civilization.

_____ **3.** Mohenjo-Daro and Harappa were
- **a.** people from central Asia.
- **b.** cities of the earliest Indian civilization.
- **c.** writings in the Vedas.
- **d.** none of the above.

_____ **4.** The Dravidians
- **a.** conquered the Indo-Aryans.
- **b.** founded the Maurya Empire.
- **c.** founded the Hindu religion.
- **d.** were conquered by the Indo-Aryans.

C. Reviewing Your Reading:

Fill in the word or term that best completes each statement below.

1. The _____ civilization was destroyed about 1500 B.C.

2. The tribal chiefs of the Aryans were known as _____.

3. The _____ were sacred books.

4. The _____ system was begun by the Indo-Aryans.

5. _____ and _____ were two religions that arose in India.

6. The _____ were defeated by the Indo-Aryans.

7. The Maurya Empire was ruled over by _____ kings.

8. The religious beliefs of the Indo-Aryans in India were written down in _____.

D. Checking for Details:

Put a T in the space next to each statement if it is true. Put an F in that space if it is false. Put an N if you cannot tell from the reading if it is true or false.

_____ **1.** The Indus River overflows each year.

_____ **2.** The Indus Valley people did not have a written language.

_____ **3.** Mohenjo-Daro was a king of the Mauryan Empire.

_____ **4.** The Indo-Aryans supported intermarriage.

_____ **5.** The Dravidians were more civilized than the Indo-Aryans.

_____ **6.** The caste system made the Indo-Aryans inferiors.

_____ **7.** Buddha was a great warrior.

_____ **8.** The Persians ruled parts of India.

_____ **9.** The Maurya Empire lasted over 500 years.

_____ **10.** The Vedic Age was a period of great art and literature in India.

_____ **11.** Alexander the Great reached the Ganges River in India.

_____ **12.** The Hindu religion developed in India during the Vedic Age.

E. Time Line Skills:

In which period of time did each of the following events occur? You may look at the time line on page 69 of this lesson to help you.

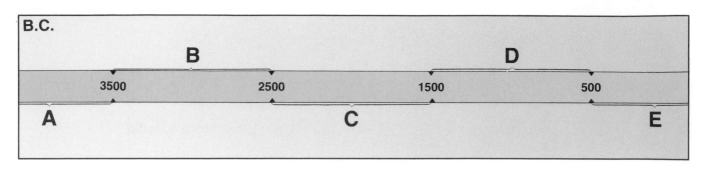

_____ **1.** Persian rule of Indian areas

_____ **2.** Indo-Aryan invasion of India

_____ **3.** Maurya Empire founded

_____ **4.** Aryan invaders rule India

_____ **5.** The armies of Alexander the Great invade the Indus Valley

_____ **6.** Buddha lives in India

_____ **7.** Indus Valley civilization develops

F. Understanding Global History:

On page 68, you read about four factors in global history. Which of these factors applies to each statement listed below? Fill in the number of the correct statement on page 68 in the space provided.

_____ **1.** Archaeologists have learned about the Indus Valley civilization from the ruins that were discovered in the early 1920s.

_____ **2.** Buddhism started in India and had a great influence in China and Japan.

_____ **3.** The Aryans conquered the Dravidians and did not allow intermarriage between the two groups. The caste system developed out of this Aryan policy.

_____ **4.** Despite the efforts of present-day Indian leaders to wipe out the caste system, it still continues to exist.

Enrichment:

Hinduism and Buddhism

Hinduism—Unlike the other religions you will be reading about, Hinduism has no single founder. Instead, it blended ancient Aryan ways with the religious beliefs of the peoples the Aryans conquered. Today, Hinduism is the religion of 85 percent of the people of India. The main Hindu beliefs are as follows:

- A supreme force unites everything in the universe.

- Every person has a soul which is part of a larger, universal soul.

- Life is filled with suffering.

- The goal of life is to free the soul from suffering and unite it with the larger, universal soul.

- A person may have to pass through many lives or re-births to reach the universal soul. This process of re-birth is called reincarnation.

- When the soul finally merges with the universal soul, then a person need never be reborn again.

According to Hindu belief, the actions of a person in this life affect his or her fate in the next life. For example, if a person follows caste rules and leads a good life, he or she may be re-born into a higher caste in the next life. Those who do not fulfill their caste duties and do not lead a good life may be born into a lower caste. You can see how the caste system is closely tied to Hindu beliefs. You can also understand how difficult it is for India's leaders to get rid of the caste system.

Buddhism—You have read about the religion begun by Siddhartha Gautama. Scholars know little about his life except that he was born into a warrior family about 563 B.C. According to legend, Gautama left home and a life of luxury to search for the causes of human suffering. After six years of wandering, Gautama came upon the answer. He then taught others. Buddhist teachings are as follows:

- Life is filled with suffering.

- The cause of suffering is desire for things that cannot last.

- The way to end suffering is to overcome desire through prayer, discipline, and self-sacrifice.

- By leading a life of self discipline and by doing good deeds, a person can attain nirvana. When Buddhists achieve nirvana, they believe they are freed from the pain and suffering of life.

- The way to escape from the causes of desire is to follow the Middle Way.

In the Middle Way, the Buddha tried to teach people to live honestly and to act kindly toward all living things. The Buddha tried to reform or change Hinduism. For example, he taught that a person's soul is re-born many times. But there are important differences between the two religions. The Buddha rejected the caste system which is a large part of Hinduism. He also believed that all people, no matter what social class they belonged to, could achieve nirvana.

75

Chapter 6

Early Civilizations of China

1 tg ˈpɑləʤil 地形学

Artists of the Shang dynasty in China made this white pottery.

[handwritten: 1 dại nàsti 1 triều vua]

Learning New Words and Terms

The following words are used in this chapter. Think about the meaning of each one.

dynasties: ruling families in China
frontiers: areas that form the edge of settled territory; borders

Think As You Read

1. How did the flooding of the Huang Ho (Yellow River) affect early Chinese civilization?
2. In what form was the Chinese written language developed?
3. What was the purpose of the Great Wall?
4. Who was Confucius and what did he seek to do?

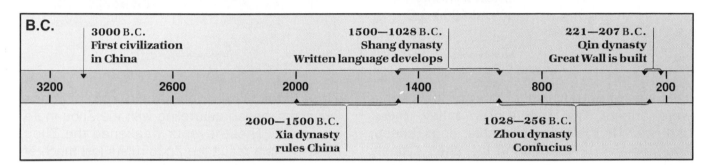

Timeline:

B.C.

3000 B.C. First civilization in China

2000—1500 B.C. Xia dynasty rules China

1500—1028 B.C. Shang dynasty Written language develops

1028—256 B.C. Zhou dynasty Confucius

221—207 B.C. Qin dynasty Great Wall is built

(scale: 3200 | 2600 | 2000 | 1400 | 800 | 200)

The Huang Ho Valley

The history of China is linked to two great rivers. These are the Chang Jiang and the Huang Ho (Yellow River). The Chang Jiang is about 3,400 miles (5,472 kilometers) long and is in central China. The Huang Ho is about 2,900 miles (4,667 kilometers) long and is located in northern China (see maps, p. 78).

The first civilizations arose in China about 3000 B.C. as people settled along the Huang Ho Valley. Like the Nile River, the Huang Ho overflows its banks each year. While the floods help enrich the soil, they also cause much damage. To prevent the river from overflowing, the Chinese began building dikes or barriers along its banks. Unfortunately, this was not an easy task. People living in the area needed to join together. Over the years they had to develop a system to make use of the water and to protect their homes from the floods.

[handwritten: 1 dại k 1 đê (đập đê) bờ sông, ụ đất]

Dynasties Rule China

The Chinese family played a major role in the development of China. Ruling families are known as **dynasties.** According to legends, the first of the dynasties was called the Xia (SHYAH). Not much is known of the Xia rulers. But it is believed

they were the first family to unite North China under their rule. The Xia dynasty lasted from about 2000 B.C. until about 1500 B.C. *[handwritten: 500]*

The next rulers were the Shang dynasty. They ruled China from about 1500 B.C. until about 1028 B.C. The Shang made important contributions to Chinese civilization. During the period of Shang rule, the Chinese learned to make metal tools and weapons. They also developed a written language. Like written languages in other parts of the world, this early language was in the form of pictures which stood for words. Although the number of pictures, or characters, has been reduced in recent times, the language serves as the basis of Chinese writing today. *[handwritten: 472]*

After 1028 B.C., the Shang dynasty was overthrown by the Zhou (JOH) dynasty. Under Zhou rulers, Chinese civilization spread southward. It stretched from the Huang Ho area in the north to the Chang Jiang in central China. These rivers formed the boundaries of the lands held by the Zhou dynasty (see map, p. 78)

Achievements of the Zhou Dynasty

The Zhou was the first of the truly great dynasties of China. For example, Zhou leaders developed systems of irrigation and flood control.

[handwritten: Hạ, Thương, Chu, Tần]

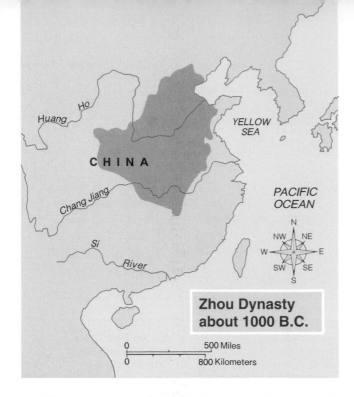

**Zhou Dynasty
about 1000 B.C.**

500 Miles
800 Kilometers

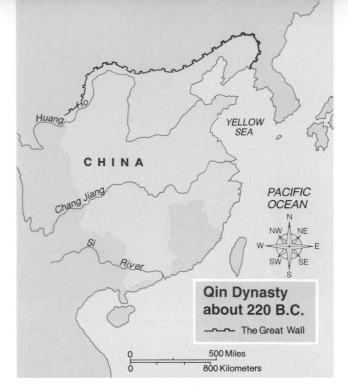

**Qin Dynasty
about 220 B.C.**

⌐⌐⌐ The Great Wall

500 Miles
800 Kilometers

This was important since most of the people were farmers. The farmers grew barley, wheat, and rice. They also raised cattle, hogs, sheep, and chickens. It was during the Zhou dynasty that peasants began raising silkworms. Peasants are poor farmers. The cocoons of the silkworms were used to make the silk for which China would later become famous.

After 700 B.C. many small kingdoms developed along the **frontiers,** or borders of the

Thousands of workers from all over China built the Great Wall. Many died during the project.

Zhou lands. The nobles, or rulers, of these kingdoms, began quarreling with the Zhou more and more. These events weakened the Zhou dynasty. As a result the Zhou rulers lost much of their power. To help them out, a scholar named Confucius (kun-FYOO-shuss) offered a bit of advice. Leaders, he said, must set an example for others to follow. At the same time, people must respect their leaders as well as their family. Confucius's advice was not taken at the time. But his ideas later became an important part of Chinese life.

Qin Rulers Give China Its Name

By 400 B.C., the kingdoms along the Zhou borders became more independent. By 256 B.C., the Zhou rulers could no longer control them. Finally, a group of people called the Qin replaced the weakened dynasty. The Qin dynasty lasted from only 221 B.C. to 207 B.C. Although this was one of the shortest dynasties, it was responsible for giving China its name.

During the Qin dynasty, warlike tribes invaded China from the north and northwest. To protect their territory the Qin rulers decided to build a wall around their lands. The result was the Great Wall of China (see map above). At its completion, the wall was 1,400 miles (2,253 kilometers) long, 25 feet (7.6 meters) tall, and 15 feet (4.5 meters) wide at its base. Despite its massive size, the Great Wall failed to keep out invaders. As a result, the Qin dynasty fell in 207 B.C.

78

Exercises

A. Finding the Main Idea:

Put a check next to the sentence that gives the main idea of what you have just read.

_____ **1.** The floods of the Huang Ho River caused much damage.

_____ **2.** Ancient China was ruled by a series of dynasties.

_____ **3.** The language of China was very complicated.

_____ **4.** Wars along China's frontiers caused the downfall of several dynasties.

B. What Did You Read?

Choose the answer that best completes each sentence. Write the letter of your answer in the space provided.

_____ **1.** The Huang Ho Valley is located in
   a. Africa.
   b. Europe.
   c. Asia.
   d. America.

_____ **2.** The Chinese built the Great Wall to
   a. prevent floods.
   b. improve transportation in China.
   c. provide work for the people.
   d keep out enemies from the north and northwest.

_____ **3.** Chinese civilization spread southward to the Chang Jiang during the
   a. Qin dynasty
   b. Shang dynasty
   c. Zhou dynasty
   d. Xia dynasty

_____ **4.** The earliest Chinese dynasty was the
   a. Zhou dynasty
   b. Qin dynasty
   c. Shang dynasty
   d. Xia dynasty

_____ **5.** The Chinese scholar Confucius taught that
   a. leaders must set an example for others to follow.
   b. the people must respect their leaders.
   c. the people must respect their families
   d. all of the above.

C. Reviewing Your Reading:

Fill in the word or term that best completes each statement below.

1. The overflowing banks of the _____ provided China with water and fertile soil.

2. The _____ dynasty was one of the shortest dynasties.

3. _____ offered advice to the Zhou rulers.

4. The _____ failed to keep out warlike tribes from the north.

5. The Chinese written language was in the form of _____ .

D. Checking for Details:

Put an F in the space next to each statement if it is a fact. Put an O in that space if it is an opinion. Remember that facts can be proved, but opinions cannot.

_____ **1.** Most Chinese welcomed the river floods.

_____ **2.** The Xia rulers were not as successful as the Shang rulers.

_____ **3.** Silkworms were difficult to raise.

_____ **4.** Irrigation was developed in China during the Zhou dynasty.

_____ **5.** After about 700 B.C., the Zhou dynasty had little power.

_____ **6.** Confucius was not trusted by the rulers of China.

_____ **7.** The building of the Great Wall was a good idea.

E. Time Line Skills:

In which period of time did each of the following occur? You may look at the text for help. Place the correct letter in the space provided.

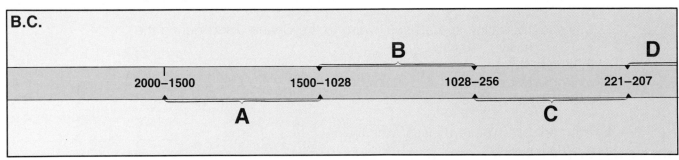

B.C.

B	D
2000–1500	1500–1028	1028–256	221–207
A		C	

_____ **1.** Metal tools were introduced in China.

_____ **2.** China was ruled by the Xia dynasty.

_____ **3.** The Great Wall was built.

_____ **4.** Silk production was started in China.

_____ **5.** The Chinese language was developed.

F. Word Meanings:

Match each word in Column A with the correct meaning in Column B. Write the letter of each answer in the space provided.

Column A

_____ **1.** frontiers
_____ **2.** peasant
_____ **3.** dynasties

Column B

a. king or emperor
b. poor farmer
c. slave owner
d. the borders, or edges, of a settled area
e. ruling families

G. Understanding Global History:

On page 76 you read about four factors in global history. Which of these factors applies to each statement listed below? Fill in the number of the correct statement on page 76 in the space provided.

_____ **1.** The flooding of the Huang Ho caused the people of the area to join together to use the water and to protect themselves.

_____ **2.** The overflowing banks of the Huang Ho provided water and fertile soil.

_____ **3.** The advice given by Confucius more than 2,700 years ago became an important part of Chinese life.

_____ **4.** Systems of irrigation and flood control allowed the Chinese to farm on a large scale and to extend their borders.

Chapter 7

The Land and the People of Japan

Understanding Global History

Think about the following statements as you read about the land and the people of Japan.
1 Contact among peoples and nations can lead to cultural changes.
2 Nations choose what they borrow and adapt from other nations.
3 The physical environment can encourage or restrict contact among people.

The statue of Buddha at Kamakura, Japan. Buddhism came to Japan from mainland Asia.

Learning New Words and Terms

The following words are used in this chapter. Think about the meaning of each one.

immigrants: people who come to a nation to settle as permanent residents
central authority: government or ruling group
clans: groups of related families

Think As You Read

1. Who were the original people of Japan?
2. Who were the people who came to Japan in ancient times?
3. What ideas and inventions did the Japanese adopt from Chinese culture?
4. What kind of government developed in Japan?

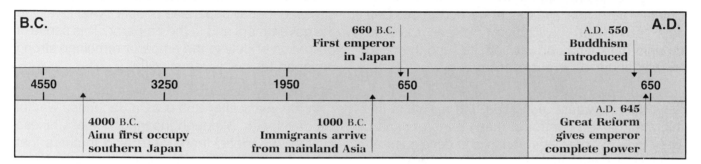

B.C.					A.D.
			660 B.C. **First emperor in Japan**		A.D. 550 **Buddhism introduced**
4550	3250	1950	650		650
	4000 B.C. **Ainu first occupy southern Japan**	1000 B.C. **Immigrants arrive from mainland Asia**			A.D. 645 **Great Reform gives emperor complete power**

The Islands of Japan

Japan is a chain of islands located off the northeast coast of Asia. (see map, this page). The islands of Japan stretch for 1,500 miles (2,414 kilometers). The four main Japanese islands are Hokkaido (ho-KI-do), Honshu (HON-shoo), Shikoku (shi-KO-koo), and Kyushu (KYOO-shoo). Many other smaller islands are also part of Japan. Most of the Japanese islands are covered with hills and mountains. However, there are also some river valley areas with fertile plains.

The People of Japan

The original people of Japan were the Ainu (AY-noo). They may have come to the islands from the Asian mainland thousands of years ago. The Ainu occupied the southern islands from about 4000 B.C. to about 1000 B.C. Sometime after 1000 B.C., groups of **immigrants** moved to Japan. The newcomers were probably from present-day China, Korea, Manchuria, Malaysia, and Indonesia. In time, this mixture of immigrants joined to form the people we know as the Japanese. As the newcomers continued to arrive, the Ainu were pushed to Hokkaido, the northernmost island of Japan.

The Influence of China

The Chinese had the greatest influence upon early Japanese civilization. During the time of the

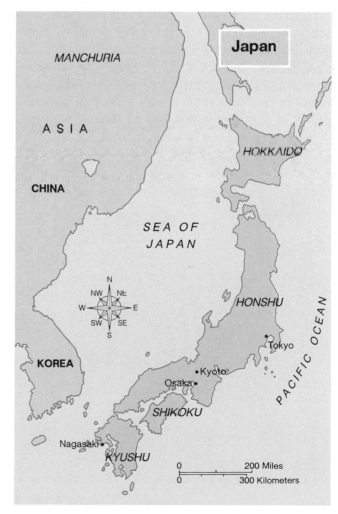

Japan

MANCHURIA

ASIA

CHINA

HOKKAIDO

SEA OF
JAPAN

KOREA

HONSHU

PACIFIC OCEAN

Tokyo

Kyoto

Osaka

SHIKOKU

Nagasaki

KYUSHU

| 0 | 200 Miles |
| 0 | 300 Kilometers |

clan /klăn/ bè đảng

Zhou dynasty (1028 B.C. to 256 B.C.) many Chinese moved to Japan. In fact, for more than 500 years, waves of mainland immigrants crossed the Sea of Japan and settled in Japan. These people brought with them skills of farming, pottery, weaving, and the raising of silkworms. They also brought knowledge of Chinese writing and Buddhism.

Japan and China were in close contact during the years after 600 B.C. Many Japanese students and government representatives traveled to China. There, the Japanese learned about China's advanced civilization. These travelers brought back ideas on religion, art, and the need for a stronger **central authority.**

Japan's Early Rulers

As their numbers increased, the mainland immigrants gained control of many parts of Japan. They took over the best lands and developed an agriculture based mainly upon rice.

The newcomers in Japan lived in **clans.** The heads of the clans formed a noble class. Each clan controlled a piece of land and the peasants who worked the land. Over time, the different clans fought each other until one became more powerful than the rest. It was from this powerful clan that the first emperors of Japan emerged sometime around 660 B.C.

Japan's first emperors had little power, however. Rival clans were always trying to take over control from the emperor. The need for a strong government finally led to the Great Reform of A.D. 645. It gave the emperor complete power. He also became the owner of all the land. The Great Reform destroyed the clan system.

In A.D. 702, a law code was written. It was based on ideas brought back from China. The code, which was called the Great Treasure, stressed that all Japanese people owed loyalty to the government and to the emperor. This sense of obligation or duty to the emperor remained strong in Japan for many years. /ʃinto/ đạo thần

A Japanese Way of Life Develops

In the years after 250 B.C., a Japanese way of life developed. Although the influence of Chinese culture was clear, there were also features that existed only in Japan. For example, Japan developed the Shinto religion. Shinto taught respect for the beauty of nature and worship of the gods. At the same time the Japanese accepted the religion of Buddhism. As you have read, the Buddhist religion began in India and then spread to China and Korea. Over the years, Shintoism and Buddhism were blended into Japanese life.

The samurai were the warriors of early Japan.

Exercises

A. Finding the Main Ideas:
Put a check next to the sentences that give the main ideas of what you have just read.

_____ **1.** Japan developed its own religion.

_____ **2.** Rice farming helped the economy of Japan.

_____ **3.** Government in Japan was influenced by the Chinese.

_____ **4.** The Ainu made many contributions to Japan.

_____ **5.** Immigrants and invaders had a great influence on Japanese life.

B. What Did You Read?
Choose the answer that best completes each sentence. Write the letter of your answer in the space provided.

_____ **1.** The Japanese developed their own religion, known as
    a. Buddhism.
    b. Shintoism.
    c. Hinduism.
    d. Confucianism.

_____ **2.** The Great Reform of A.D. 645
    a. took power away from the ruling dynasty.
    b. allowed Japanese students to travel to China.
    c. dealt with religion in Japan.
    d. gave greater power to the emperor.

_____ **3.** The original people of Japan were the
    a. Koreans.
    b. Chinese.
    c. Ainu.
    d. Malaysians.

_____ **4.** The Chinese brought to Japan
    a. a written language.
    b. the Buddhist religion.
    c. skills in farming
    d. all of the above.

C. Chronology Skills:

In the space provided, write the letter of the event that took place first. You may use the time line on page 83 for help.

_____ **1. a.** earliest Japanese emperor
   b. Buddhism
   c. Stone Age

_____ **2. a.** Great Reform
   b. growth of Japanese culture
   c. earliest Japanese emperor

_____ **3. a.** immigrants from Southeast Asia
   b. Ainu
   c. Buddhism

_____ **4. a.** growth of Japanese culture
   b. Great Reform
   c. Buddhism

_____ **5. a.** Great Reform
   b. earliest Japanese emperor
   c. Buddhism

D. Checking for Details:

Read each statement. Put a T in the space next to each statement if it is true. Put an F in that space if it is false. Put an N if you cannot tell from the reading if it is true or false.

_____ **1.** More Japanese followed Buddhism than Shintoism.

_____ **2.** The Japanese adopted the Chinese form of writing.

_____ **3.** The Ainu were the first people in Japan.

_____ **4.** Japanese students did not support the Great Reform.

_____ **5.** The Great Treasure made loyalty to the emperor an important part of Japanese life.

_____ **6.** Korean immigrants settled in Japan.

_____ **7.** Japan and China were in close contact after 1100 B.C.

_____ **8.** Japanese emperors always had great power.

_____ **9.** Silkworms were raised in Japan before the arrival of any immigrants.

_____ **10.** The Japanese are a mixture of many peoples from Asia.

E. Word Meanings:

Look up the following words in the glossary. Write the meaning next to each word.

IMMIGRANTS _____

_____

CENTRAL AUTHORITY _____

_____

CLANS _____

_____

F. Understanding Global History:

On page 82, you read about three factors in global history. Which of these factors applies to each statement listed below? Fill in the number of the correct statement on page 82 in the space provided. If no factor applies, fill in the word NONE.

_____ **1.** The islands of Japan stretch for 1,500 miles (2,414 kilometers). Most of the islands are covered with hills and mountains.

_____ **2.** In the years after 250 B.C. Japanese life was influenced by Chinese culture. But at the same time, it developed some of its own characteristics.

_____ **3.** Japanese emperors had little power.

_____ **4.** The immigrants who moved to Japan brought much of their own culture.

Chapter 8

The Land and the People of Southeast Asia

Understanding Global History

Think about the following statements as you read about the land and the people of Southeast Asia.
1. Location, topography, and resources affect interaction among people.
2. Interaction among people can lead to cultural changes.
3. Present culture is shaped by the past.

The people of Cambodia built this huge temple. It is called Angkor Wat.

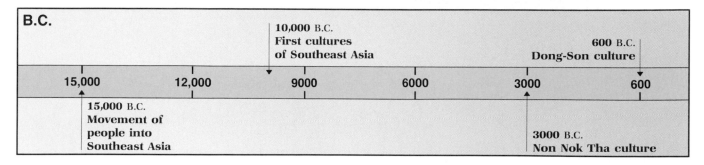

Learning New Words and Terms

The following words are used in this chapter. Think about the meaning of each one.

origins: places where things are started
populated: filled with people
migrations: movements of people from one place to another

Think As You Read

1. Which areas are included in Southeast Asia?
2. How does its location make Southeast Asia a crossroads of the world? How has this affected the culture of Southeast Asia?
3. What were the early cultures of Southeast Asia?

B.C.

10,000 B.C.
First cultures of Southeast Asia

600 B.C.
Dong-Son culture

15,000   12,000   9000   6000   3000   600

15,000 B.C.
Movement of people into Southeast Asia

3000 B.C.
Non Nok Tha culture

The Land of Southeast Asia

There are two land areas in Southeast Asia. One area is made up of islands in the Pacific Ocean. The other area is the southeast portion of the Asian mainland. Southeast Asia is shaped like a triangle. India, China, and Australia form the outer boundaries of the triangle. Within the triangle are the islands that make up the present-day nations of Indonesia and the Philippines. The mainland areas of Southeast Asia include the present-day nations of Myanmar (Burma), Thailand (TI-land), Cambodia, Laos (LA-os), Vietnam (vee-et-NAHM), Malayasia, and Singapore (see map, p. 90).

The location of Southeast Asia makes it a crossroads of the world. Australia and the nations of Europe, Africa, and mainland Asia, trade along its waters and across its lands.

The People of Southeast Asia

Many groups of people have moved across Southeast Asia. The **origins** of the earliest people are not really known. It is believed, however, that Southeast Asia was **populated** by groups who came from the northern areas of Asia. Such **migrations** of people took place thousands and thousands of years ago.

The earliest humans in Southeast Asia were probably ancestors of the people who today live in the islands of the Pacific Ocean. Later, people from the area of Mongolia moved into parts of Southeast Asia. The movement of these people into the region may have begun more than 12,000 years ago. Scientists have found evidence of people living in Southeast Asia as far back as 15,000 B.C.

Remains of the Dong-Son culture of Southeast Asia.

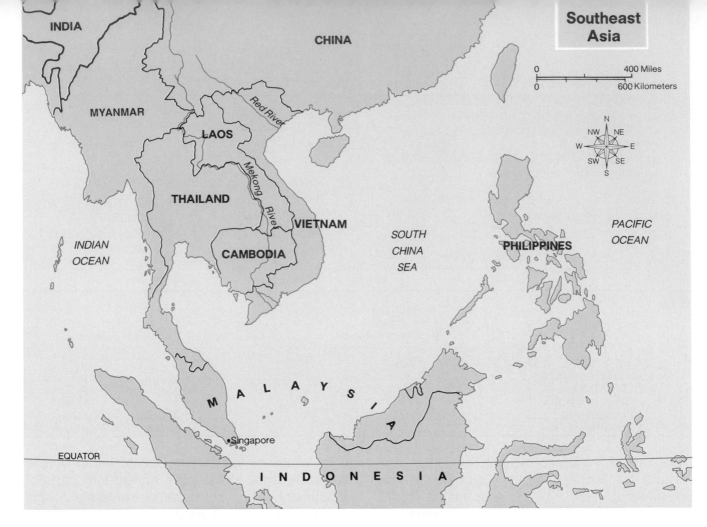

Different Ways of Life Develop

The groups who eventually settled in Southeast Asia developed different ways of life. Some of the larger and stronger groups settled in the rich, fertile river valleys on the mainland. They often controlled the areas in which they settled. The smaller and weaker groups of people were forced to live in the hill country and the forests. Today, the people of the hill country live much like their ancestors. Like the people before them, they have little contact with others. Many highland peoples of Southeast Asia have languages and cultures that are quite different from that of their neighbors in the lowland areas.

Civilizations of Southeast Asia

Several early civilizations arose in the mainland areas of Southeast Asia. One of the earliest was the Non Nok Tha culture. This culture started in Thailand. Experts believe the Non Nok Tha culture existed around 3000 B.C. People of the Non Nok Tha culture used stone tools, raised rice, and made canoes. They also kept domestic animals.

A later Southeast Asian civilization arose in the highland areas of present-day Vietnam. This is known as the Dong-Son culture. Its remains have been dug up and examined for many years. The Dong-Son culture made some use of iron, but it is best known for its bronze objects. A great number of bronze kettledrums have been found in the Dong-Son area. These drums may have been used for some religious purpose. Figures that appear on the kettledrums show that women played an important part in the Dong-Son culture.

The people of the Dong-Son culture used domestic animals including the ox. They also irrigated their fields and grew rice. In addition, the Dong-Son people were skilled boat builders. They were involved in trade and traveled to many parts of Asia.

The remains of these ancient Southeast Asian cultures tell only part of the story. However, they show that many different groups lived in the island and mainland areas of Southeast Asia between 3000 B.C. and 600 B.C. Chinese influence became very strong around 111 B.C. The Chinese ruler conquered parts of Southeast Asia at that time.

Exercises

A. Finding the Main Ideas:

Put a check next to the sentences that give the main ideas of what you have just read.

_____ **1.** Southeast Asia is made up of island and mainland areas.

_____ **2.** Southeast Asia is shaped like a triangle.

_____ **3.** The early Southeast Asian cultures were developed by people who moved there from other areas.

_____ **4.** Many different languages are spoken in Southeast Asia.

_____ **5.** The highland areas of Southeast Asia developed a separate culture.

B. Checking for Details:

Read each statement. Put a T in the space next to each statement if it is true. Put an F in that space if it is false. Put an N if you cannot tell from the reading if it is true or false.

_____ **1.** Singapore is one of the island areas of Southeast Asia.

_____ **2.** Weaker tribes in Southeast Asia were forced to move to the river valley areas.

_____ **3.** Myanmar is one of the mainland areas of Southeast Asia.

_____ **4.** The earliest people in Southeast Asia were related to people now living on islands in the Pacific Ocean.

_____ **5.** The earliest group in Southeast Asia was the people of the Dong-Son culture.

_____ **6.** Women played a minor part in the Dong-Son culture.

_____ **7.** Indonesia is one of the island areas of Southeast Asia.

_____ **8.** Vietnam is one of the mainland areas of Southeast Asia.

_____ **9.** People of the highland areas of Southeast Asia had many contacts with other cultures.

_____ **10.** Dong-Son peoples traded with peoples in many parts of Asia.

_____ **11.** The Chinese had little influence in Southeast Asia.

C. Map Skills:

Write the letter of each place in the correct box on the map.

A. Vietnam

B. Japan

C. Indonesia

D. China

E. Philippines

F. India

G. Cambodia

H. Thailand

I. Malaysia

J. Laos

K. Myanmar

L. Singapore

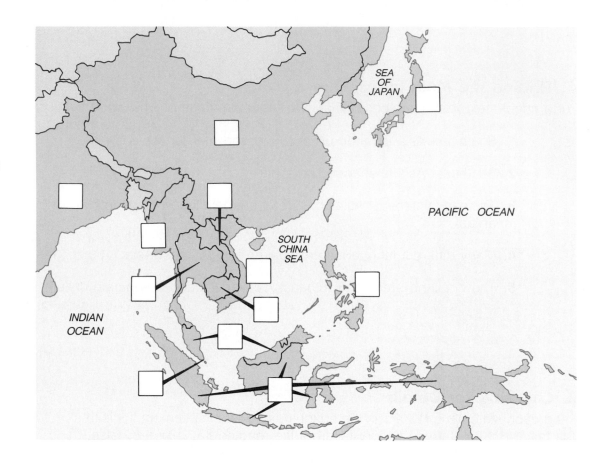

D. Matching:

Match each item in Column A with the correct cultures listed in Column B. Items in Column B can be listed more than once.

Column A

_____ **1.** made some use of iron
_____ **2.** developed in Thailand
_____ **3.** carried on trade and travel
_____ **4.** used stone tools
_____ **5.** made bronze kettledrums

Column B

A. Non Nok Tha culture
B. Dong-Son culture

E. Thinking it Over:

On a separate piece of paper answer the following question in two or three sentences.

Why is Southeast Asia known as the "crossroads of the world"?

F. Word Meanings:

Match each word in Column A with the correct meaning in Column B. Write the letter of each answer in the space provided.

Column A

_____ **1.** populated
_____ **2.** migrations
_____ **3.** origins

Column B

a. movements of people from one place to another
b. to be alarmed
c. filled with people
d. places where things are started
e. to rule or control others

G. Understanding Global History:

On page 88 you read about three factors in global history. Which of these factors applies to each statement listed below? Fill in the number of the correct statement on page 88 in the space provided. If no factor applies, fill in the word NONE.

_____ **1.** Many highland people of Southeast Asia have languages and cultures that differ from their neighbors in the lowland areas.

_____ **2.** The various groups moving into Southeast Asia developed different ways of life.

_____ **3.** Australia and the nations of Europe, Africa, and Mainland Asia trade along the waters and across the lands of Southeast Asia.

_____ **4.** The people of the Southeast Asian hill country live much like their ancestors. They have little contact with their lowland neighbors and have cultures of their own.

Chapter 9

The First People of the Americas

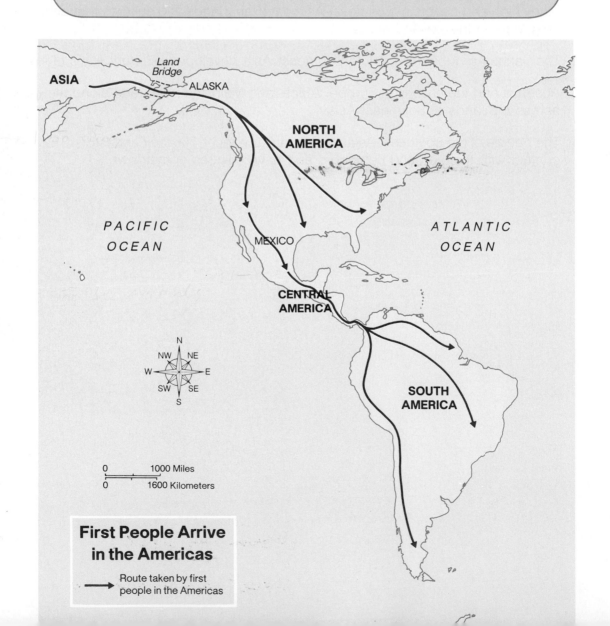

First People Arrive in the Americas

→ Route taken by first people in the Americas

Learning New Words and Terms

The following words are used in this chapter. Think about the meaning of each one.

clue: a guide to solving a problem or mystery
descendants: people who are born of a certain group or family; offspring

Think As You Read

1. How did the first people come to the Americas?
2. Who were the first people to come to the Americas?
3. What do we know about the way the first Americans lived?

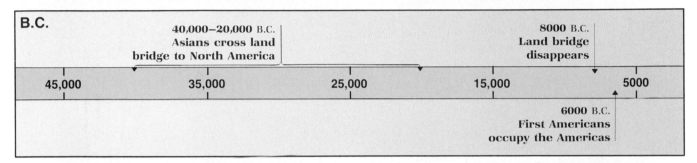

B.C.

40,000–20,000 B.C.
Asians cross land bridge to North America

8000 B.C.
Land bridge disappears

45,000   35,000   25,000   15,000   5000

6000 B.C.
First Americans occupy the Americas

The First People Arrive in the Americas

Two great oceans separate the continents of North and South America from the rest of the world. They are the Atlantic Ocean and the Pacific Ocean. Look at the map on page 94. Notice how close the northwest tip of North America (Alaska) is to the northeast tip of Asia (Siberia). The closeness of the two continents provides a **clue,** or guide, to the probable origins of the first people to settle in the Americas.

Tens of thousands of years ago, Asia and North America were connected. A wide bridge of land joined the two continents. As a result, it was possible for people to cross between Asia and North America. After many years the shape of the earth changed. The land bridge between the two continents disappeared. Today, this land bridge between Asia and North America is under water.

Some time between 40,000 and 20,000 years ago, the first people began to move from Asia to the Americas. They probably came across the land bridge in search of herds of animals. Several waves of different peoples moved back and forth across the land bridge for a period of thousands of years.

Many of the groups were related to the Mongol people of Asia. Because they had no written language, it is difficult to learn much about their history. Social scientists have uncovered many of the tools, weapons, and carvings of these early

people. Some of the remains date back to around 30,000 years ago. Although they tell us a great deal about the story of the first Americans, there is still much more that needs to be learned.

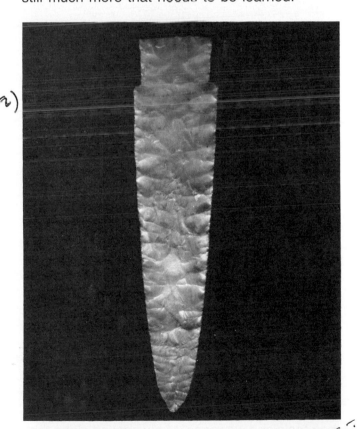

The first people to live in the Americas made spear points like these. They used the points in hunting.

95

/ˈbɔisən/ bò rừng The early Native Americans drew these pictures of animals on rocks.

The first peoples to come to the Americas
- each spoke a different language.
- lived in caves and made use of fire.
- hunted the giant bison, or buffalo, and gathered fruits and berries from the land.
- did not farm or—with the exception of dogs— have domesticated animals. sə(—)rʌ

thuần lự animals

People Move South

For thousands of years, many groups of people moved between Asia and the Americas. In time, a number of the people remained in North America and began to move south. Some traveled along the route east of the Rocky Mountains. Others drifted through Mexico and Central America. By 6,000 to 10,000 years ago, groups of people had reached all the way to the tip of South America.

As these people moved south they improved their tools and weapons. Many passed along their skills to the people they met moving across the

continent. Scientists have discovered well-made stone spear points in what is today the state of New Mexico. These spear points are about 20,000 years old. Thousands of miles to the south, at the tip of South America, scientists have found similar kinds of spear points. These remains may be nearly 7,000 years old. The spear points tell the story of the southward movement of the first people in the Americas.

The land bridge connecting Asia and North America disappeared about 10,000 years ago. As a result, the movement of people between the two continents came to an end. By this time many of the groups that had crossed to America over a period of thousands of years had moved southward. Their **descendants** were scattered throughout all of the Americas. Experts believe that the last people to cross the land bridge remained in the northern Arctic regions. These people are called the Inuits. They are also called by another name—Eskimos. Jt cực

/ˈɛskəmo/
151

Exercises

A. Finding the Main Ideas:

Put a check next to the headings that give the main ideas of what you have just read.

_____ **1.** The great migrations between Asia and North America

_____ **2.** The first people in the Americas and where they came from

_____ **3.** How the first Americans used tools and weapons

_____ **4.** How people traveled in the Americas in ancient times

_____ **5.** The travels of the descendants of the first Americans

B. What Did You Read?

Choose the answer that best completes each sentence. Write the letter of your answer in the space provided.

_____ **1.** The Inuits
   a. settled in South America.
   b. were the first people to cross the land bridge from Asia.
   c. vanished about 10,000 years ago.
   d. were the last people to cross the land bridge from Asia.

_____ **2.** The spear points found in New Mexico are
   a. the only ones found in the Americas.
   b. about 7,000 years old.
   c. older than the spear points found in South America.
   d. similar to ones found in Africa.

_____ **3.** People were able to move to the Americas from Asia because
   a. the northwest tip of Asia is near the northwest tip of North America.
   b. the southwest tip of Asia is near the northwest tip of North America.
   c. the northeast tip of Asia is near the northwest tip of North America.
   d. the southeast tip of Asia is near the northeast tip of North America.

_____ **4.** The first Americans did all of the following *except*
   a. go hunting.
   b. use iron weapons and tools.
   c. use fire.
   d. use spoken languages.

C. Checking for Details:

Read each statement. Put a T in the space next to each statement if it is true. Put an F in that space if it is false. Put an N if you cannot tell from the reading if it is true or false.

_____ **1.** Each of the first groups of people to come to the Americas spoke a different language.

_____ **2.** The southern tip of Asia lies close to North America.

_____ **3.** The first people to come to America grew wheat and corn.

_____ **4.** The land bridge between Asia and North America still exists today.

_____ **5.** The first people to come to the Americas lived in a Stone Age culture.

_____ **6.** The last people to cross the land bridge traveled south to the tip of South America.

_____ **7.** Asia and North America were connected tens of thousands of years ago.

D. Matching:

Match each word in Column A with the word or term associated with it in Column B.

Column A

_____ **1.** Alaska
_____ **2.** Rocky Mountains
_____ **3.** Siberia
_____ **4.** Arctic area

Column B

a. Asia
b. Inuits
c. North America
d. South America
e. Atlantic Ocean

E. Thinking it Over:

On a separate piece of paper answer the following question in three or four sentences.

What problems were faced by the people who crossed the land bridge from Asia to North America?

F. Word Meanings:

Look up the following words in the glossary. Write the meaning next to each word.

CLUE _____

_____

DESCENDANTS _____

_____

_____

G. Understanding Global History:

On page 94, you read about three factors in global history. Which of these factors applies to each statement listed below? Fill in the number of the correct statement on page 94 in the space provided. If no factor applies, fill in the word NONE.

_____ **1.** The land bridge connecting Asia and North America disappeared into the sea and ended almost all movement of people between the two continents.

_____ **2.** The skills of making tools and weapons were passed along from one group to another.

_____ **3.** The first people to come to the Americas had no system of agriculture, but hunted, fished, and gathered food.

seat /sit/   sheet /ʃit/   shit /ʃit/

Enrichment:
The Land Bridge

For about 500 years people have been trying to solve a mystery. The mystery was how and why people first came to North America. Many scientists now think that they have solved that mystery. /ʃit/

The clue was the Ice Age. During the Ice Age huge sheets of ice covered parts of Asia, Europe, and North America. The sheets of ice made the temperature drop.

Now scientists know that the ice did something else. It locked up a great deal of water from the oceans. When so much ocean water was frozen, the level of the seas and oceans dropped. What happened was something like what happens when the ocean tide goes out. A great deal of land that used to be under water was open, dry land.

Thousands of years passed before the water came back to cover the land bridge. During that time, plants began to grow on the land. Animals came to eat the plants. People came to hunt animals and gather plants. As they fol-lowed the animals, the people crossed from Asia into North America. They didn't know they were crossing into another continent. They just knew they were following good sources of food.

The people were also going where the weather was better. Scientists believe that the parts of Europe, Asia, and North America that were covered with ice sheets were much colder than they are now. The area between what is now Siberia and Alaska was much warmer than it is now. It was good climate for people.

About 10,000 years ago, the sheets of ice began to disappear. The water level slowly rose. The land bridge grew narrower and narrower. Once it was probably 1,000 miles (1,600 kilometers) wide. As it grew narrower, the land grew colder. Fewer people crossed over. After many years, ocean water again covered the land that had once connected Asia and North America.

The Inuit People of North America

> **Understanding Global History**
>
> Think about the following statements as you read about the people called the Inuits.
> 1 People use the environment to achieve economic goals.
> 2 The culture in which we live influences our view of other people.
> 3 Basic human needs are influenced by our environment and our culture.

This Inuit family lives in Alaska. Note their clothing. Many Inuits wear coats made from sealskin. Inuits also wear clothing bought in stores.

[handwritten notes in the margins:]
1 Tcai xk 1 xương đồ nhẹ bọc da chó biển 08 λ eskimo
1 nɔɾs 1 tiếng Na uy (p6) λ Na uy

Learning New Words and Terms

The following words are used in this chapter. Think about the meaning of each one.

Norse: people from Norway
caribou: North American reindeer
igloos: Inuit homes built with ice and snow
kayak: Inuit canoe made of a frame covered with animal skins

Think As You Read

1. When did the Inuit people come to the Americas?
2. How did the Inuit people adjust to their environment?
3. How did the life of the Inuits differ from the life of people in the Siberian Arctic region?

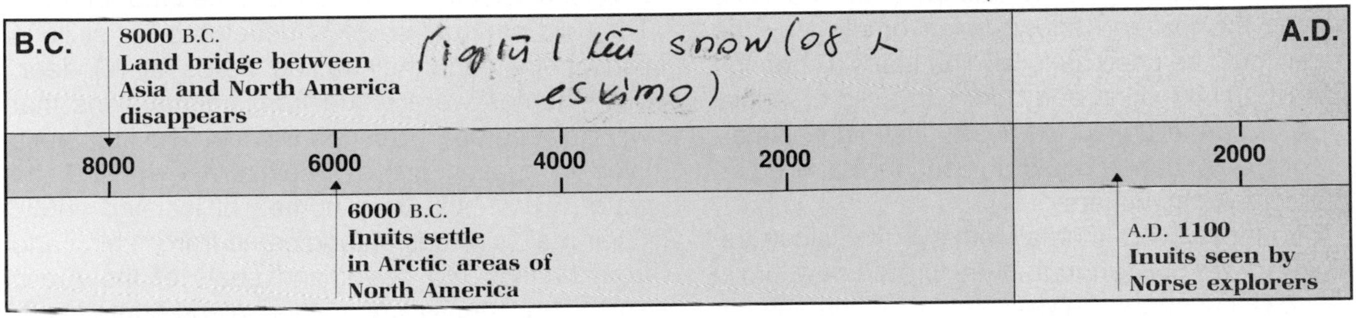

B.C.	8000 B.C. Land bridge between Asia and North America disappears					A.D.
	8000	6000	4000	2000		2000
		6000 B.C. Inuits settle in Arctic areas of North America				A.D. 1100 Inuits seen by Norse explorers

[handwritten note across timeline:] *1 igluː 1 lều snow (08 λ eskimo)*

The Inuits

As you have read, the Inuits were probably the last group of people to cross the land bridge from Asia to North America. After the land bridge disappeared under the sea, the Inuits remained in North America. Those who settled in the Arctic regions moved from Alaska across northern Canada and on to Greenland. Experts believe that during the Ice Age some Inuits moved as far south as the St. Lawrence River in Canada.

Like many early humans, the Inuits had no special name for themselves. In their own language they were "Inuits," or "the people." However, a group of migrating Native Americans, called the Ojibwa, saw the Inuits eating raw fish. After that, they referred to the Inuits as "Eskimos"—the Ojibwa word for "eaters of raw flesh."

Not only were the Inuits the last people to cross the land bridge, they probably were also the first people in America to be seen by Europeans. Around A.D. 1100, some **Norse** explorers reported seeing people who must have been Inuits. This event occurred almost 400 years before Columbus landed in America.

There were never many Inuits in North America. When Europeans first arrived almost 500 years ago, fewer than 100,000 Inuits were settled there. For a time the number of Inuits continued to decline. Today, only about 40,000 Inuits (Eskimos) live in North America.

The Inuit Way of Life

Because the Inuits settled in the Arctic regions, they had to adjust to extremely cold weather. These areas had no grasses to feed herd animals and very few trees. To survive, the Inuits had to make use of things they could find easily in their

These Inuits are building an igloo.

environment. For example, for food they had to depend upon the fish, seals, **caribou,** and large bears of the area.

By using ice, animal bones, animal skins, and stones the Inuits were able to build their homes, make their clothing, and carve their tools. Snow and ice were used to build homes, called **igloos.** Animal bones and stones were sharpened to make spearheads and harpoons. The Inuits even solved the difficulty of crossing the wastelands of ice and snow. They used animal bones and skins to make sleds. Dogs were trained to pull the sleds across the ice and snow. In an emergency the dogs could be used as food. The Inuits also made use of animal skins and bones to build a special type of canoe called a **kayak.** This light, water-proof type of canoe could be used for traveling on the cold Arctic waters.

The Inuits lived in small family units. When the children were old enough, they formed new family units. Because food was scarce, villages and cities never developed. People had to travel to find food. Thus, the Inuits never settled in one place. The Inuits had no chiefs or tribes and there was no organized system of government.

Coastal and Inland Ways of Life

The Inuits, or Eskimos, who came to North America are related to the people of Siberia. This region is found in eastern Asia. Despite this common background, the two groups developed very different ways of life. The main reason for this difference was the environment. For example, the people of Siberia turned toward the land for food. They did not hunt seals or develop great skills in fishing. Instead, they raised herds of reindeer. Their homes were made from animal skins that were placed upon wooden frames. The first Inuits lived in coastal areas. They turned toward the water. They built their homes of ice and snow. Their main sources of food came from fishing and from hunting the bears and seals of the Arctic area. Those Inuits who settled inland hunted caribou and fished in lakes.

vŏṇŋ ăai

The Inuit kayak has a sort of collar around its opening. The collar keeps water from getting inside the kayak.

Exercises

A. Finding the Main Ideas:
Put a check next to the sentences that give the main ideas of what you have just read.

_____ **1.** The Inuits were the last group of Asians to cross the land bridge to North America.

_____ **2.** Food was scarce among the Inuits.

_____ **3.** The Inuits were probably the first people in the Americas to be seen by Europeans.

_____ **4.** The caribou were important to the Inuits.

_____ **5.** The Inuits made use of the environment of the Arctic region.

B. What Did You Read?
Choose the answer that best completes each sentence. Write the letter of your answer in the space provided.

_____ **1.** The Inuit people are also referred to as
  a. Siberians.
  b. Asians.
  c. Norse.
  d. Eskimos.

_____ **2.** The Inuits depended upon all of the following for food *except*
  a. seals.
  b. wheat.
  c. fish.
  d. caribou.

_____ **3.** Inuit tools and weapons were made of
  a. iron.
  b. steel.
  c. animal bone.
  d. all of the above.

_____ **4.** The Inuits traveled by
  a. sled and igloo.
  b. kayak and caribou.
  c. sled and kayak.
  d. caribou and sled.

C. Checking for Details:

Read each statement. Put an F in the space next to each statement if it is a fact. Put an O in that space if it is an opinion. Remember that facts can be proved, but opinions cannot.

_____ **1.** The Inuits in North America lived a better life than the people in Siberia.

_____ **2.** Caribou could be used for food.

_____ **3.** There were never many Inuits in North America.

_____ **4.** Dogs were more important to the Inuits than tools or weapons.

_____ **5.** The Inuits would have been better off if they had been led by chiefs.

_____ **6.** The Inuits received the name "Eskimo" from Native Americans.

D. Thinking it Over:

On a separate piece of paper, answer the following question in three or four sentences.

How did the Inuits make use of the Arctic environment?

E. Word Meanings:

Match each word in Column A with the correct meaning in Column B.

Column A

_____ **1.** kayak
_____ **2.** igloo
_____ **3.** caribou
_____ **4.** Norse
_____ **5.** Eskimos

Column B

a. North American reindeer
b. Inuit home made of ice and snow
c. Inuit canoe
d. Ojibwa name for Inuits
e. land without trees or plants
f. people from Norway

F. Understanding Global History:

On page 100, you read about three factors in global history. Which of these factors applies to each statement listed below? Fill in the number of the correct statement on page 100 in the space provided. If no factor applies, fill in the word NONE.

_____ **1.** The Inuits made use of their environment to provide themselves with homes, clothing, and food.

_____ **2.** The Inuit manner of eating raw flesh led the Ojibwa people to refer to them as "Eskimos."

_____ **3.** The Inuits had no special name for themselves.

_____ **4.** The environment led to the development of different life styles in coastal and inland areas.

104

Enrichment:
Change Comes to the Inuits

For many centuries, the Inuit way of life remained unchanged. Then, the last part of the 20th century brought about a great deal of change.

Some Inuits still build igloos for winter homes. Some still live in summer homes made of animal skins. But most Inuits of today live in homes made of more modern materials.

While there are still Inuits who use sleds and sled dogs, most now use snowmobiles.

Some Inuits still make by hand the warm, waterproof jackets of animal skins. Now most Inuits wear store-bought down jackets.

Even the Inuit snow goggles are being replaced. Light shining on the snow creates a strong glare. The goggles let people see without going snow blind. The old goggles used by the Inuits were made from walrus ivory and had thin slits to see through. They are now being replaced with goggles made in factories.

All the old things the Inuits used were made from things found in the environment. Most new things come from other places. The Inuits now need money and earn it. Many Inuits work in fish canning factories. Many of them work for people who are not Inuit. Some Inuit groups, however, have started their own businesses. Many of these businesses make things found in the environment.

Most Inuit children now go to school. They learn what other North American children learn.

The Inuits have borrowed ideas and ways of doing things from non-Inuits. Non-Inuits have also learned from the Inuits. For example, they have learned how to survive in an environment that is always cold. The Inuits know how to travel and survive in a frozen land.

In the changing Inuit world, there are now television sets and radios. There is food in cans and packages. There are modern cooking tools and games. In the winter, though, supplies cannot always be flown in. The rivers are frozen. Bringing supplies in over the frozen land is too expensive and too difficult. The Inuits and their non-Inuit neighbors then have to rely on many of the skills and customs that the Inuits have known for centuries.

Some Inuits now use airplanes and snowmobiles to carry supplies.
The Inuits shown here live in Canada.

The Early Native American People of North America

> **Understanding Global History**
>
> Think about the following statements as you read about the Native Americans in North America.
>
> **1** People use the environment to achieve economic goals.
>
> **2** Each of the social sciences focuses on different factors in the environment.
>
> **3** People should learn to understand and appreciate cultures different from their own.

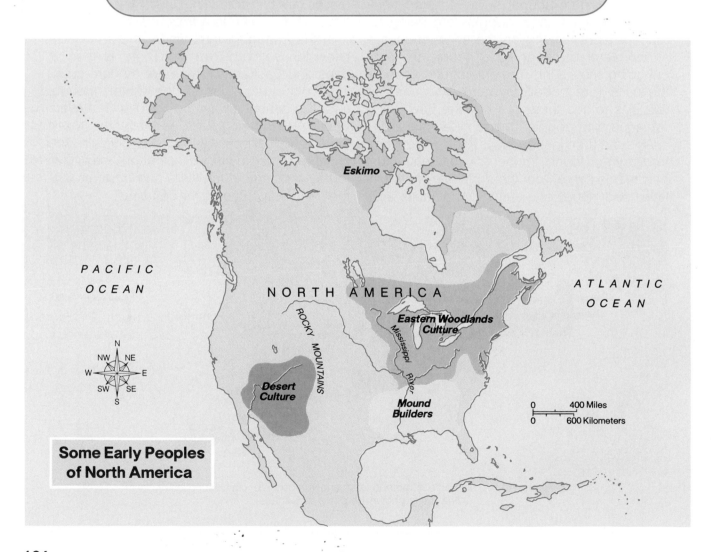

Some Early Peoples of North America

Learning New Words and Terms

The following words are used in this chapter. Think about the meaning of each one.

extinct: no longer existing
erosion: gradual wearing away of the soil

Think As You Read

1. What caused the hunting cultures of North America to disappear?
2. What were the purposes of the mounds built by the Eastern Woodlands people?
3. Who were the Cahokians and what were some elements of their civilization?

B.C.						A.D. 1200 Cahokian civilization flourishes	A.D. 1300 Anasazi move from their cliff houses A.D.
7500 B.C. Desert Culture develops			4000 B.C. Hohokam settle in Southwest				
7500	6000	4500	3000	1500			1500
							A.D. 1500 Cahokian civilization disappears

/dĭ zĕn/

Early North Americans

You have read that the first people in North America probably came from northeastern Asia. Their descendants are the people we know as Native Americans, or Indians. The Native Americans never developed a written language. Nor did they leave any written records. Therefore, we must depend upon the work of social scientists, especially archaeologists, to uncover their past.

You should recall that the Ice Ages lasted from about 1 million B.C. to about 25,000 B.C. The people who crossed from Asia arrived during the ending of the last Ice Age. The cool, wet climate that resulted left much of North America covered with thick, tall grass. Very large animals that are now **extinct** grazed upon the grass. Their skeletons have been found in many parts of the North American continent.

The early North American Indians lived by hunting these very large animals. Archaeologists have been able to identify different hunting cultures by the types of spear points they used. Similar kinds of spear points have been found in all parts of North and South America. This suggests trade and cultural diffusion, or spreading, among the different Indian cultures.

Desert Culture

The hunting cultures died out when the Ice Age glaciers moved back, far to the north. The climate changed and the large animals became extinct. As the hunting cultures died out, new cultures developed. These were the Desert Culture and the Eastern Woodlands Culture.

The Desert Culture existed in the areas that are now the western and southwestern sections of the United States. It developed about 7500 B.C. and was still in existence after A.D. 1500. The people of the Desert Culture depended mainly upon plant seeds and roots for food. They used baskets to carry these items from place to place. The Indians made stone tools to grind the roots and seeds into flour.

Two important Indian groups made their homes in the southwestern deserts. One group, the Hohokam, lived in the Arizona area from about 4000 B.C. to about 1100 B.C. They knew how to irrigate the land to grow crops in the dry desert.

The other group, the Anasazi, lived in the desert area of present-day New Mexico, Colorado, and Arizona. They lived in rooms carved out of cliffs and used irrigation for farming. They created pottery, wove cloth, and made baskets.

/ˈfæktəri/ ɖɔ gɔ̃w

107

The Anasazi of the Desert Culture carved out apartments from the sides of cliffs.

Some time around A.D. 1300 the Anasazi moved from their cliff homes. Experts believed that **erosion,** or the wearing away, of nearby river beds made irrigation impossible. With their system of farming destroyed, the Anasazi were forced to move to new lands.

Eastern Woodlands Culture

The Eastern Woodlands Culture was located in the midwestern and eastern regions of the present United States (see map, p. 106). These people are often called Mound Builders because of the huge mounds of earth they built throughout the area. Most of the mounds were used as burial places or for religious purposes. Archaeologists have found thousands of these burial mounds. Inside the mounds they found jewels, tools, and weapons. These hand-made objects show us that the Mound Builders had highly developed artistic skills.

Building large earthen mounds obviously required a great deal of effort by many people. First, earth had to be scraped out by hand. The Native Americans had no picks or shovels. Then, the earth had to be carried in a basket to the area where the mound was being built. There were no wagons or carts. You can imagine why it must have taken many years to build each mound.

This picture shows the Great Serpent Mound in Ohio. It was built by the people of the Eastern Woodlands Culture.

The Hohokam were able to farm the dry lands of the Southwest region.

Many different kinds of mounds were built. Some are in the shape of animals. One in Ohio, the Great Serpent Mound, is more than 1,300 feet (396 meters) long and about 150 feet (45 meters) high. It has the shape of a snake. Building such a mound required a great deal of cooperation. At least some form of government probably resulted from such teamwork.

The Cahokians

The last Mound Builder culture developed in the Mississippi River area. It seems to have been more advanced than earlier Mound Builder settlements. One of the main groups in this culture was the Cahokian (ka-HO-ki-an) civilization. It was located in the area that is now the city of East St. Louis, Illinois.

The first Cahokians probably lived in small villages. Each one was ruled by a local chief. From about A.D. 700 to A.D. 900 more people moved into the area. Over the years, they developed more advanced methods of farming. Eventually, a civilization arose.

The Cahokian people built a large capital city. The "Great Pyramid" was located in its central plaza. A temple was located at the flattened top of this huge structure. Many other mounds were also built within the city. Cahokian leaders placed their homes and their temples on these mounds. By A.D. 1100, thousands of people lived in the capital city. This was 400 years before Europeans first came to the Americas.

Cahokian Tools and Trade

Cahokian tools were crude, but they included scrapers, hoes, and axes. Tools, spear tips, and arrowheads were made of stone. The Cahokians used canoes but had no wheeled carts or wagons. Nor did they use animals to carry goods. People had to carry things on their backs.

The Cahokians traded tools, weapons, jewelry, and food with people who lived hundreds of miles away. While trading with different Indian groups the Cahokians also exchanged a number of ideas and inventions.

The Cahokian civilization reached its high point during the 1200s A.D. Then it began to decline. By A.D. 1500, the civilization disappeared completely. Nothing remained but the mounds of this once great civilization. The decline and disappearance of the Mound Builders is an unsolved mystery of the North American continent.

Exercises

A. Finding the Main Ideas:
Put a check next to the sentences that give the main ideas of what you have just read.

_____ **1.** Mound building was an important part of the eastern culture of North America.

_____ **2.** Temples were built on mounds.

_____ **3.** The Great Serpent mound is located in Ohio.

_____ **4.** The first people to come to the Americas led a nomadic life.

_____ **5.** The Cahokians had an advanced Mound Builder civilization.

B. What Did You Read?
Choose the answer that best completes each sentence. Write the letter of your answer in the space provided.

_____ **1.** The Mound Builders were found
   a. mainly in the southwestern areas of North America.
   b. in the midwestern and eastern regions of the present-day United States.
   c. in all parts of the Americas.
   d. mainly in desert areas.

_____ **2.** The Desert Culture people depended mainly upon
   a. fishing and hunting.
   b. trade and tool making.
   c. farming and hunting.
   d. gathering plant seeds and roots.

_____ **3.** For transportation the Cahokians used
   a. animals.
   b. canoes.
   c. wheeled vehicles.
   d. kayaks.

_____ **4.** The mounds built by Indians were used as all of the following *except*
   a. burial places.
   b. bases for temples and homes.
   c. religious structures.
   d. schools.

C. Checking for Details:
Read each statement. Put a T in the space next to each statement if it is true. Put an F in that space if it is false. Put an N if you tell from the reading if it is true or false.

_____ **1.** The Cahokians built homes and temples on the mounds in their city.

110

_____ **2.** The first Cahokians were ruled by local chiefs.

_____ **3.** Building a mound took many years.

_____ **4.** The early North American Indians were farmers, not hunters.

_____ **5.** The Great Pyramid of the Cahokians was located in a central plaza of their capital city.

_____ **6.** The largest number of Mound Builders lived in the midwestern region of the United States.

_____ **7.** The Cahokians traded a great deal.

D. Remembering What You Have Read:

Use the following words to complete each sentence below.

cliff   Cahokian   shovels   Eastern Woodlands   wagons   canoes

1. The _____ Cultures are known today as the Mound Builders.

2. The Cahokians used _____ for transportation.

3. The Mound Builders had no _____, picks, or _____.

4. The _____ civilization existed in the area that is today East St. Louis.

5. The homes of the Anasazi were _____ dwellings.

E. Vocabulary Skills:

Match each word or name in Column A with the correct meaning or identification in Column B. Write the letter of each answer in the space provided.

Column A   Column B

_____ **1.** extinct   **a.** wearing away of the soil

_____ **2.** erosion   **b.** lived in what is today Arizona

_____ **3.** Anasazi   **c.** home

_____ **4.** Hohokam   **d.** no longer in existence

                                          e. lived in present-day New Mexico, Colorado, and Arizona

F. Understanding Global History:

On page 106, you read about three factors in global history. Which of these factors applies to each statement listed below? Fill in the number of the correct statement on page 106 in the space provided. If no factor applies, fill in the word NONE.

_____ **1.** Archaeologists can identify different hunting cultures by the spear points they used.

_____ **2.** The Cahokians built a large number of earth mounds in which they buried their dead.

_____ **3.** The Anasazi people lived in cliff dwellings and used irrigation for farming.

The Mesoamerican Maya Civilization

> ## Understanding Global History
>
> Think about the following statements as you read about the Mayas.
>
> 1. The physical environment can encourage or restrict contact among people.
> 2. The culture in which we live influences our view of other people.
> 3. Contact among peoples and nations can lead to cultural changes.

The Mayas built many cities in the Yucatan. This picture shows a pyramid with a temple at the top. The pyramid is in the Maya city of Uxmal.

Learning New Words and Terms

The following words are used in this chapter. Think about the meaning of each one.

peninsula: a piece of land nearly surrounded by water

social structure: basis of personal and family relations in society

Think As You Read

1. Where was the civilization of the Mayas located?
2. What form of government existed among the Mayas?
3. What forms of transportation were used by the Mayas?
4. How did the Spaniards view the Mayas?

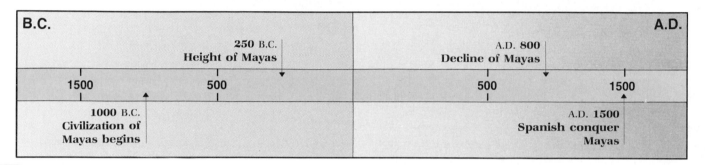

B.C.						A.D.
		250 B.C. **Height of Mayas**		**A.D. 800** **Decline of Mayas**		
1500	500		500		1500	
1000 B.C. **Civilization of Mayas begins**					**A.D. 1500** **Spanish conquer Mayas**	

The Mayas in Mesoamerica

Mesoamerica refers to the land that is today Mexico and Central America. As you can see from the map on page 114, this area connects North and South America. Several Indian civilizations developed in this part of the Americas. One group was the Mayas (MY-yuhz). They settled in the Yucatán **peninsula** in southern Mexico (see map, p. 114). The civilization of the Mayas began sometime before 1000 B.C. However, it was strong between the years 250 B.C. and A.D. 800. During this period there were nearly two million Mayas.

The Mayas built great stone cities in the jungle areas where they settled. They created a stepped-pyramid similar to the ziggurats of Sumer. The Mayas were also skilled in mathematics. They developed a calendar to help them set accurate dates for planting crops. Like some other early peoples, the Mayas had a system of writing. They used symbols and pictures to write in books and to carve on stone. Unfortunately, nearly all of their books were destroyed by the Spanish conquerors who invaded the region. Thus only part of the Mayas' written language is understood by social scientists today.

Maya City-States

The Mayas did not have a single kingdom or empire. Instead, they lived in a number of city-states ruled by chiefs and priests. Most of the people were in the lower classes, however. They worked as corn farmers or as crafts workers in the cities. The lower classes received almost no education. Their task was to serve the well-educated rulers. *1 ʃtæʃū I eʒovɔ*

The people of Mesoamerica worshipped their own gods. This is a statue of a Maya god.

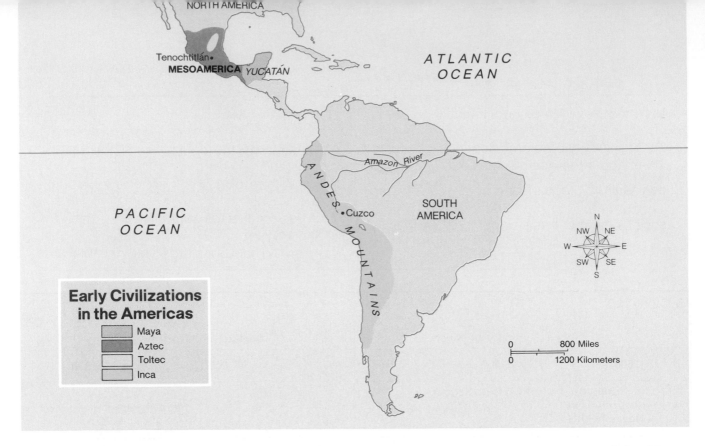

Early Civilizations
in the Americas

- Maya
- Aztec
- Toltec
- Inca

The Maya city-states were connected by wide, well-built stone roads. These roads were used only by people traveling on foot. There were no wheeled vehicles although the Mayas did know about the wheel. They even put wheels on children's toys. Still, they did not use wagons or carts because they had no animals to pull them.

Travel and Trade

Much of the travel done by the Mayas was by canoe. Small canoes were used for river travel. Larger canoes were used when going out to sea for longer voyages. The Mayas traded with one another and with people who lived far from the Yucatán peninsula. Since they had no wagons or carts they had to depend on water for transportation. As the Mayas sailed the seas for adventure and trade, they learned about the cultures of many neighboring lands.

The Rise and Fall of the Mayas

The civilization of the Mayas went through several stages. As you know, it began before 1000 B.C. and reached a peak about 250 B.C. For more than a thousand years (250 B.C. to about A.D. 800) the civilization of the Mayas prospered. This time was known as the Classic Period. It was during this period that the Mayas built groups of buildings, developed a system of mathematics, and created an accurate calendar.

Around A.D. 800, the civilization of the Mayas began to decline. For reasons that remain unclear, people began to leave the great cities. They moved inland toward the highland areas. During the next 700 years the Maya civilization changed. Many new ideas were introduced from the people of present-day Guatemala and Mexico. At the same time, there were frequent periods of civil war. Harsh weather conditions, such as hurricanes or periods of reduced rainfall, also may have led to the decline of the Mayas.

The Spanish Conquer the Mayas

In the early 1500s, Spanish explorers conquered the Mayas. They quickly destroyed what remained of this once proud Indian civilization. The Spanish settlers looked down upon the Mayas and their culture. They judged the Mayas on the basis of European standards. And they made no effort to understand their way of life.

The Spanish regarded the religions and customs of the Indian civilizations as inferior. They wanted to replace these practices with Christianity. As a result, the Spanish destroyed the languages and the **social structure** of the Native Americans. Two very different cultures had met in the Yucatán peninsula. The European Spanish culture flourished while the culture of the Mayas was destroyed.

Exercises

A. Finding the Main Ideas:

Put a check next to the sentences that give the main ideas of what you have just read.

_____ **1.** There are many rivers in the Yucatán peninsula.

_____ **2.** The Mayas made many contributions to society.

_____ **3.** The written language of the Mayas was very advanced.

_____ **4.** The civilization of the Mayas prospered for many years but eventually was destroyed.

B. What Did You Read?

Choose the answer that best completes each sentence. Write the letter of your answer in the space provided.

_____ **1.** The Classic Period of the Mayas was from about
   a. 1000 B.C. to 250 B.C.
   b. 800 B.C. to A.D. 800.
   c. 250 B.C. to A.D. 800.
   d. A.D. 250 to A.D. 800.

_____ **2.** After A.D. 800, most Maya cities were located in
   a. the highlands of Yucatán.
   b. the lowlands of Yucatán.
   c. the Guatemala area.
   d. all parts of Mexico.

_____ **3.** At its peak, the population of the Mayas reached as high as
   a. one million.
   b. two million.
   c. four million.
   d. five million.

_____ **4.** The civilization of the Mayas made use of all of the following *except*
   a. a reliable calendar.
   b. wheeled vehicles.
   c. a written language.
   d. canoes.

_____ **5.** The Spanish regarded the culture of the Mayas as
   a. better than their own.
   b. worth preserving.
   c. inferior to their own.
   d. none of these.

C. Checking for Details:

Read each statement. Put a T in the space next to each statement if it is true. Put an F in that space if it is false. Put an N if you cannot tell from the reading if the statement is true or false.

_____ **1.** The Mayas had few wise rulers.

_____ **2.** The wheel was important to the Mayas.

_____ **3.** Lower-class Mayas received almost no education.

_____ **4.** Most Mayas were happy with their system of government.

_____ **5.** The Mayas depended upon water transportation to carry on their trade.

_____ **6.** The Mayas did not understand the importance of democracy.

_____ **7.** The Mayas respected the cultures of other Indian groups.

_____ **8.** The Spanish destroyed the culture of the Mayas.

_____ **9.** The Mayas were ruled by a powerful king.

_____ **10.** Mayan roads were wide, well-built, and made of stone.

D. Word Meanings:

Match each word in Column A with the correct meaning in Column B. Write the letter of each answer in the space provided.

Column A

_____ **1.** Mayas
_____ **2.** peninsula
_____ **3.** social structure

Column B

a. a piece of land nearly surrounded by water
b. a domesticated animal
c. a people of Mesoamerica
d. basis of personal and family relations in society

E. Understanding Global History:

On page 112, you read about three factors in global history. Which of these factors applies to each statement listed below? Fill in the number of the correct statement on page 112 in the space provided.

_____ **1.** After A.D. 800, the Mayas were influenced by the people of present-day Guatemala and Mexico.

_____ **2.** The Mayas used canoes for travel on the nearby rivers and oceans.

_____ **3.** Nearly all the books written by the Mayas were destroyed by Spanish conquerors.

Enrichment:
The Great City of Tikal

Tikal (te-KAL) was the greatest of all Maya cities. Tikal, like most Maya cities, was built and rebuilt several times. The great time for Tikal, though, was in the 700s A.D. Then something happened by A.D. 900. The great city of Tikal had almost disappeared.

Tikal is in what is now the country of Guatemala. At its greatest period, the city may have been one of the finest cities in the entire world. People from all over the Maya empire came to Tikal to buy and sell goods. Cacao beans (which are used to make chocolate today) were used for money. People bought and sold food, cloth, and wood. But some people traded one kind of goods for another. They also traded animals and handmade goods.

Tikal's buildings probably amazed the traders visiting the city for the first time. There were temples and ball courts. There were government buildings and palaces. There were also pyramids. In addition, Tikal had several large market places and a great plaza used for ceremonies. The city had several reservoirs to supply drinking water to the people that lived there.

Just outside the city of Tikal were small farms for some of the people who grew food for the city. The city itself had a ruler and priests and noble families. Tikal also had architects and builders and artists.

Most of what we know about Tikal and other Maya cities comes from the Mayas themselves. They wrote their own history. The Mayas carved their history on stone pillars and used picture symbols called glyphs. They carved pictures of their rulers and the dates of rule on their pyramids and other buildings.

The Mayas also kept a calendar. People who study the Mayas today know how to read their calendar. People also know what year in our time a year in the Maya calendar represents. That is how scientists know that the last stone pillar carved in Tikal was carved in the year A.D. 811.

What happened to Tikal and the nearly 40,000 people who lived there? Why did people stop living in and near this great city? Why was Tikal covered with jungle growth until scientists started to dig and discover? Scientists are still trying to discover the answers to these questions about Tikal.

The Mayas were skilled builders. This picture shows the stonework in a Maya building.

The Mesoamerican Aztec Civilization

Understanding Global History

Think about the following statements as you read about the Aztecs.

1. The culture in which we live influences our view of other people.
2. Nations borrow and adapt ideas and institutions from other nations.
3. Physical surroundings, community, and culture make up the total environment.

The snake was a symbol of life to the Aztecs. This snake is made of turquoise, a semi-precious stone.

Learning New Words and Terms

The following words are used in this chapter. Think about the meaning of each one.

tribute: forced payment by one nation to another

supreme: highest in importance or rank

legend: a story handed down over the years

ruthless: without pity; cruel

heathens: people who do not believe in God

Think As You Read

1. Who were the Aztecs and when was their civilization founded?
2. What was the basis of Aztec power?
3. Why was Aztec power too weak to hold out against the Spanish invaders?
4. Who was the leader of the Spanish conquerors?
5. How did the Spanish view the culture of the Aztecs?

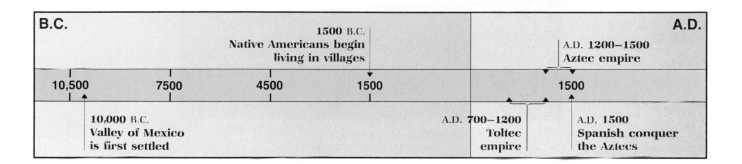

The Aztecs in Mesoamerica

You have already read about the civilization of the Mayas in the Yucatán peninsula. Another Indian civilization was to develop farther north in the valley area of Mexico. This area of Mexico was first settled around 10,000 B.C. by groups of Native Americans. Small farm villages developed along the valley sometime around 1500 B.C.

By A.D. 300, one Indian group had developed its own civilization. Experts know little about this early civilization except that it was destroyed around A.D. 700.

At about the same time, an Indian group called the Toltecs (tol-TECKS) established themselves in the central part of Mexico. The Toltecs flourished until their territory was invaded by the Aztecs (AZ-tecks) around A.D. 1200. The Aztecs were Native Americans who had pushed their way into central Mexico from the north. They had no lands they could occupy and had to settle on an island in Lake Texcoco. It was here that they built their capital city of Tenochtitlán (tay-nohk-tee-TLAHN) around A.D. 1325.

Aztec Life

The Aztecs were very warlike people. Their weapons included spears, bows and arrows, and wood swords with sharp stone edges. With these weapons, and their good military organization, they defeated their neighbors, including the Toltecs.

The Aztecs were feared and hated by those whom they conquered. Despite this, the power of the Aztecs grew until they were able to force their way of life upon others. The Aztecs collected **tribute** from the people they conquered. This tribute took the form of gold, turquoise (a semi-precious stone), corn, animals, and slaves. Gold played an important part in the Aztec culture. But, as you will read, it also helped bring about their downfall.

Aztec life was organized around a number of clans. Each clan had its own chief and council of elders. The government of the Aztecs was led by an emperor and a **supreme** council. One person from each clan was a member of the supreme council. The council advised the emperor and

119

Aztec artists were skilled in carving and sculpting. This statue is of an Aztec god.

helped select a new leader when there was a vacancy. The Aztec emperor was the highest military and religious leader.

When the Aztecs defeated the Toltecs they took over belief in one of the Toltec gods. Unlike the fierce gods of the Aztecs, this was a gentle god. There was a **legend** that this gentle god had been driven from the land but would return some day from the eastern sea. The god was said to have fair skin, blue eyes, and a long white beard. The Aztecs believed the legend was true.

The Spanish in Mexico

The Aztec empire was at its height when Spanish explorers entered Mexico in the early 1500s. Luck was with the Spanish. The Aztecs were puzzled when they saw the generally light-skinned Spanish for the first time. Perhaps the leader of these strangers might be the gentle god returning after many years. In fact, the leader of the Spanish was Hernando Cortés (kor-TEZ), a **ruthless** adventurer.

Cortés had only a small force of soldiers, a few cannons, and several horses. The Aztec emperor, Montezuma (mahn-tuh-ZOO-muh), commanded forces that greatly outnumbered the Spanish. But Montezuma was unsure of himself. He finally decided to send Cortés gifts. Unfortunately for the Aztecs, he sent presents made of gold. Cortés and his men were greedy for as much gold as they could get. Thus, they made plans to capture Tenochtitlán with its vast wealth in gold.

The Spanish were few in number, but they had two important weapons. One was gunpowder. It terrified the Aztec warriors who had never seen guns of any kind. The second weapon was the horse—an animal never seen before in the Americas. To make matters worse, the Aztecs had many enemies. The surrounding peoples who had been paying tribute to the Aztecs eagerly joined Cortés and his men. Montezuma was unable to act and was finally taken prisoner by Cortés. The Spanish seized the treasure of the Aztecs and captured their capital city.

The Defeat of the Aztecs

For a time it seemed the Spanish would have no trouble controlling the Aztecs. However, an Aztec revolt resulted in the death of Montezuma. The new emperor was eager to renew the fight with the Spanish. Cortés was forced to flee, but he returned later with a small army. Again the enemies of the Aztecs rose in revolt and helped Cortés. The result was again the defeat of the Aztecs. The Spanish forces then proceeded to destroy the entire Aztec civilization.

The Spanish never understood the Aztec culture. They regarded it as inferior to the Spanish way of life. In the minds of Spanish explorers, the Aztecs were **heathens,** who were to be either converted or destroyed.

The Spanish, on the left, had horses, guns and cannons. They were able to defeat the Aztecs, on the right. The Native American allies of the Spanish are shown in the middle.

Exercises

A. Finding the Main Ideas:

Put a check next to the sentences that give the main ideas of what you have just read.

_____ **1.** The Aztecs established their power in the valley area of Mexico.

_____ **2.** The Aztec and Spanish cultures clashed in Mexico.

_____ **3.** Montezuma was the religious and political leader of the Aztecs.

_____ **4.** Aztec religious beliefs influenced the Aztecs' attitude toward the Spanish invaders.

_____ **5.** Tenochtitlán was the capital city of the Aztec empire.

B. What Did You Read?

Choose the answer that best completes each sentence. Write the letter of your answer in the space provided.

_____ **1.** The Aztecs took over part of central Mexico from the
  a. Spanish.
  b. family clans.
  c. Toltecs.
  d. supreme council.

_____ **2.** Tenochtitlán was
  a. the god of the Aztecs.
  b. a Toltec city.
  c. the capital city of the Aztecs.
  d. none of the above.

_____ **3.** The Aztec emperor was chosen by the
  a. warriors.
  b. priests.
  c. Spanish.
  d. supreme council.

_____ **4.** The Spanish victory over the Aztecs was aided by
  a. the use of horses by Cortés.
  b. Montezuma's poor leadership.
  c. the use of gunpowder by Cortés.
  d. all of the above.

C. Chronology and Time:

Choose the event that happened first in each group below. Write the letter of your answer in the space provided.

_____ **1. a.** the Toltec empire
   b. Native Americans settle in central Mexico
   c. the Aztec civilization

_____ **2. a.** early civilizations in Mexico
   b. the Toltec empire
   c. valley of Mexico settled

_____ **3. a.** Spanish conquer Aztecs
   b. the Toltec empire
   c. early civilizations in Mexico

D. Checking for Details:

Read each statement. Put an F in the space next to each statement if it is a fact. Put an O in that space if it is an opinion. Remember that facts can be proved, but opinions cannot.   :

_____ **1.** Cortés was able to defeat the Aztecs because his men used horses.

_____ **2.** Cortés's army was small in size.

_____ **3.** Montezuma was not a brave leader.

_____ **4.** The Aztecs were wrong to have invaded the territory of the Toltecs.

_____ **5.** Spain was mainly interested in Aztec gold.

_____ **6.** Spain never understood the Aztec culture.

_____ **7.** The Aztec civilization was in many ways more advanced than Spain's culture.

_____ **8.** The Aztecs had a poor system for selecting an emperor.

E. Behind the Headlines:

Each headline has a story behind it. Write three or four sentences that support or tell about each headline.

GODS OR MEN? WHO ARE THESE STRANGERS?

_____

_____

_____

EMPEROR SENDS GIFTS TO VISITORS

_____

_____

_____

GENERALS CLAIM NEW WEAPONS CAUSED DEFEAT

_____

_____

_____

CORTÉS GETS HELP FROM AZTEC ENEMIES

_____

_____

_____

F. Word Meanings:

Match each word in Column A with the correct meaning in Column B. Write the letter of each answer in the space provided.

Column A

_____ **1.** supreme
_____ **2.** legend
_____ **3.** ruthless
_____ **4.** heathen

Column B

a. an unbeliever
b. highest in importance or rank
c. filled with people
d. a story handed down over the years
e. without pity or mercy; cruel

G. Understanding Global History:

On page 118, you read about three factors in global history. Which of these factors applies to each statement listed below? Fill in the number of the correct statement on page 118 in the space provided.

_____ **1.** When they defeated the Toltecs, the Aztecs took over belief in one of the Toltec gods.

_____ **2.** The Aztecs finally settled on an island in the valley area of Mexico. Over the years, they extended their empire from this island area.

_____ **3.** The Spanish never understood the Aztec culture. They viewed it as inferior to their own culture.

Enrichment:
The Spanish and the Aztecs

Bernal Díaz del Castillo (DE-ath del kas-TE-lyo) was a Spanish historian who traveled with Hernando Cortés to Mexico in 1519. He wrote a history of the Spanish conquest of Mexico. A great deal of what we know about the Aztecs comes from the writings of Díaz del Castillo.

He reports that the Spanish were amazed at their first sight of Tenochtitlán. Some of the soldiers believed that the great city they saw before them was a dream. None of them had expected to see anything like the great towers of Tenochtitlán. They did not expect to find palaces and gardens of great riches. Even though the Spanish had heard of the gold of the Aztecs, they were not prepared for the actual sight of it.

While Díaz del Castillo and the other Spaniards were amazed by the Aztec riches, they were also shocked by human sacrifice. Although the Spanish were accustomed to death in war and to some kinds of cruelty in their own country, they could not believe the numbers of human skulls the Aztecs had piled up in some places. Díaz del Castillo guessed that he saw more than 100,000 human skulls in one place.

The Aztecs kept their own records, but nothing in them explains why they believed in human sacrifice. Aztec records show that they were a people who conquered others in war, but they did not really make the other people a part of their empire. Aztec rule brought wealth to the Aztecs, but it brought nothing to the conquered people. Of course, the conquered people hated the Aztec rule.

The Aztecs had not ruled very long when the Spanish came and conquered them. Montezuma was only the ninth Aztec to rule the empire. At first, the Spanish were surprised when the people ruled by the Aztecs helped the Spanish. Once they learned about how the Aztecs had treated the conquered people, they were no longer surprised.

Aztec records have told us some of what Bernal Díaz del Castillo did not know. Maps of Aztec farms tell us a lot about their system of irrigated farming. These irrigated farms could often produce about seven crops a year. Aztec paintings tell us a great deal about Aztec ceremonies and religion.

Together, the Spanish and the Aztecs have given us an excellent picture of the world of the Aztecs before it was destroyed.

The Spanish fighting the Aztecs.

Chapter 14

The South American Inca Civilization

Understanding Global History

Think about the following statements as you read about the Incas.

1 Physical surroundings, community, and culture make up the total environment.
2 People use the environment to achieve economic goals.
3 The culture in which we live influences our view of other people.
4 Contact among peoples and nations can lead to cultural changes.

This picture shows the ruins of the Inca city of Machu Picchu. Notice the high peaks of the Andes Mountains.

Learning New Words and Terms

The following words are used in this chapter. Think about the meaning of each one.

totalitarianism: a system in which the government has total power over the lives of the people

terraced farming: farming on a flat, raised piece of land

Think As You Read

1. Where was the Inca civilization located?
2. How were the Inca people organized?
3. What caused the downfall of the Inca civilization?
4. How did the Spanish regard the Native American civilization?
5. How did the Spanish treat the defeated Incas?

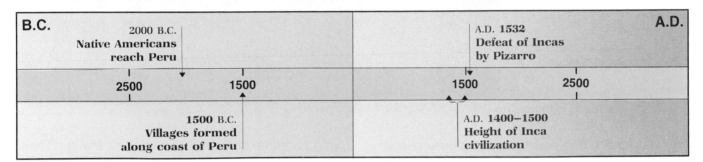

B.C.				A.D.

2000 B.C.
Native Americans reach Peru

A.D. 1532
Defeat of Incas by Pizarro

2500   1500   1500   2500

1500 B.C.
Villages formed along coast of Peru

A.D. 1400–1500
Height of Inca civilization

The Inca Empire

While the Aztecs were building an empire in Mexico, another group of Indians was creating an empire in South America. This group was the Incas. The Inca empire stretched for about 2,500 miles (4,023 kilometers) from what is today Ecuador, through Peru, Bolivia, Chile, and Argentina.

The Incas built great cities high on top of the Andes mountains. One of the cities was Machu Picchu. It was built more than 8,000 feet (about 2,438 meters) above sea level. Only the ruins of this ancient city remain today.

The Inca civilization developed in the fertile valleys of the Andes Mountain range. The first Incas probably came to Peru about 2000 B.C. By about 1500 B.C., people were beginning to live in villages along the coast of Peru.

Over the years, the civilization of the Incas grew. By the late 1400s A.D, the empire had become large and prosperous. Its center was located around the capital city of Cuzco. This city rested in a mountain area 11,000 feet (2,352 meters) above sea level.

Inca Religion and Government

The Incas worshipped many gods but the sun god was the most important. The ruler of the Incas was viewed as a child of the sun god. His title—the ruler was always a man—was *Inca*. The Inca was an absolute ruler. He had complete power.

The Inca, center, was the name of the ruler of the Incas. His cloak has a sun symbol. The symbol of the sun also appears on his helmet.

The Temple of the Sun was sacred to the Incas.

Because an Inca had several wives and many children choosing a new Inca often created a problem. Only one son could become the new ruler. Not surprisingly, the sons of the Inca often fought bitterly with each other for control. These constant disputes helped lead to the downfall of the Incas.

The Inca empire was governed by a small group of nobles. Some of the nobles were related to the Inca. Others were former leaders of areas that had been conquered by Inca armies.

Inca Society

Below the nobles in the Inca empire were the great mass of people. They had no power and had to obey the orders of the Inca and his nobles. Life for most of the Incas was difficult. They were told where and when to plant crops and what share they had to give to the Inca and the nobles. The people were required to build roads, bridges, palaces, and temples. In addition, they were forced to serve as warriors in times of war.

Every person in the empire was supposed to work. In return, the government made sure that each person had food, clothing, and shelter. This system of total control by a government is called **totalitarianism.** The Incas lived in a totalitarian society that left little room for personal freedom.

Most people in Inca society remained in the class into which they were born. Still, some women were able to improve their status. They could become priests along with men. Or they might become the wife of a nobleman. Many young women were also trained as weavers of fine fabrics. These fabrics were used by the Inca and the wealthy nobles.

Inca Achievements

The Incas were skilled farmers and engineers. They used the hillsides to carry on **terraced farming.** The terraces were built one above the other for thousands of feet. Inca farmers grew mainly corn and white potatoes. Both of these foods were unknown in Europe until they were brought back by explorers.

The Incas built great cities. They put up fortresses and laid down wide roads. Temples and palaces were built on the sides of the steep slopes of the Andes. The Incas used huge stone blocks and fitted them together without the use of cement. Because the Incas did not use wheeled vehicles, the huge stones were probably moved along on log rollers by slaves and workers.

Although the Inca empire stretched for hundreds of miles, the rulers were able to maintain complete control. One reason was that excellent roads and bridges linked the capital city of Cuzco to all parts of the empire. These roads were used by special runners since the Incas had no carts or wagons. A series of runners could carry messages from one end of the Inca empire to the other.

In addition to the system of rapid communication, the stone fortresses built by the Incas helped give them control over the areas they conquered. Throughout the day and night, someone stood guard along the top of each structure. When an enemy approached the fortress, the Incas prepared for attack.

Inca Power Grows

The power of the Incas grew as they took over neighboring lands. They soon extended their skills as farmers, weavers, and builders to many new areas. Within the empire the Incas trained large numbers of young men to serve as artisans. Over the years, they became skilled in the use of copper, silver, and gold. To keep them supplied with enough gold, the Inca demanded that large amounts of the precious metal be brought to Cuzco from all parts of the empire.

The Incas used gold to decorate palaces and to make art objects. They even ate from gold plates and drank from gold cups. As you will read, this treasure in gold later excited the greed of the Spanish explorers.

The Defeat of the Incas

By the time the first Spanish arrived in 1528, the ruler of the Incas was losing his power. Four years later, a small force led by Francisco Pizarro (pi-ZAR-o), crushed the huge Inca army. The horses, guns, and cannons of the Spanish terrified the Incas. They had never seen such things before. To make matters worse, two sons of the Inca upset the government as they fought bitterly for the right to the throne.

Finally, Pizarro killed the Inca and many of his nobles. Without an Inca to give orders, the entire system of government fell apart. The Spanish swiftly crushed the once great Inca empire.

As you have read, the Spanish regarded the Native Americans as inferiors. They forced the Incas to do the worst kinds of work. They even forced the Incas to become slaves.

Inca goldsmiths created many beautiful objects out of gold. This is a gold mask.

Exercises

A. Finding the Main Ideas:

Put a check next to the sentences that give the main ideas of what you have just read.

_____ **1.** Cuzco was the Inca capital.

_____ **2.** The Inca was an absolute ruler.

_____ **3.** Some Inca women married nobles.

_____ **4.** The Incas lived in a totalitarian society.

_____ **5.** Spain destroyed the Inca culture.

B. What Did You Read?

Choose the answer that best completes each sentence. Write the letter of your answer in the space provided.

_____ **1.** People obeyed the Inca because he
   a. was an old man.
   b. had little power.
   c. had absolute power.
   d. was cruel.

_____ **2.** The ordinary people of the Inca civilization had to
   a. serve as warriors.
   b. plant crops where and when they were told to.
   c. build roads and bridges.
   d. do all of the above.

_____ **3.** The Inca people were all of the following *except*
   a. farmers.
   b. road builders.
   c. conquerors.
   d. hunters.

_____ **4.** Pizarro used all of the following to defeat the Incas *except*
   a. guns.
   b. horses.
   c. cannons.
   d. fire.

C. Who Were These People?

Name the person or people described in each of the following sentences. Write your answer in the space provided.

_____ **1.** I was called the child of the sun god.

_____ **2.** We helped govern the Inca state.

_____ **3.** We served as warriors for the Inca.

_____ **4.** We carried messages from place to place.

_____ **5.** We were skilled in the use of gold, silver, and copper.

_____ **6.** We were trained as skilled weavers.

_____ **7.** We wanted all the gold in the Inca empire.

D. Checking for Details:

Read each statement. Put a T in the space next to each statement if it is true. Put an F in that space if it is false. Put an N if you cannot tell from the reading if the statement is true or false.

_____ **1.** The Incas were more advanced than the Aztecs.

_____ **2.** The Incas built fortresses and roads.

_____ **3.** The Incas learned about corn and potatoes from the Europeans.

_____ **4.** The Incas lived in a totalitarian society.

_____ **5.** Machu Picchu was an Inca city.

_____ **6.** The death of the Inca was one reason for the collapse of the Inca empire.

_____ **7.** Cuzco was larger than any city in Spain.

_____ **8.** The youngest son of the Inca inherited the throne.

_____ **9.** The stone fortresses of the Incas helped them control the areas they conquered.

_____ **10.** The Incas used the wheel to help move huge stones.

E. Word Meanings:

Match each word in Column A with the correct meaning in Column B.

Column A

_____ **1.** totalitarianism
_____ **2.** absolute ruler
_____ **3.** terrace

Column B

a. to become less powerful
b. a system in which the government has total power
c. someone who has complete control
d. flat, raised piece of land

F. Understanding Global History:

On page 126, you read about four factors in global history. Which of these factors applies to each statement listed below? Fill in the number of the correct statement on page 126 in the space provided.

_____ **1.** The Inca civilization arose in the fertile valleys of the Andes Mountains.

_____ **2.** The Inca conquerors spread their ideas and their customs to the people of the eastern coast of South America.

_____ **3.** The Incas used the hillsides for terraced farming.

_____ **4.** The Spanish destroyed the Inca civilization—a civilization they regarded as pagan and inferior to their own culture.

Enrichment:
The Mystery of the Inca Quipus

The Incas built a great series of roads through their land. Many of these roads were high above the land. Special messengers carried information from one stopping place to another. When a messenger reached a stopping place, he would turn over his information to the next messenger. The messengers had a special form of message to carry. The message was in the form of a *quipu* (KE-poo).

The quipu was set of cords or strings. The knots in each cord were a kind of code. The code kept records of amounts. Sometimes the amounts were of food or other supplies. Sometimes they were records of the number of people available to do a kind of work. The quipu were kept in storage places and in government buildings. They were considered to be of great importance.

The code message of the quipu was very complicated. Smaller cords or strings were attached to a main cord. Different colors and sizes of string were part of the code. The position of the string on the main cord was also part of the code. Then, of course, the knots were an important part of the code.

We do not know too much about these Inca codes. But we do know that most of the Inca's record-keeping was based on the decimal system.

The Inca runners who carried the quipus did not know how to read the codes. Their job was to carry the messages, not to read them. Only special officials were trained to read the quipus' secrets. Since there was no written Inca language, the quipus were the most important records the Inca rulers had. The officials who could read the quipus were very important people.

Although some scientists have tried, they have not yet discovered the code of the Inca quipus. Some old quipus still remain, but nobody has been able to read all their secrets.

People who live in the Andes today use something like a quipu. They live in places where the Incas once ruled. The farmers who live in the region use some form of knotted ropes to keep their own records. Perhaps by studying the ways of the Andean farmers today, scientists may be able to unlock the mystery of the Inca quipus.

The Incas built roads throughout their empire. Some of the Inca roads still remain. This picture shows a road in present-day Cuzco. Inca messengers probably carried quipus along this road.

Unit 3

The Emergence of the
Modern World

Ways of thinking and acting changed from the time of the earliest civilizations. In time, a modern world emerged. You will read about the beginning of the modern world in Unit 3.

As you read about life in ancient Greece, you will learn why our world owes so much to the early Greeks. Democracy—"rule by the people"—began in the Greek city-state of Athens.

The next civilization you will explore is that of ancient Rome. You will learn how Rome grew from a city-state into a vast empire. You will also learn how the influence of Rome continues today.

After the fall of Rome, Europe entered a time called the Middle Ages. As you read, you will learn why Europe was divided into many small kingdoms. You will also explore why contacts between people were limited at this time.

While Europe was disunited, a new force rose up in the Middle East. This was the religion of Islam. You will learn about the beliefs and teachings of Islam in this unit.

During the 1400s and 1500s, a rebirth of learning took place in Europe. This time was called the Renaissance. People took a new interest in the world around them. Schools grew as more people sought learning. One school is shown in the picture opposite. New faiths also emerged during the 1500s.

Slowly, Europe moved into modern times. Cities grew as trade and industry expanded. The interest in trade led to an Age of Discovery. You will learn how, in the late 1400s, and early 1500s, explorers discovered lands outside of Europe.

In Unit 3, you will read the following chapters:

Chapter 1

The Civilization of Ancient Greece

Understanding Global History

Think about the following statements as you read about the civilization of the early Greeks.

1 The physical environment can encourage or limit contact among people.

2 Present culture is shaped by the past.

3 Contact among peoples and nations can lead to cultural changes.

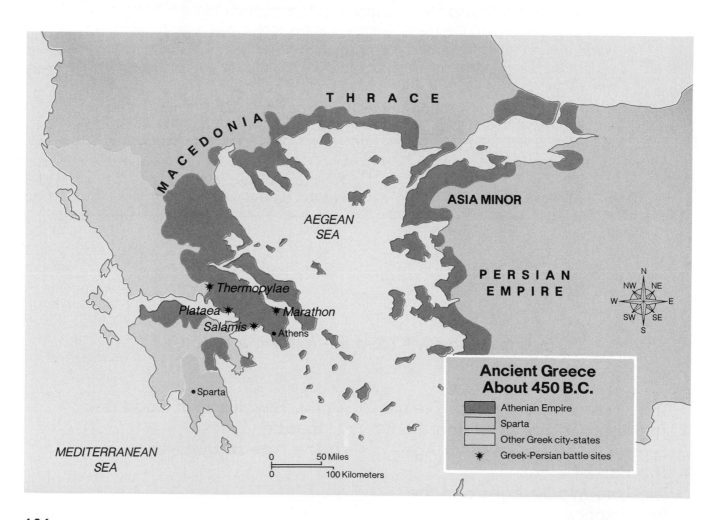

THRACE

MACEDONIA

ASIA MINOR

AEGEAN SEA

PERSIAN EMPIRE

* Thermopylae

Plataea * * Marathon
Salamis * • Athens

• Sparta

MEDITERRANEAN SEA

| 0 | | 50 Miles |
| 0 | | 100 Kilometers |

Ancient Greece About 450 B.C.

- Athenian Empire
- Sparta
- Other Greek city-states
- * Greek-Persian battle sites

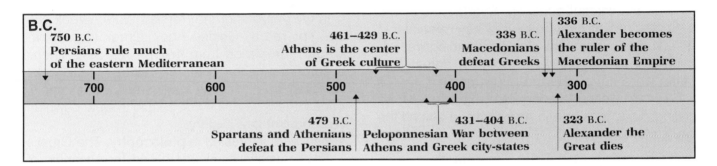

B.C.

750 B.C.
Persians rule much of the eastern Mediterranean

461–429 B.C.
Athens is the center of Greek culture

338 B.C.
Macedonians defeat Greeks

336 B.C.
Alexander becomes the ruler of the Macedonian Empire

700   600   500   400   300

479 B.C.
Spartans and Athenians defeat the Persians

431–404 B.C.
Peloponnesian War between Athens and Greek city-states

323 B.C.
Alexander the Great dies

A Civilization Develops in the Eastern Mediterranean

By now you have read about the rise of the first civilizations. These civilizations grew up in the river valleys of the Middle East, Africa, and Asia. Now you will read about another area—the eastern part of the Mediterranean Sea. You will find out about the civilization that grew up there—in Greece.

After about 750 B.C., a group of people called the Persians ruled much of the eastern Mediterranean. Their empire spread from Asia Minor to the Indus Valley. About 200 years later, a number of wars broke out between the Persians and the Greeks. The Greeks won these wars. During the 400s B.C. they built a great civilization.

The Geography of Early Greece

Early Greece was not a single, united country (see map, p. 136). Greece is made up of many small islands and peninsulas. The land is rugged and covered by mountains. Because of its geography, contacts between the people within Greece were limited. But Greece is located on the crossroads between Europe, Asia, and Africa. As a result, the Greeks took to the sea around them. They traded with other peoples and were influenced by different cultures.

Mountains separated the people of Greece. Cut off from each other, the early Greeks grouped themselves around city-states. The most important city-states were Athens and Sparta.

Two City-States—Athens and Sparta

Athens—The people of Athens had great thinkers, artists, business people, and traders. They also developed a form of government called **democracy.** The word democracy comes from the Greek words meaning "rule by the people." Every citizen of Athens had the right to vote and the right to speak at public meetings.

Citizens of Athens had responsibilities as well as rights, however. They had to promise to defend the city against its enemies. Citizens were also called upon to serve on juries or act as elected officials. Athenian youth were trained to become good citizens. They studied grammar, history, and the art of public speaking. A free exchange of ideas is one aspect of a democracy. Citizens of Athens were expected to take part in discussions and share their ideas on many issues.

But democracy in Athens was limited in many ways. It applied only to men who were citizens of Athens. Women did not have the right to vote, hold office, or own property. Slaves had no rights at all.

Sparta—The Spartans were very different from the people of Athens. Their government was not a democracy. Instead, the government was led by a small group of men. These men wanted Sparta to be a strong, military state. They wanted to rule the people they had taken over. To meet this end, they set down strict rules for all citizens.

Spartan boys left home at the age of seven to start army training. Their training was very hard. Spartan boys were given only a few pieces of clothing and a little food. They were expected to be strong and brave. They were also expected to take orders without question. Spartan men were kept in a kind of army reserve. They remained in reserve from youth until old age. Winning was all-important to the Spartans. Soldiers defeated in battle were not allowed to return home.

Spartan women were also expected to be strong. They took part in army drills to defend the city-state.

Greeks Unite Against the Persians

Around 550 B.C., the Persians began to add to their empire. They took over the Greek city-states along the coast of Asia Minor. Then, they attacked the mainland Greeks. In the first battle, the Athenians crushed the larger Persian force. But they knew the Persians would attack again. To survive, the Greek city-states would have to join together. So they put aside their differences, and the Spartans and the Athenians united to fight the Persians. These wars were called the Persian Wars. In 479 B.C., the Greeks completely defeated the mighty Persians. Persian armies never again invaded mainland Greece.

Greek Contributions

In the years after the Persian Wars, Greek culture entered a "Golden Age." Greek ideas flowered in the period from 461 to 429 B.C. Athens became the center of Greek culture. The Greeks achieved great things in many areas. For example,

- the Greeks were the first people to write down an account of their history.
- they were interested in **philosophy.** The Greeks asked questions about life and the meaning of human actions.
- the Greeks were skilled builders and sculptors.

Inside a Greek home. What kinds of activities are shown in the picture?

138

The Parthenon is one of the most famous buildings in the world. It was built in honor of Athena. She was the patron god of Athens.

The Parthenon (PAR-thuh-NAHN) in Athens is their most famous building. Greek statues show the human body in its most beautiful form.

- the Greeks studied mathematics and science.
- they were among the first people to study the causes of sickness.
- Greek scientists developed ideas about the stars and the planets. Although some of these ideas were later proved wrong, they were accepted for many years.
- the Greeks were the first people to write plays about how people think and act. The plays of the early Greeks are still performed today.

Athens and Sparta Fight

Athens became the leader of Greece as a result of the Persian Wars. It had provided a navy and good leadership. After the defeat of the Persians, however, Athenian leaders began to dream of riches and glory in other lands. They wanted to spread their power to the Middle East.

Other Greek city-states were against Athenian power. In 431 B.C., war broke out between Athens and its supporters and the other Greek city-states. This was called the Peloponnesian (pehl-uh-puh-NEE-shuhn) War. Sparta led the city-states that were fighting Athens. The war ended in 404 B.C., when an exhausted Athens gave up. By this time, all of Greece was disunited. Even though the Spartans had won, they could not bring all the city-states under their control.

Alexander Spreads Greek Culture

The Greek city-states were weakened because of their many wars. Also, at this time, a new power threatened Greece. North of Greece was a land called Macedonia (MASS-uh-DOH-nee-uh). (see map, p. 136.) In 359 B.C., Philip II became its king. After taking over many lands, Philip moved his army into Greece. For a while the Greeks were able to hold off the invaders. But in 338 B.C., the Greeks were finally conquered. Greece now became part of the Macedonian Empire. Two years later, Philip was killed. The job of spreading his empire fell to his 20-year-old son, Alexander.

In 334 B.C., Alexander brought his army together to fight the Persian Empire. After the defeat of the Persians, he marched his soldiers more than 11,000 miles (17,703 kilometers) east-ward into India. But Alexander's tired soldiers would go no further. Alexander was forced to turn back. He fell ill and died before he could return to Greece. He was 33 years old.

Before his death in 323 B.C., Alexander had conquered Asia Minor, Egypt, the Fertile Crescent, and Persia. During the 13 years of his rule Alexander spread Greek learning and culture to Eastern lands. He also adopted Eastern ways and customs. A new civilization developed from this blend of East and West.

Exercises

A. What Did You Read?
Choose the answer that best completes each sentence. Write the letter of your answer in the space provided.

_____ 1. The geography of Greece gave rise to
  a. clans.
  b. villages.
  c. city-states.
  d. farms.

_____ 2. The first democracy was in
  a. Egypt.
  b. Sparta.
  c. Athens.
  d. Persia.

_____ 3. In Athens, citizens were expected to
  a. serve on juries.
  b. discuss political matters.
  c. defend the city-state.
  d. do all of the above.

_____ 4. The Spartans were best known as
  a. philosophers.
  b. soldiers.
  c. artists.
  d. scientists.

B. Checking for Details:
Read each statement. Put a T in the space next to each statement if it is true. Put an F in that space if it is false. If the statement is false, rewrite it so that it is true.

_____ 1. The Greek city-states became closer to each other after the defeat of the Persians.

_____

_____ 2. The Athenians wanted to spread their power all through the Middle East.

_____

_____ 3. The Peloponnesian War took place between Greece and Macedonia.

_____

_____ 4. After 338 B.C., Greece was ruled by Macedonia.

_____

_____ 5. Alexander conquered the Persian Empire.

_____

_____ 6. Athens and Sparta joined together to defeat Persia.

_____

_____ 7. Macedonia was south of Greece.

_____

140

_____ **8.** Men and women were treated equally in Athens.

C. Complete the Sentence:
Fill in the word or term that best completes each statement below.

1. Victory over_____brought power to Athens.

2. Athens fought_____for control of Greece.

3. Greece was challenged by_____in the north.

4. The Greeks grouped themselves around _____.

5. The_____wanted to spread their power throughout the Middle East.

6. Philip II led_____to victory over Greece.

7. The leaders of_____wanted a strong state.

8. _____spread Greek culture to the lands he took over.

9. Spartan men served as_____from youth to middle age.

10. A form of government in which all citizens take part is known as a_____.

D. Behind the Headlines:
Write two or three sentences that support or tell about each of the following headlines. Use a separate piece of paper:

ATHENS AND SPARTA JOIN TOGETHER AGAINST PERSIA

ALEXANDER DIES AT THE AGE OF 33

ATHENS SEEKS TO SPREAD ITS POWER

E. Understanding Global History:
On page 136, you read about three factors in global history. Which of these factors applies to each statement listed below? Fill in the number of the correct statement on page 136 in the space provided. If no factor applies, fill in the word NONE.

_____ **1.** The Greeks contributed many ideas and inventions to later civilizations.

_____ **2.** Alexander brought Greek culture to the lands he took over.

_____ **3.** Athens and Sparta joined together to defeat Persia.

_____ **4.** Because of its rugged mountains, Greece was divided into many city-states.

Chapter 2

The Rise and Fall of Ancient Rome

Understanding Global History

Think about the following statements as you read about the rise and fall of ancient Rome.

1 Events occurring in one part of the world have influenced developments in other parts of the world.

2 Present culture is shaped by the past.

3 Contact among peoples and nations can lead to cultural changes.

4 Nations borrow and adapt ideas and institutions from other nations.

A man and woman of ancient Rome. The woman is holding a stylus. This was used to carve letters on tablets made of wax. The man is holding a scroll.

Learning New Words and Terms

The following words are used in this chapter. Think about the meaning of each one.

republic: a system of government in which citizens who have the right to vote choose their leaders.

Senate: the group of patrician Romans who passed the laws in the Roman Republic.

patricians: rich landowners who ran the government of Rome

plebeians: the common people of Rome

Think As You Read

1. What did the Romans learn from the Greeks, the Phoenicians, and the Etruscans?
2. Which groups of people made up Roman society? Which group held the most power? Why did they hold power?
3. What were some of the problems of Rome that led to its decline and fall?
4. How did Rome contribute to civilization?

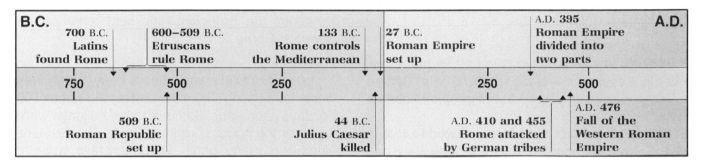

B.C.				A.D. 395	A.D.
700 B.C. Latins found Rome	**600–509 B.C.** Etruscans rule Rome	**133 B.C.** Rome controls the Mediterranean	**27 B.C.** Roman Empire set up	**Roman Empire divided into two parts**	
750	500	250		250	500
	509 B.C. Roman Republic set up	**44 B.C.** Julius Caesar killed	**A.D. 410 and 455** Rome attacked by German tribes	**A.D. 476** Fall of the Western Roman Empire	

Rome Is Founded

Around 1000 B.C., many peoples living in central Europe moved into the Italian peninsula (see map on this page). The Latins were the most important of these groups. They settled near the Tiber River and founded the city-state of Rome around 700 B.C.

Rome's location was a good one for trade and contacts with other peoples. It was on the west coast of Italy where land was good for farming. Ships could make their way up the Tiber River to drop off and pick up food. The Romans met Greeks and Phoenicians who had trading colonies in Sicily and Italy. From them the Romans learned about growing grapes and olives.

The Roman Republic

The Latins, or Romans, were farmers and herders. They were not warlike. As a result, they were defeated by a people called the Etruscans (ih-TRUHS-kuhnz). The Etruscans had settled north of the Tiber. About 600 B.C. they took over Rome. Etruscan kings ruled the Romans until 509 B.C. During this time, the Romans adopted the Etruscan alphabet and learned Etruscan building and farming skills.

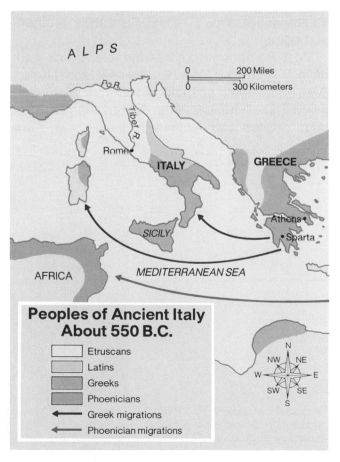

Peoples of Ancient Italy About 550 B.C.

- Etruscans
- Latins
- Greeks
- Phoenicians
- → Greek migrations
- → Phoenician migrations

After 509 B.C. Rome set up a **republic**. A republic is a system of government in which citizens who have the right to vote choose people to run the government. Two elected consuls headed the republic. They led the army and government. But consuls served only one year and therefore had little power. The real power was held by the **Senate.** Senators, the members of the Senate, were appointed by the consuls for life. The Senate passed the laws in the republic.

After freeing themselves from the Etruscans, the Romans built up a strong army. Soon they had control of all Italy. They then spread their power to other parts of the world. For more than 500 years, Rome defeated and ruled many lands and many groups of people.

Roman Society

Millions of people were ruled by Rome. However, not everyone was a citizen of Rome. Roman citizenship was only given to the people of certain defeated places.

Only adult male citizens were allowed to vote in Rome. Women had few rights, though they had more freedom than Greek women. Some even had great influence over their husbands, brothers, and sons.

Most Romans worked as farmers. In the early days of Rome the farms were small. Most farmers lived and worked on their own land. In later years, much of the land was taken over by the rich. Their huge estates were worked by slaves or by farmers who rented the land from the rich owners. As the number of people in Rome grew, so did its need for food. About one million people living in or near Rome had to get food and other goods from conquered lands.

As you have read, early Rome was a republic. Rich landowners, called **patricians** (puh-TRIHSH-uhnz), ran Rome. Only patricians were allowed to serve as consuls or sit in the Senate. They also held most of the government jobs. The common people were known as **plebeians** (pluh-BEE-uhnz). They had little voice in government. As time went on, the plebeians began to demand more rights. By about 250 B.C., the plebeians won the right to vote and to hold office in the republic. However, the patricians still held most of the power in Rome.

Daily Life

Daily life in Rome was always busy. When they were not working, Romans celebrated about 100 holidays each year. Some of these holidays were to honor the gods. Like the Greeks, the Romans worshiped many gods. Other holidays were to honor military heroes or conquests. Holiday fun often included chariot races. Over the years, these games became more violent. Some games had fighting. Trained fighters, called gladiators (GLAD-ee-AY-turz), sometimes fought animals. But they often fought each other. Crowds of Romans cheered as the fights ended with the death of one or both of the gladiators.

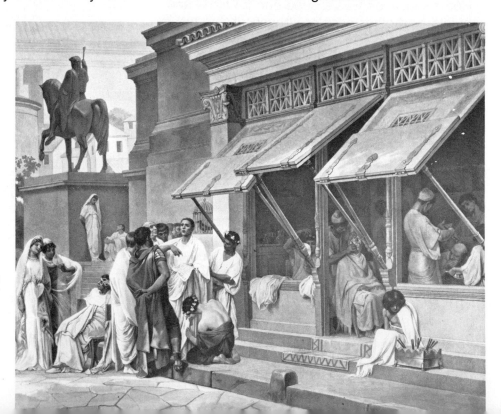

A street in ancient Rome. The building in the picture is a barber shop.

Problems of Rome

Romans believed their power would last forever. By 133 B.C., Roman armies had taken over all the lands in the western and eastern Mediterranean (see map, p. 147). But serious problems still troubled Rome. In politics, the plebeians wanted more rights. This led to quarrels that often became violent.

Rome also faced the problem of paying for its large army. The government was always in need of money. As a result, Roman farmers and city workers had to pay high taxes. Patricians won land and riches in wars. But the average Roman gained little. In fact, many Romans had no jobs. Slaves brought back from conquered lands took over many jobs in Rome. The Romans were becoming poorer even as their armies were taking over the world. By 100 B.C., Rome had become disunited.

The Republic Ends—The Empire Begins

Roman generals and politicians fought one another to see who would rule Rome. One of the most famous generals was Julius Caesar (JOOL-yus SEEZ-ur). He won the fight and was made ruler for life. Caesar tried to bring about changes but many were against him. He was killed by a group of senators in 44 B.C. Civil war broke out in Rome and several leaders fought for power. Finally, a young patrician named Octavian (ock-TAY-vee-UN) won control. He was given the name Augustus and made leader of the Roman armies. Augustus was the first emperor. From 27 B.C. on, Rome stopped being a republic. Instead, it became an empire, ruled by a series of emperors.

A New Religion

During the time of the first emperors, a growing number of people in the empire turned to a new religion. This religion was Christianity. It was started by Jesus, a Jew living in the Roman part of Palestine (see map, p. 147). His followers became known as Christians. Jesus taught people to believe in one God and to love other people.

The first emperors tried to crush Christianity. They failed. The Christians refused to treat the emperor as a god. Because of this, the emperors thought the Christians were trying to make trouble. Many Christians were killed for their faith. Fi-

Julius Caesar was a famous general before he became ruler of Rome. He led Roman armies into Gaul (present-day France and Belgium) and Germany. He even landed in Britain.

nally, in A.D. 313, a Roman emperor named Constantine allowed Christians to follow their faith. In A.D. 395, another emperor made Christianity the official religion of the Roman Empire. However, the acceptance of Christianity as a national religion came too late to bring together the Roman people.

The Pax Romana

The emperor Augustus ruled from 27 B.C. to A.D. 14. During this time, he tried to improve the government within the empire. One of his goals was to make the governments in the defeated territories more honest. That way, the people would have less reason to turn against Roman rule. Augustus succeeded in his plan. For almost 200 years, the Roman Empire was peaceful, strong, and prosperous. This time was known as the Pax Romana, or Roman peace.

Augustus was the first Roman emperor.

Emperors After Augustus

Some of the emperors who came after Augustus were also good rulers. They ruled Rome wisely. Other emperors did not rule well. Conflicts took place within the empire in the 100 years after A.D. 180. The army grew weaker and non-Romans were allowed to become soldiers. Some non-Romans even rose as high as officers and generals in the army. This weakened the army because non-Romans had fewer reasons to fight for Rome.

The Empire is Divided

One emperor after another failed to solve Rome's problems. In A.D. 395, the empire was divided into two parts, with two capitals. The western part of the empire was ruled from Rome. The eastern part was ruled from Constantinople (KON-stan-tuh-NOH-pul). But this action also failed to get rid of the problems of the empire. Rome was steadily weakened by fighting within the empire and by attacks from people from central and northern Europe. For years, these tribes had been pushing into the border lands of the Roman Empire. Then, they began to spill over into the empire itself.

The Fall of Rome

Around A.D. 360, the Huns, a fierce people from Asia, invaded Europe. The German tribes in central Europe poured into the Roman Empire to be safe from the Huns. As each of these tribes came into the empire, they destroyed buildings and other property. When the Huns came into Roman lands, the Romans were able to defeat them. But other invaders continued to pour into the empire. Rome was attacked by the German tribes in A.D. 410 and again in A.D. 455.

The final blow to Rome came in A.D. 476. In that year one of the German chiefs took control of the Western Roman Empire. This action is often taken to signal the fall of Rome.

Civil wars and other problems helped to destroy the empire from within. Attacks from the German tribes further weakened the empire. Gradually the Western Empire fell apart. Many small kingdoms rose up in its place.

The Contributions of Rome

As you have read in Chapter 1, Greek culture was carried to Eastern lands by Alexander the Great. Greek culture also made its way to Italy. There, the Romans borrowed and adapted Greek ideas, art, building styles, and religion. For example, the Romans worshiped the same gods as the Greeks. They called them by different names, however. As Rome took over new lands, Roman armies and traders brought Greek culture to far parts of the empire.

Rome also made its own contributions to life in Europe, North Africa, and the Middle East. Early Rome contributed to civilization in the following areas:

- *Government*—The Roman Empire lasted for over 500 years—from 27 B.C. to A.D. 476. It governed for a long time over a huge area. Many different peoples were part of the Roman Empire. The main government in Rome held the most important powers. But the empire did not try to run the governments of conquered lands or change the customs of the people. Many of the forms of Roman government continued to exist long after the fall of Rome. In some ways, the United States Senate is patterned after Rome's Senate.
- *Law*—The Romans developed laws and a system of justice. Their one law system was used everywhere in the empire. Also, Roman laws

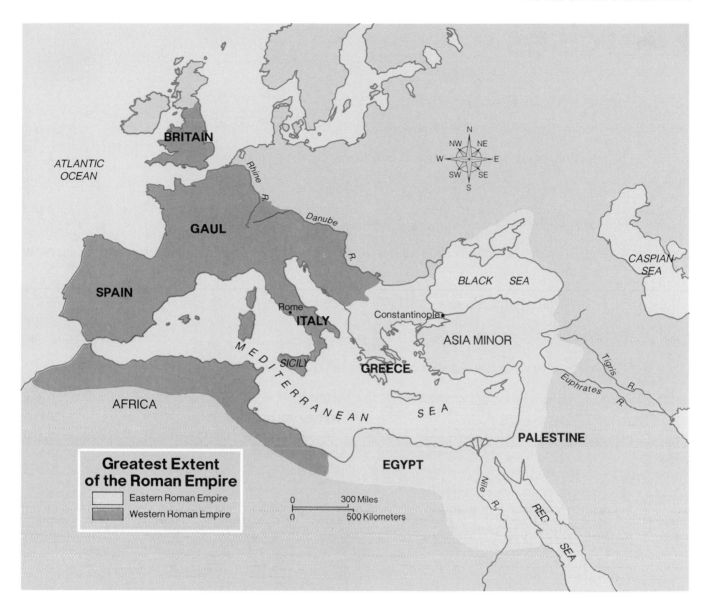

Greatest Extent of the Roman Empire
- ☐ Eastern Roman Empire
- ☐ Western Roman Empire

were written down for all to see. Many of our ideas of law and justice are based on the laws of Rome. For example, under Roman law, an accused person was thought to be innocent until proven guilty.

- *Architecture*—Roman engineers built roads, bridges, aqueducts (these were structures used to carry water), and buildings in all areas of Europe, North Africa, and the Middle East. Many of these structures remain today.

- *Language*—The Romans brought their language, Latin, to many parts of Europe. Out of the Latin language arose the Roman, or Romance, languages. These include Italian,

French, Spanish, Portuguese, and Romanian. In addition, much of the English language is built around Latin words.

- *Literature*—The Romans wrote plays, poems, and histories. The most famous Roman poet was Virgil. His poem tells the story of Rome's beginning.

The influence of Rome, like that of early Greece, is felt to this day. The Romans contributed to the language and culture of the nations of Europe, and North and South America. The Romans' ideas, like those of the Greeks, reached parts of the world that were never in direct contact with early Greece or early Rome.

Exercises

A. Finding the Main Ideas:
Put a check next to the sentences that give the main ideas of what you have just read.

_____ **1.** The patricians were powerful in Rome.

_____ **2.** The Romans came into contact with many different peoples.

_____ **3.** In the early days of Rome, farms were small.

_____ **4.** The Romans borrowed from different cultures and also made their own contributions to civilization.

_____ **5.** There were many reasons for conflict in early Rome.

_____ **6.** Life in Rome was not easy for all people.

_____ **7.** There were many reasons for the downfall of Rome.

B. What Did You Read?
Choose the answer that best completes each sentence. Write the letter of your answer in the space provided.

_____ **1.** Rome's many wars brought
  a. glory to the plebeians.
  b. freedom to the slaves.
  c. high taxes to the Romans.
  d. none of the above.

_____ **2.** A serious problem facing Rome was
  a. the lack of good roads.
  b. the lack of good generals.
  c. its form of government.
  d. the growing number of slaves who took the jobs of Roman workers.

_____ **3.** During the end of the republic, Roman generals and politicians
  a. worked closely together.
  b. fought each other to rule Rome.
  c. were liked by the people.
  d. tried to bring Christianity to Rome.

_____ **4.** German tribes helped to bring about the
  a. spread of Christianity.
  b. freedom of all slaves.
  c. fall of the Etruscans.
  d. fall of Rome.

C. Checking for Details:

Read each statement. Put a T in the space next to each statement if it is true. Put an F in that space if it is false. Put an N if you cannot tell from the reading if it is true or false.

_____ **1.** Rome became a republic after it gained its freedom from the Etruscans.

_____ **2.** The plebeians made too many demands for their rights.

_____ **3.** Christianity was accepted at once by the Roman emperors.

_____ **4.** Christianity failed to hold the Roman Empire together.

_____ **5.** Roman citizenship was not given to all who were ruled by Rome.

_____ **6.** Roman women had few rights.

_____ **7.** Rome began as a republic run by patricians.

_____ **8.** Most Romans were against wars in other lands.

_____ **9.** The Huns were better soldiers than the Romans.

_____ **10.** Rome and Constantinople were capitals of the Roman Empire.

D. Map Study Skills:

Look at the outline map of the Roman Empire below. Identify the following areas shown by the letters on the map. Place the correct letter in the space provided.

_____ **1.** Spain

_____ **2.** Greece

_____ **3.** Egypt

_____ **4.** Gaul

_____ **5.** Britain

_____ **6.** Asia Minor

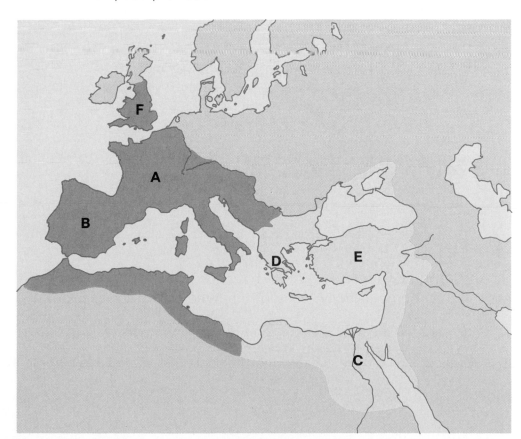

E. Time Line Skills:

In which period of time did each of the following events occur? You may look at the text and the time line on page 143 of this lesson to help you. Place the correct date in the space provided.

_____ **1.** Latins move into the Italian peninsula.   _____ **4.** Plebeians win the right to vote.

_____ **2.** Etruscans take over Rome.   _____ **5.** Romans set up a republic.

_____ **3.** Roman Empire begins.   _____ **6.** Rome is founded.

F. Understanding What You Have Read:

Tell whether each of the following events involved Rome in a military (M), political (P), or economic (E) way. Write the correct letter in the space provided.

_____ **1.** Huns attack Roman lands.   _____ **5.** Rome has two capitals.

_____ **2.** Slaves take over many jobs in Rome.   _____ **6.** An emperor rules Rome.

_____ **3.** Roman farmers and workers pay high taxes.   _____ **7.** Many Romans are without work.

_____ **4.** A republic is set up in Rome.   _____ **8.** Patricians are rich landowners.

G. Behind the Headlines:

Write two or three sentences that support or tell about each of the following headlines.

PLEBEIANS DEMAND MORE RIGHTS

_____

_____

CHRISTIANS TO BE ALLOWED FREEDOM OF WORSHIP

_____

_____

GERMAN TRIBES ATTACK ROME

_____

_____

H. Thinking It Over:

Answer each of the following questions in three or four sentences. Use a separate piece of paper.

1. What were the main problems facing Rome after it gained its freedom from the Etruscans?

2. How might Rome have avoided the problems that led to its fall in A.D. 476?

I. Word Meanings:

Match each word in Column A with the correct meaning in Column B. Write the letter of each answer in the space provided.

Column A

_____ **1.** republic
_____ **2.** consuls
_____ **3.** senators
_____ **4.** gladiators
_____ **5.** Pax Romana

Column B

a. trained fighters
b. a government led by elected officials
c. elected to a one-year term in the Roman republic
d. the first Roman emperor
e. a time of peace and well-being in the empire
f. they passed the laws in Rome

J. Who Were They?

Name the person or group of people described in each sentence. Write the answer in the space provided.

_____ **1.** They ruled Rome until 509 B.C.

_____ **2.** They were the only Romans allowed to serve in the Senate.

_____ **3.** They brought a new religion to Rome.

_____ **4.** He was a Roman ruler who was killed in 44 B.C.

_____ **5.** They came from Asia and invaded Europe around A.D. 360

_____ **6.** They were the common people of Rome.

K. Understanding Global History:

On page 142, you read about four factors in global history. Which of these factors applies to each statement listed below? Fill in the number of the correct statement on page 142 in the space provided.

_____ **1.** The Romans worshiped many of the same gods as the early Greeks. The Romans gave the gods different names, however.

_____ **2.** Our belief that an accused person is innocent until proven guilty was part of the Roman system of law.

_____ **3.** The early Romans learned about growing grapes and olives from the Greeks and Phoenicians who had colonies in Italy.

_____ **4.** The Roman Empire was weakened when its lands were invaded by German tribes. These tribes were fleeing the fierce Asian Huns.

151

Chapter 3

Europe in the Early Middle Ages

Understanding Global History

Think about the following statements as you read about Europe after the fall of the Roman Empire.
1. Interaction among people can lead to cultural changes.
2. Providing for individual and group needs is a common goal of all peoples and cultures.

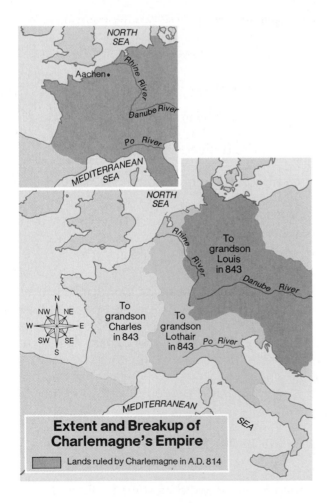

Extent and Breakup of Charlemagne's Empire

Lands ruled by Charlemagne in A.D. 814

Charlemagne (Charles the Great) built a great empire in Europe.

Learning New Words and Terms

medieval: the period of the Middle Ages

vassal: a person who receives land from a lord and gives loyalty and service in return

feudalism: a system of rule that came into being from the arrangement between lords and vassals

barter: the exchange of goods and services

manor: the lands, including a village and the surrounding lands, held by a noble

serfs: peasants tied to the manor

self-sufficient: able to meet all of one's needs by oneself

parish: the town or village looked after by a priest

pope: the head of the Roman Catholic church

patriarchs: heads of churches in the Eastern Orthodox church

Think As You Read

1. In feudal society, what did vassals owe their lords? What did lords give their vassals in return?
2. How did the fall of the Roman Empire affect economic life in Europe?
3. What classes of people made up medieval society?
4. What was another name for the Eastern Roman Empire?

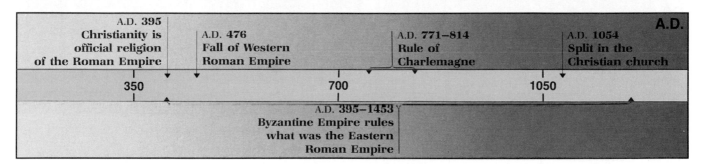

A.D. 395 Christianity is official religion of the Roman Empire	A.D. 476 Fall of Western Roman Empire	A.D. 771–814 Rule of Charlemagne	A.D. 1054 Split in the Christian church	A.D.
350	700		1050	

A.D. 395–1453 Byzantine Empire rules what was the Eastern Roman Empire

Medieval Times

As you have read in Chapter 2, the western part of the Roman Empire fell in A.D. 476. As a result, life in Europe changed greatly. Sometimes, the 1,000 years after A.D. 476 are divided into two periods. These are the early Middle Ages (A.D. 450 to A.D. 850) and the later Middle Ages (A.D. 850 to A.D. 1450). Often, the entire period is called **medieval** times. Medieval times are the years between early times and modern times.

In the following pages you will read about the way of life during the early Middle Ages.

New Kingdoms

The Roman Empire fell apart in Europe after A.D. 476. Bands of warlike German tribes from central and northern Europe swept into Roman lands. As they moved in, they broke down the system of Roman control. These new people then set up their own kingdoms. By the 800s there were many small kingdoms all over Europe.

The most powerful ruler of the early Middle Ages was Charlemagne (SHAR-luh-mayn). He ruled from A.D. 771 to 814. His kingdom included what is today France, Germany, and part of Italy. Charlemagne set up a strong central government. He made laws and had local judges carry them out. He spread the Christian faith and furthered learning. Both Roman and German ways of life were brought together in Charlemagne's kingdom. A new culture then came into being. It was a European culture.

After his death, Charlemagne's kingdom was divided among his three grandsons. One part included most of France; another included most of Germany. A third part ran from Italy to the North Sea. The countries of present-day Europe slowly grew out of these three parts.

Feudalism

Not all medieval rulers were as strong as Charlemagne. Many could not defend their lands

153

Medieval knights wore heavy armor and suits of chain mail as protection in battle.

against invaders. When kings had to defend their lands they called upon other nobles for help. These nobles would join their armies with those of the king. Armies were made up of soldiers on horseback. These were called knights. Together, king and nobles could defeat their enemies. But kings had no money to pay their nobles for help in time of war. The only thing they had was land.

In return for their help in battle, the king would give his nobles land for their own use. The person who received land in this way became a **vassal.** He owed loyalty and service to his lord. The lord also had certain duties. He had to give protection to his vassals.

The practice of granting land in return for service became common in Europe. A system of rule soon came into being from the arrangement between lords and their vassals. It was called **feudalism.** The feudal system brought order to Europe after the fall of the Roman Empire.

At the top of feudal society was the king. Then came his chief lords. These chief lords were vassals of the king. The chief lords also had their own vassals. Then came the knights. They were also vassals to some lord. All belonged to the noble class. At the bottom of feudal society were the peasants.

Trade Slows Down

The fall of Rome brought about less trade and commerce in Europe. Cities and roads in Europe were destroyed by invading tribes and by wars. The cities that remained built high walls to help protect them against enemies. The loss of trade meant there was less need for money. People often used **barter** in place of money. Barter is the direct exchange of goods and services. For example, a farmer might exchange eggs for shoes, or a bushel of oats for a calf. In such exchanges there was no need for money.

154

The Manor System

Farming was the main way of earning a living during the Middle Ages. Most of the land belonged to nobles. As you remember, the nobles received their land from a lord. The land owned by the nobles was called the **manor.** The manor might have a village and the land around it. Or it might have two or three villages.

Nobles did not work the land on their manor. They were usually off fighting and had no time to farm. The work on the manors was done by peasants. In earlier times, these peasants gave their land to a lord and he in turn would protect them. Peasants had no way to defend themselves in times of war or disorder. Over the years, these peasants became tied to the land of the manor. They were known as **serfs.** Serfs could not move away from the manor. Because of the manor system, there was very little chance for contacts between people during early medieval times.

A lord usually divided his manor among his serfs. But he also kept some of the land for himself. In order to be protected by the lord, the serfs had to work his land. Also, each peasant family had to pay rent for the land they farmed themselves.

The people of a medieval manor were largely **self-sufficient.** They took care of all their own needs. For example, peasants grew wheat for food. They also raised sheep and made thread from wool. Village workers made tools. However, people of the manor had to trade for things they could not make. Some of these things were salt and iron.

A medieval manor. The serfs are planting vines and harvesting grapes.

The Church

Christianity became the religion of the Roman Empire in A.D. 395. It was the religion of Europe during the Middle Ages. After about A.D. 500, the Roman government lost control over many parts of the Western Empire. In such cases, the people began to look to the Roman Catholic church to protect them.

The Church played a large role in medieval life.
- the Church kept records of births, deaths, and the sale of lands.
- the Church taught reading and writing to those training to be priests. However, the Church also offered learning to others. The monasteries were important centers of learning. These were places where people could live apart from the world and pray.
- the Church cared for the sick and poor.

The organization of the Church grew during the Middle Ages. Priests took care of a **parish.** A bishop ruled over many parishes. The **pope** in Rome was the leader of the Christian church. He was in charge of all the bishops.

Classes of People

People in medieval Europe were divided into three main classes. These were the nobles, serfs, and the free men and women. The nobles were few in number. They had most of the power, however. The serfs made up the greatest number of people. But they had almost no power or rights. Free people in medieval Europe were few in number. They were either peasants or townspeople. They had more rights than the serfs. However, they had fewer rights than the nobles.

The Life of the Nobles

The way of life of the nobles was very different from that of the serfs and the free men and women. Because they were knights in service to their lord, nobles spent much of their time at war or in training for war. At an early age young nobles trained to become knights. A noble child might start out as a helper to a lord. Then at 14 or 15 years of age, he learned how to ride a horse and use weapons. When he finished his training, a young noble might be knighted.

When not fighting, the nobles had their own way of living. They hunted and took part in tournaments. These were games of military skill. Nobles also entertained visitors.

The life of the nobles was centered on the castle. This was a building with high towers and thick walls. The castle was built to protect the lord, his family, and his serfs from attack. Even though the medieval castle protected them, it was not a comfortable home. It was cold, dark, and damp.

The Life of the Common People

The serfs and free men and women had a much simpler way of life. They worked from sunrise to sunset. Their homes were plain huts made from straw and mud. Peasant life followed the seasons. In the spring the peasants planted seed for grain. Summer and early fall was the time to harvest the crops. During the winter, peasants stayed indoors. They made candles, wove cloth, and did other tasks.

The Byzantine Empire

While feudalism developed in Europe, the eastern part of the old Roman Empire continued. As you remember from Chapter 2, the Roman Empire was divided into two parts in the 4th century A.D. While the Western Roman Empire grew weaker, the Eastern part stayed strong. Its capital, Constantinople, became rich through trade.

The Eastern Roman Empire is often called the Byzantine Empire. It gets its name from the old city of Byzantium. This city was later called Constantinople. The Byzantine Empire lasted from A.D. 395 to 1453. Greece and Asia Minor were part of it. The people of the Byzantine Empire spoke Greek. They were also Christians.

Empress Theodora of the Byzantine Empire.

Byzantine rulers carried on some of the Roman ways of life. One of these was the system of law started by the Romans. During the early Middle Ages, Roman law was forgotten in Europe. But it stayed alive in the Byzantine Empire. The Eastern Empire also had ways of life that were different from those of Rome. For example, the Byzantine ruler did not accept the pope as head of the Christian church. In the Byzantine Empire, the ruler made **patriarchs** the heads of the churches in different cities. Also, the kind of church worship differed in the Eastern Empire. Greek became the language of the Eastern church instead of Latin. Differences over forms of worship led to a split in the Christian church in 1054. In the West, the Christian church was known as the Roman Catholic church. In the East, it was known as the Eastern Orthodox church.

156

Exercises

A. Finding the Main Ideas:
Put a check next to the sentences that give the main ideas of what you have just read.

_____ **1.** Europe was made up of many small kingdoms in medieval times.

_____ **2.** A system of feudalism developed in Europe in medieval times.

_____ **3.** The Church kept learning alive during the Middle Ages.

_____ **4.** Nobles owned the land during the Middle Ages.

_____ **5.** Castles were built for protection in medieval times.

B. What Did You Read?
Choose the answer that best completes each sentence. Write the letter of your answer in the space provided.

_____ **1.** The fall of Rome led to
  a. the decline of cities.
  b. a slowdown in trade and commerce.
  c. the beginning of many small kingdoms.
  d. all of the above.

_____ **2.** Barter is a term used in dealing with
  a. trade.
  b. religion.
  c. warfare.
  d. political life.

_____ **3.** During the Middle Ages, many of the duties once carried out by Roman government were taken over by the
  a. manors.
  b. Church.
  c. cities.
  d. invaders.

_____ **4.** During the Middle Ages, a lord would give land to a noble who served him in time of war. This noble became the lord's
  a. merchant.
  b. serf.
  c. vassal.
  d. free man.

C. Checking for Details:

Read each statement. Put a T in the space next to each statement if it is true. Put an F in that space if it is false. Put an N in the space if you cannot tell from the reading if the statement is true or false.

_____ **1.** The Roman Empire fell apart after A.D. 476.

_____ **2.** Nobles ruled many kingdoms during the Middle Ages.

_____ **3.** The Church had little influence during the Middle Ages.

_____ **4.** Cities grew larger during the Middle Ages.

_____ **5.** Nobles had more rights than free people.

_____ **6.** Church services were an important part of life in the Middle Ages.

_____ **7.** Kings were able to pay their armies with money.

_____ **8.** Farming was the main activity on the manor.

_____ **9.** Serfs were under the control of the Church.

_____ **10.** There was no learning at all during the Middle Ages.

D. Who Were They?

Name the group of people who might have said the following during the Middle Ages. Write the answer in the space provided.

_____ **1.** We owed our lord loyalty and service in time of war.

_____ **2.** We kept records during medieval times.

_____ **3.** We were not nobles, but we had more rights than serfs.

_____ **4.** We took care of the poor.

_____ **5.** We were the horse soldiers of the Middle Ages.

_____ **6.** We did the work on the manors.

E. Understanding What You Have Read:

Tell whether each of the following involves (P) political, (E) economic, (R) religious, or (S) social aspects of medieval life. Place the correct letter in the space provided.

_____ **1.** Because there was little money, people in the Middle Ages traded goods for services.

_____ **2.** Charlemagne set up a strong central government.

_____ **3.** There was very little trade during the Middle Ages.

_____ **4.** Serfs were the lowest class of people in the Middle Ages.

_____ **5.** The Church offered learning to people during the Middle Ages.

_____ **6.** Manors provided for almost all their own needs.

_____ **7.** The Byzantine ruler did not accept the pope as head of the Christian church.

_____ **8.** Charlemagne made the laws and had judges carry them out.

F. Word Meanings:

Match each word in Column A with the correct meaning in Column B. Write the letter of each answer in the space provided.

Column A

_____ **1.** barter
_____ **2.** vassal
_____ **3.** pope
_____ **4.** manor
_____ **5.** parish
_____ **6.** patriarch

Column B

a. church leader in the Eastern Orthodox church
b. head of the Roman Catholic church
c. land held by a noble
d. person holding land received from a noble or a king
e. exchange of goods without the use of money
f. local church area
g. person forced to work land in service of another

G. Understanding Global History:

On page 152 you read about two factors in global history. Which of these factors applies to each statement listed below? Fill in the number of the correct statement on page 152 in the space provided.

_____ **1.** German customs were blended with the traditions of the Roman Empire in the kingdom of Charlemagne. Out of this blending, a new culture emerged.

_____ **2.** Medieval lords and peasants made their living on the manors. Most of their needs were provided for. Lords had to give protection to the serfs and the serfs had to farm the lord's land holdings.

Chapter 4

The Rise of Islam

Understanding Global History

Think about the following statements as you read about the rise of Islam.
1. Nations borrow and adapt ideas and institutions from other nations.
2. Present culture is shaped by the past.
3. Contact among peoples and nations can lead to cultural changes.

Mecca, the holiest city in Islam. Muhammad was born in Mecca.

Learning New Words and Terms

Islam: an Arabic word meaning "submitting to the will of God"; the religion founded by Muhammad

hegira: Muhammad's flight from Mecca to Medina

prophet: someone who presents religious beliefs as given by God

alms: money or goods given to the poor

Koran: the holy book of Islam
mosque: the Islamic place of worship

Think As You Read

1. Where did Islam start?
2. What are the teachings of Islam?
3. Why did Islam spread so fast?

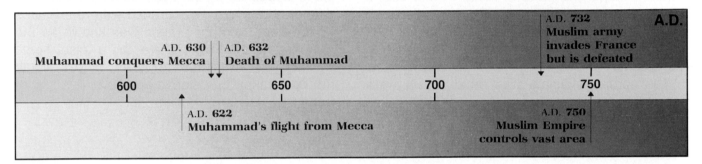

A.D. **630**
Muhammad conquers Mecca

A.D. **632**
Death of Muhammad

A.D. **732**
Muslim army invades France but is defeated

A.D.

600   650   700   750

A.D. **622**
Muhammad's flight from Mecca

A.D. **750**
Muslim Empire controls vast area

Muhammad Founds a New Religion

The first religion to teach belief in one God was Judaism. Another faith, Christianity, grew out of Judaism. It came into being around the time of the first Roman emperors. It, too, put forward a belief in one God. Christianity spread to most of Europe by A.D. 600. It had a smaller following in many parts of the Middle East, however. Old religions remained strong there. For example, the people of Arabia believed in many gods. It was in Arabia, however, that a new religion arose in the early 600s A.D. This religion taught belief in one God.

The founder of the new religion was a man named Muhammad (muh-HAHM-id). He was born in Arabia, in the city of Mecca. Sometime around the age of 40, Muhammad turned against the belief in many gods. He asked the people to believe in a single God, Allah. Muhammad's ideas were based in part on the teachings of Judaism and Christianity. But many of his ideas were new. Mohammed called the new religion **Islam.** This is an Arabic word meaning submitting, or giving in, to the will of God. Followers of Islam are called Muslims.

Muhammad Escapes

Those who worshiped the old gods were against Muhammad. He was forced to escape from Mecca in A.D. 622. Muhammad and his followers went to the city of Medina (muh-DEE-nuh). The flight from Mecca to Medina is called the **hegira** (hih-jy-ruh). The year of the flight, A.D. 622, became the first year of the Muslim calendar.

In A.D. 630, Muhammad returned to Mecca with an army. He took over the city and destroyed the idols of the old faith. Mecca and Medina became the holy cities of Islam. But Mecca is the holiest city of the religion.

Teachings of Islam

The Muslims did not worship Muhammad as a god. They called him a **prophet.** Muhammad presented the religious beliefs of Islam as given to him by Allah.

The teachings of Islam are as follows:

- To believe there is no God but Allah, and Muhammad is the prophet of God
- To pray five times a day facing the direction of Mecca
- To give **alms** to the poor
- To go without food from sunrise to sunset during one holy month of the year. This month is called Ramadan.
- To make a trip to the holy city of Mecca at least once

The teachings of Islam are written down in the **Koran.** This is the holy book of Islam. It has all the religious rules Muslims must follow. Muslims believe that the Koran is the sacred word of God.

The Spread of Islam

Muhammad died in A.D. 632. This was two years after he had taken over Mecca. By that time his army had taken over most of Arabia. In the next 100 years, Islam spread from Arabia to all of the Middle East, Egypt, northern Africa, and Spain (see map below). It also made its way to central Africa, Persia, and parts of India. In A.D. 732, a Muslim army invaded France. But it was defeated by Christian forces. The defeat of the Muslims in France stopped the spread of Islam into Western Europe.

The spread of Islam was rapid. There were many reasons why people were in favor of it. For example, Muslims held that all believers were equal. They did not need priests or a church to practice their religion. Also, Islam brought the Arabs together for the first time. They fought for one God and to spread Islam.

Disputes Within Islam

By A.D. 750, Muslim armies had taken over a very large area. But there were problems within the Muslim empire. Some leaders fought about who should be the successor to Muhammad. This led to bloodshed. In the 700s, Islam broke up into different branches. One branch were the Shiites (SHEE-ites). Another branch was known as the Sunnites (SOON-its). There were also fights within these branches of Islam. These fights helped weaken the Islamic empire.

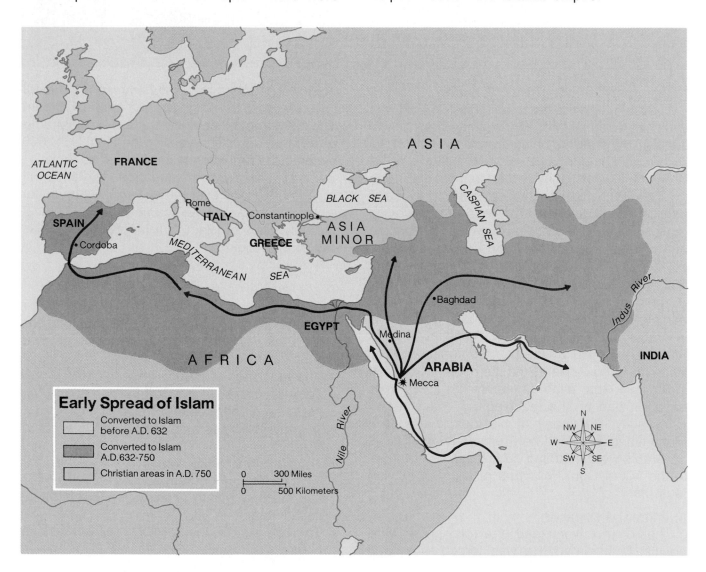

Early Spread of Islam

- ☐ Converted to Islam before A.D. 632
- ☐ Converted to Islam A.D. 632–750
- ☐ Christian areas in A.D. 750

0   300 Miles
0   500 Kilometers

Contributions of Islam

Islam was a powerful force when Europe was in disorder. During Europe's early Middle Ages, Muslim culture bloomed. Through trade, people in Europe learned much about Muslim science, art, and products. Islamic peoples achieved great things in many areas. For example,

- Muslim scholars kept the ideas of the early Greek philosophers alive. They also studied the writings of the Romans.
- Muslim doctors studied diseases and found ways to treat them. One doctor, Avicenna (AV-ih-SEHN-uh), explained how illness could spread by dirty water.
- Muslims adopted the system of numbers from India. This system later came to be known as "Arabic numerals."
- Muslims were very much in favor of learning. They started schools where medicine, law, and religion could be studied.
- Muslims built **mosques** and palaces. These buildings were often covered with beautiful drawings.
- Muslim merchants carried on trade in Africa, Asia, and Europe. Arab cities were filled with fine cloths, rugs, leather goods, and other riches.

A Muslim teaching the Koran to the people.

The Alhambra in Spain. This palace was built by Muslims. They invaded Spain in the 700s A.D.

Exercises

A. Finding the Main Ideas:

Put a check next to the sentences that give the main ideas of what you have just read.

_____ **1.** Before Muhammad, the people of the Middle East worshiped many gods.

_____ **2.** Islam came into being and grew during the 600s and 700s.

_____ **3.** Muhammad escaped to Medina in A.D. 622.

_____ **4.** Islam teaches belief in one God.

_____ **5.** After Muhammad's death, Islam split into different branches.

_____ **6.** Mecca is the holiest city in Islam.

B. What Did You Read?

Choose the answer that best completes each sentence. Write the letter of your answer in the space provided.

_____ **1.** Muhammad was born in
    a. Egypt.
    b. Arabia.
    c. Spain.
    d. none of the above.

_____ **2.** The Koran is the name of
    a. a holy Islamic city.
    b. an Islamic religious leader.
    c. the holy book of Islam.
    d. an Islamic prophet.

_____ **3.** In A.D. 732, a Muslim army invaded
    a. Spain.
    b. Persia.
    c. Egypt.
    d. France.

_____ **4.** The Muslims think of Muhammad as
    a. a military leader.
    b. a prophet.
    c. the founder of Islam.
    d. all of the above.

C. Checking for Details:

Read each statement. Put a T in the space next to each statement if it is true. Put an F in that space if it is false. Put an N if you cannot tell from the reading if it is true or false.

_____ **1.** The Islamic religion started in Arabia.

_____ **2.** Judaism was the first religion to teach belief in one God.

_____ **3.** What Muhammad taught was accepted at once by the people of Mecca.

_____ **4.** Problems arose in Islam because of its rapid spread to all parts of the world.

_____ **5.** Giving alms to the poor is not one of the beliefs of Islam.

_____ **6.** Muslims formed ideas about the causes of diseases.

_____ **7.** Most of the people of the Middle East were unhappy with their religion at the time of Muhammad.

_____ **8.** Warfare did not play an important part in the spread of Islam.

_____ **9.** Muslims were interested in education.

_____ **10.** The fights between the Shiite and Sunnite groups divided Islam.

D. Behind the Headlines:

Write two or three sentences that support or tell about the following headlines. Use a separate piece of paper.

MECCA FALLS TO MUHAMMAD

MUSLIMS DEFEATED IN FRANCE

RELIGIOUS DISPUTES WITHIN ISLAM

E. Word Meanings:

Match each word in Column A with the correct meaning in Column B. Write the letter of each answer in the space provided.

Column A

_____ **1.** Allah
_____ **2.** mosque
_____ **3.** prophet
_____ **4.** alms
_____ **5.** hegira

Column B

a. Muhammad's flight from Mecca to Medina
b. the one God
c. money or goods given to the poor
d. Muslim place of worship
e. person who presents beliefs as given by God
f. holy book of Islam

F. Understanding Global History:

On page 160 you read about three factors in global history. Which of these factors applies to each statement listed below? Fill in the number of the correct statement on page 160 in the space provided.

_____ **1.** People in Europe learned much about mathematics, science, and medicine from Muslim traders.

_____ **2.** The different branches of present-day Islam came into being after the death of Muhammad.

_____ **3.** Like the teachings of Judaism and Christianity, Islam teaches belief in one God.

Chapter 5

The Late Middle Ages and the Renaissance

Understanding Global History

Think about the following statements as you read about Europe during the late Middle Ages and the Renaissance.
1 Present culture is shaped by the past.
2 Nations borrow and adapt ideas and institutions from other nations.
3 Contact among peoples and nations can lead to cultural changes.
4 Events occurring in one part of the world have influenced developments in other parts of the world.

Medieval and Renaissance towns were busy places.

Learning New Words and Terms

Crusades: the wars carried out to free the Holy Land from Muslim control

manufacturing: the making of goods by hand or machine

humanists: the name given to the scholars of the Renaissance; they were interested in all aspects of human life

Renaissance: the period from around the 1300s to the 1600s; a term meaning "re-birth" of civilization

reform: to bring about a change for the better

patrons: people who back the arts

Think As You Read

1. Why did towns begin to grow during the late Middle Ages?
2. What were the Crusades? How did they change Europe?
3. What does the word "Renaissance" mean?
4. What was the Protestant Reformation?
5. What changes were brought about by the Renaissance?

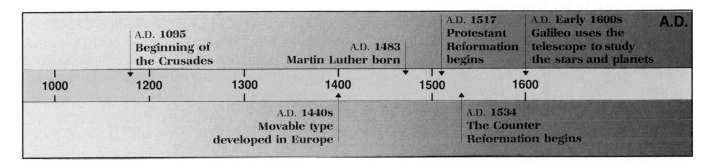

A.D. **1095** Beginning of the Crusades

A.D. **1483** Martin Luther born

A.D. **1517** Protestant Reformation begins

A.D. **Early 1600s** Galileo uses the telescope to study the stars and planets

A.D.

1000   1200   1300   1400   1500   1600

A.D. **1440s** Movable type developed in Europe

A.D. **1534** The Counter Reformation begins

Town Life Begins Again

During the early Middle Ages, there was just about no town life in Europe. People stayed near the manors of nobles. There, they were protected from the wars and dangers of the age.

By around 900, towns slowly began to grow. They often sprang up where people gathered to trade. Many towns were founded near rivers. In river towns, it was easy for merchants to ship and sell their goods. Towns also grew up around or near castles.

As you read in Chapter 3, castles were built to protect lords and their households. Soon, people of the castle needed more room. They began to spill outside of the castle walls. In times of danger, however, they would come back to the castle to be protected.

Something else caused the towns to grow. The population of Europe began to grow between A.D. 500 and A.D. 1000. This meant that more people would be looking for work. Because there were more workers, not as many peasants were needed to farm the land. Some peasants made

their way to the towns. Their skills in weaving and other jobs helped build commerce in the towns. Trade grew all over Europe as more people from the towns made and sold goods.

The Crusades

All during the Middle Ages, Christians went back and forth from Europe to the Middle East. They visited the land where Jesus lived and preached. They called this part of the world the Holy Land. It was sacred to Christians.

As you remember from Chapter 4, the Middle East came under Arab Muslim control by the 700s. But Arab Muslims were open-minded about the Christians. They allowed Christians to come and go freely in the Holy Land. This changed in 1071. In that year, the Holy Land was taken over by the warlike Seljuk (SEL-jook) Turks.

The Muslim Turks were not open-minded about the Christians. Pilgrims returning to Europe from the Holy Land told how Christians were being killed and holy places destroyed. The Turks were also close to taking over Constantinople. This was the capital of the Byzantine Empire. The patriarch of Constantinople asked the pope in Rome for help. In 1095, Pope Urban II called for a holy war against the Muslims. He hoped to capture the Holy Land and save the Byzantine Empire.

Thousands of people took part in the **Crusades.** This was the name given to the wars to free the Holy Land. The Crusades lasted for about 150 years. There were many reasons why people took part in the Crusades. Some people were truly religious. They hoped to free the Holy Land. Others were looking for adventure and glory. Serfs ran away to the Crusades to escape their hard life. Nobles took part in Crusades to gain land, riches, and power.

The Crusades Bring Change

The Crusades did not win back the Holy Land for very long. But they had important results. For example,

- Many nobles died in the battles of the Crusades. Without them to compete for power, the kings gained more power.
- Europeans began to take an interest in other parts of the world.
- Crusaders brought back spices and other luxuries from the Middle East. These improved life in Europe. The spices made food taste better. Perfumes, rugs, and glass mirrors were brought to Europe from the Middle East.
- **Manufacturing** began to grow in Europe. Armies needed weapons and supplies to keep up the fighting.
- Some cities grew rich because of trade between Europe and the Middle East. The most famous trading city was Venice. Venice is found in northern Italy.
- The increase in manufacturing and trade affected learning. Growing merchant classes in Europe needed workers who could read and write. It was important to know arithmetic, too. Without these skills it was impossible to trade.

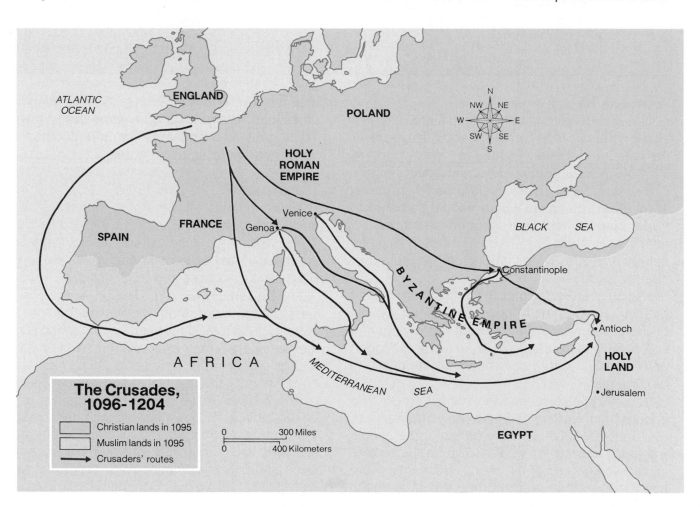

The Crusades, 1096-1204

- Christian lands in 1095
- Muslim lands in 1095
- → Crusaders' routes

0   300 Miles
0   400 Kilometers

Desire for Knowledge Grows

During the 1300s, some Europeans wanted to learn more than the skills of trade and commerce. They also wanted to learn more about the world in which they lived. They wanted to know about the past. Some people thought that learning about the past would help them to better understand their own lives.

The interest in the past led scholars to study the writings of the Greeks and Romans. These scholars called themselves **humanists.** They were interested in everything about human beings. The humanists studied books and letters from early Greece and Rome. These had been saved by Muslim and Byzantine scholars when Europe was in decline. Early writings could also be found in monasteries, castles, and in the libraries of the rich.

It became important to know Greek and Latin. Those who had the money hired teachers to teach them the early languages. In this way, they could discuss the ideas of the past. Through reading and discussing, the ideas and beliefs of early times came alive again. This period in history is called the **Renaissance** (REN-uh-SAHNS). The word means "rebirth." It refers to the rebirth of Greek and Roman ideas.

Humanists Start the Renaissance

The Renaissance was started by the humanists. They were interested in people. They wanted to know more about nature and the world around them. The humanists brought this desire to learn into European life. In the Middle Ages, people were more concerned with religion and life after death. The Church was the center of life. During the Renaissance, the individual person became the center of attention.

The humanists set the Renaissance in motion. The Renaissance began in the cities of northern Italy in the 1300s. It reached its peak in the 1500s. The ideas of the humanists spread throughout Europe during the 1500s and 1600s.

Modern Languages Develop

During the Renaissance, culture and learning in Europe were born again. However, people read more than the books from early Greece and Rome. Books were collected from the Middle East

Erasmus was a famous humanist. He was born in the Netherlands.

and from different parts of Europe. These books were translated into Italian, English, Spanish, and French. In this way, more and more people could learn in their own language. They didn't have to know Greek or Latin.

Languages of everyday life were used in poems and government papers. Tales and comedies were also written in many languages. In Spain, for example, Miguel de Cervantes (suhr-VAN-teez) wrote a novel about an old knight. This novel was *Don Quixote.*

The Printing Press Spreads Learning

The desire to learn was an important part of the Renaissance. Hundreds of books and papers were translated and copied. However, the old system of copying books by hand was too slow. Also, books cost too much money. Some new way to make copies of books had to be found.

The art of making paper first began in China. It had been brought to Europe by way of Arabia. By the 1400s, there were also new kinds of ink. During this time a printing press—a way of pressing paper onto inked type—had also been found. The problem was that printing was a clumsy process. The words of a page had to be cut into the surface of a block of wood before the page could be printed. This took a long time.

By the 1440s, movable type had been developed in Europe. The idea was simple. Separate metal letters were made. The letters were placed side by side to form words and sentences. They were then put into a frame. The frame made a page of type to be printed. Later, the type could be used again to make up pages of other books. This system made it possible to reproduce a book for a fairly low price.

It is not known who first thought of the idea of movable type. However, we do know that Johann Gutenberg, a German printer, first made a kind of metal that could be used to make movable type. In this way, type could be set quickly and easily. Gutenberg was also the first person to print a complete edition of the Bible. He is thought of as the founder of modern printing.

New Ideas Emerge

Learned Europeans discovered more than the works of the early Greeks and Romans. They also discovered new ideas in science, mathematics, philosophy, and medicine.

Two of the most famous scientists of the Renaissance were Copernicus (koh-PUR-nih-kuhs) and Galileo (GAL-uh-LEE-oh). Copernicus was a Pole. In 1543, he said the earth moved around the sun. Before that time, people believed the earth was the center of the universe.

In the early 1600s, Galileo, an Italian, made some more discoveries. He improved an earlier Dutch invention—the telescope. Galileo used his improved telescope to study the stars and planets. He found that the planets were not perfect bodies. Instead, they had rough surfaces. In early times, scientists thought the planets and stars were perfect. Galileo's findings helped support the theories of Copernicus.

A Call for Reform

The Renaissance brought a change to life in Europe. People began to question the world around them. Religion also began to change. As you have read, the Roman Catholic church had become powerful during medieval times. Many people in Europe were pleased with the Church. They accepted what it taught. But there were others who wanted the Church to **reform,** or change. During the Renaissance, some people began to question certain Church practices. One of those people was Martin Luther.

Martin Luther, center, led the Protestant Reformation.

Martin Luther

Martin Luther was born in Germany in 1483. He became a monk and a teacher. Luther won praise for his teaching at the University of Wittenberg in Germany. But he was unhappy with what was going on in the Church. Luther was against the Church selling indulgences. An indulgence was the lessening of the punishment a sinner would suffer after death. Indulgences were not supposed to be sold. But many persons gave money to the Church in return for indulgences. Luther and others in the Church felt that this was wrong. In 1517, Luther nailed a list of his ideas on the door of the church in Wittenberg. He attacked the sale of indulgences. Luther stated that only God could forgive sins, not the Church.

The Protestant Reformation

Luther's actions upset Church leaders in Rome. Luther was called to Rome to explain his actions to the pope. After several years of debate, the Church leaders made Luther leave the Church. The Church could not settle its differences with Luther. Luther and his followers set up a new church. They asked Christians in Europe who agreed with them to join this new church. Before long, people who agreed entirely with Luther, or even in part, formed new churches in many parts of Europe.

Martin Luther and his followers had demanded the reform of the Roman Catholic church. Because of their protests, followers of Luther were called Protestants. The movement that began with Martin Luther became known as the Protestant Reformation.

Results of the Reformation

The Protestant Reformation caused a split in the Christian world. By 1600, there were two church groups in Western Europe. One group was the Roman Catholic church. The new group was made up of many smaller Protestant groups. The Lutherans and Anglicans are two of these Protestant groups. These groups are still around today. Other Protestant churches began years later.

The Reformation had another result. It brought about a change in the Roman Catholic church. The Church decided to reform itself. Also, a religious order called the Society of Jesus was formed. Its members were called Jesuits. The Jesuits tried to win back people to the Roman Catholic church. This reform movement was called the Counter Reformation. It began in 1534 and lasted into the 1600s.

Achievements in the Arts

The Renaissance was a time of great advances in art and literature. Renaissance artists made many beautiful paintings, statues, and buildings. These works of art are among the most well known in the world.

During the Renaissance art changed. Artists no longer limited themselves to paintings and statues of religious subjects. They began to show real-life people as they really looked.

Leonardo da Vinci was one of the most outstanding artists of the Renaissance. He was a painter, engineer, inventor, and musician.

Writers also did great things during the Renaissance. In England, William Shakespeare wrote plays for his theater in London. These plays are still acted out today. They are the greatest plays in the English language.

The work of Renaissance artists and writers was made possible by **patrons.** These were rich people who wanted to beautify their palaces and churches. They backed the artists and writers of the day. In this way, the artists could use all their time to make beautiful things. The first patrons were the rich families of the Italian cities. As the Renaissance spread in Europe, kings and queens also became patrons of the arts.

How Life Changed

Perhaps the greatest change during the Renaissance was in the way people were thinking. More people could read and learn because there were more books. Ideas spread faster. People began to think about different subjects such as science and medicine.

Imagine, if you can, that you fell asleep in the year 1300 and woke up in the year 1600. Only 300 years would have passed. But you would have awakened to a new world. In those 300 years the people of Europe had changed. They were no longer tied to the ways of early times. More and more they looked like modern people of our own time.

The "Mona Lisa" is Leonardo da Vinci's most famous painting.

Exercises

A. Finding the Main Ideas:

Put a check next to the sentences that give the main ideas of what you have just read.

_____ **1.** Town life began to grow during the late Middle Ages.

_____ **2.** The Renaissance changed life in Europe in many ways.

_____ **3.** Books were an important part of life during the Renaissance.

_____ **4.** The Crusades had a big impact on life in Europe.

_____ **5.** People began to write in their own everyday languages during the Renaissance.

_____ **6.** Leonardo da Vinci was a famous person of the Renaissance.

B. What Did You Read?

Choose the answer that best completes each sentence. Write the letter of your answer in the space provided.

_____ **1.** By around 900, towns in Europe began to
  a. slowly appear.
  b. grow up near rivers and castles.
  c. trade with other towns.
  d. do all of the above.

_____ **2.** Something important that came out of the Crusades was the
  a. discovery of the Holy Land.
  b. defeat of the Muslims.
  c. beginning of Europeans' interest in other places.
  d. defeat of Christians in Spain.

_____ **3.** During the Renaissance, people were interested in
  a. studying religion.
  b. learning more about the world around them.
  c. life after death.
  d. none of the above.

_____ **4.** The inventor of the printing press was
  a. Copernicus.
  b. Leonardo da Vinci.
  c. Gutenberg.
  d. Shakespeare.

C. Checking for Details:

Read each statement. Put an F in the space next to each statement if it is a fact. Put an O in that space if it is an opinion. Remember that facts can be proved, but opinions cannot.

_____ **1.** The Renaissance brought happiness to the people of Europe.

_____ **2.** During the Renaissance, people could buy and read books written in their own languages.

_____ **3.** The Crusades helped manufacturing to grow in Europe.

_____ **4.** Renaissance artists were well paid for their work.

_____ **5.** Renaissance merchants were more interested in money than in spreading learning.

_____ **6.** Crusaders brought back spices and luxuries to Europe from the Middle East.

_____ **7.** People who wanted to read the writings of early times had to know Greek and Latin.

_____ **8.** The Renaissance started in the cities of northern Italy.

_____ **9.** The growing merchant class in Europe needed workers who could read and write.

_____ **10.** Life in the medieval towns was better than life on the manor.

_____ **11.** Martin Luther began the Protestant Reformation.

D. Word Meanings:

Look up the following words in the glossary. Write the meaning next to each word.

1. humanists_____

2. manufacturing_____

3. Renaissance_____

E. Understanding Global History:

On page 166, you read about four factors in global history. Which of these factors applies to each statement listed below? Fill in the number of the correct statement on page 166 in the space provided.

_____ **1.** The ideas of the Renaissance spread from northern Italy throughout Europe during the 1500s and 1600s.

_____ **2.** Events in the Holy Land during the Crusades led to many changes in Europe in the 1300s.

_____ **3.** During the Renaissance, people in Europe wanted to know more about people and events of the past.

_____ **4.** Europeans learned about making paper from China and Arabia.

The Revolution in Trade and Industry

Understanding Global History

Think about the following statements as you read about the growth of trade and industry in Europe from the 1100s to the 1400s.

1 Nations are linked by a network of economic interdependence.

2 People use the environment to achieve economic goals.

A medieval banker and his wife.

Learning New Words and Terms

commercial cities: cities whose main business is trade and banking
mint: to make coins and paper money
tariff: a tax placed on imported goods
guilds: groups of merchants and crafts workers
apprentice: a person learning a craft or trade with the help of a master teacher
profit: the money made by business owners from running their businesses

capital: money used to start a business
factories: places where goods are made

Think As You Read

1. How did the Crusades help business and trade in Europe?
2. Why did gold and silver replace land as the main form of wealth?
3. Why did business people want a strong form of government?
4. What were the guilds? The middle class?

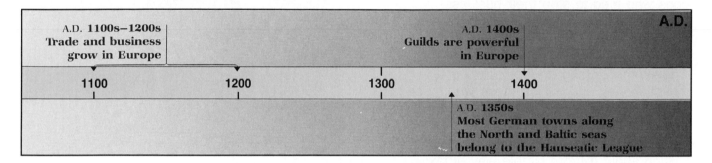

A.D.

A.D. **1100s–1200s**
Trade and business grow in Europe

A.D. **1400s**
Guilds are powerful in Europe

1100   1200   1300   1400

A.D. **1350s**
Most German towns along the North and Baltic seas belong to the Hanseatic League

Trade and Commerce Grow in the Cities

As you have read in Chapter 5, the Crusades brought about a change in trade in Europe. During the 1100s and 1200s, trade and business grew. This was because of the new contacts between Europe and the Middle East. The first important trading cities were Venice, Genoa, and Pisa in northern Italy. They traded across the Mediterranean. Florence was a manufacturing and banking center. It did business with many nations in Europe. All of these Italian cities became rich and powerful.

Trade was also growing in northern Europe. Many people left the farms and manors. They moved to the cities to find new work. The large landowners had fewer workers to farm their land. They then had to sell or rent some of it. In return they received money. The landowners needed this money to buy the many new goods that were appearing in the markets of towns and cities.

There were also people in the towns who could help landowners get money. These were the moneylenders. They made loans of money. But they charged high interest rates. Before long some moneylenders and moneychangers became bankers.

A New Kind of Wealth

During the early Middle Ages, land was the measure of a person's wealth. During the 1200s, money slowly replaced land as a sign of wealth. Money was needed to buy goods and to pay workers. The money used was usually gold or silver. These metals are valuable because they are hard to find and because people desire them.

Some merchants held great wealth in gold and silver. They even lived better than nobles did on their manors.

Merchants Demand Change

There were some major problems in being a merchant in the 1200s. One was that they could be robbed. Someone could steal their gold and silver. Another problem was finding a way to move goods across Europe and the Mediterranean. Europe was made up of many small kingdoms. Each kingdom was supposed to take care of its own roads and bridges, but few did. Merchants began to push for better kinds of trans-

175

portation. They also wanted some sort of central government. Such a government would take care of roads and bridges and improve the forms of transportation.

Merchants also wanted their ships to be protected from attack by pirates. In order to protect themselves against pirates, a number of **commercial cities** along the Baltic and North seas formed the Hanseatic (HAN-see-AT-ik) League. This league of about 80 cities had its own armed forces. It got rid of the pirates in the North Sea. Once this was done, merchants could safely ship their goods. The league also watched over the land routes between Germany and Italy. Sometimes, cities in the league went to war against kings who tried to stop their business.

But the Hanseatic League did not take care of all the problems of the merchants. Merchants still felt there should be one central government. Such a government could do the following:

- **Mint** money and punish those who made fake money
- Build and fix roads and bridges
- Protect travelers and merchants from robbers
- Bring about a more simple way of taxing
- Set aside tax money to pay for an army and navy. The armed forces could then protect citizens and their property.
- Set up one set of laws for everyone
- Limit cheap goods being shipped from other lands. These goods sold for less than the local goods. Merchants wanted a tax placed on goods being imported. This kind of tax is called a **tariff.** Tariffs help local manufacturers.

Crafts Workers and Merchants Organize Themselves

The growth of trade and industry led to the rise of new classes of people from the 1100s to the 1400s. The number of skilled crafts workers living in the cities grew steadily. Crafts workers might be weavers, tailors, or shoemakers. These workers formed **guilds.** Guilds were groups of people who worked at the same trade. The worker guilds, or crafts guilds, set a high standard for skilled work. They also set prices, wages, and hours of work. The guilds checked all work to make sure it was of a high quality. There were also merchant guilds.

These guild members are settling their accounts.

They protected commerce in the towns. They also placed limits on the foreign merchants.

Training to Be a Guild Member

Guild members were called masters. They were highly skilled in their trades. These master crafts workers ran the shops. They also hired young people to serve under them.

Most of the skilled workers of the time were men. A young boy of seven or eight who wanted to learn a trade was sent to a master crafts worker. The young worker was called an **apprentice.** The apprentice usually received a room, food, and some clothing from the master. He did not receive any payment, however. An apprentice might study under his master for anywhere from 3 to 12 years. He then became a journeyman.

The word journeyman comes from the French word *journée,* which means "day." A journeyman was a worker who was paid by the day. He still worked with the help of a master, however. After a time, a journeyman could take a test to become a master crafts worker. He had to show a sample of his work to the guild masters. The journeyman who passed the test became a master crafts worker and guild member. He could open his own shop and maybe teach his sons the trade. Most guilds did not allow women to join. But many women were crafts workers.

The guilds were very powerful in the 1400s. They set high standards, promised good work, and limited the number of people who could become guild members. This kept the quality of goods high. But it also limited the amount of goods that were made. The result was that prices were kept high.

The Middle Class

In the meantime, another class was beginning. This was the middle class. Members of the middle class did not own land and were not crafts workers. They were people who planned the production of goods. Their major goal was to make a **profit.** The more profits they made, the richer they would become.

The middle class brought together those that produced the goods and those that bought the goods. They raised the **capital** to buy raw materials such as wool, lumber, and leather. And they hired people to make goods from these materials. When producing goods, the merchants of the middle class often broke the rules of the guilds. Little by little, the guilds had less power as large-scale, middle-class production grew.

Many middle-class people lived in cities. The middle class was called by different names in different countries. In the Netherlands, they were called burghers. In France, they were called the bourgeoisie (bur-zhwa-ZEE). In England, they were known as factors. Later on, the buildings the English factors used for making and storing goods were called **factories.** You will read about the change in factories in Unit 5.

The middle class of Europe brought great changes to trade and commerce. Guild rules that held back production were removed. The middle class had money, talent, and business knowledge. They helped trade and industry to grow in Europe.

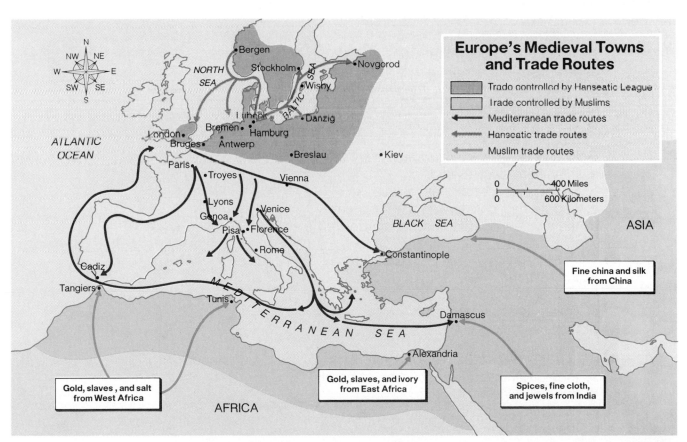

Europe's Medieval Towns and Trade Routes

Trade controlled by Hanseatic League
Trade controlled by Muslims
Mediterranean trade routes
Hanseatic trade routes
Muslim trade routes

Fine china and silk from China

Gold, slaves, and salt from West Africa

Gold, slaves, and ivory from East Africa

Spices, fine cloth, and jewels from India

Exercises

A. Finding the Main Ideas:
Put a check next to the sentences that give the main ideas of what you have just read.

_____ **1.** Merchants wanted tariffs so that goods from other places would not be sold for less.

_____ **2.** The guilds were an important part of business life in European cities.

_____ **3.** The Crusades helped trade and commerce grow in Europe.

_____ **4.** Gold and silver were minted into money during the 1200s.

_____ **5.** European merchants wanted a central government that would protect trade.

B. What Did You Read?
Choose the answer that best completes each sentence. Write the letter of your answer in the space provided.

_____ **1.** As trade grew during the 1100s and 1200s
    a. land became a sign of wealth.
    b. money was used less often.
    c. money became a measure of wealth.
    d. fewer goods were bought and sold.

_____ **2.** Gold and silver were used as money because
    a. they were easy to find.
    b. people knew what they looked like.
    c. people had only limited use for them.
    d. they were valuable and people desired them.

_____ **3.** The crafts guilds
    a. set hours of work.
    b. protected commerce.
    c. limited foreign merchants.
    d. minted money.

_____ **4.** All the following are true about the rising middle class *except:*
    a. they organized the production of goods.
    b. they followed guild rules.
    c. they hired people to make goods.
    d. they raised money to buy raw materials.

C. Understanding What You Have Read:

Tell whether each of the following involved political (P), social (S), or economic (E) aspects of life. Place the correct answer in the space provided.

_____ **1.** Europe was made up of many small kingdoms in the 1200s.

_____ **2.** Some people left the farms and manors to find new work in the cities.

_____ **3.** Trade was growing in northern Europe during the 1100s and 1200s.

_____ **4.** From the 1100s to the 1400s, the number of skilled crafts workers living in the cities grew.

_____ **5.** The guilds checked all work to make sure it was of high quality.

_____ **6.** A central government could set up one set of laws for everyone in the country.

_____ **7.** The middle class wanted to make profits.

D. Thinking it Over:

Answer the following question in three or four sentences. Use a separate piece of paper.

How did an apprentice become a master crafts worker?

E. Word Meanings:

Match each word in Column A with the correct meaning in Column B. Write the letter of each answer in the space provided.

Column A

_____ **1.** apprentice
_____ **2.** capital
_____ **3.** mint
_____ **4.** profit
_____ **5.** factories

Column B

a. to make coins and paper money
b. places where goods are made
c. someone who is learning a trade or craft
d. someone who makes false money
e. money used by the middle class to start a business
f. the money a business owner makes from running a business

F. Understanding Global History:

On page 174, you read about two factors in global history. Which of these factors applies to each statement listed below? Fill in the number of the correct statement on page 174 in the space provided.

_____ **1.** The cities of northern Italy had ties with many parts of the world. Venice carried on trade with the Middle East. Florence served as a banker for European nations.

_____ **2.** Because of their closeness to the sea, many north German cities turned to trade. These cities eventually formed the Hanseatic League. They wanted to protect their shipping across the North and Baltic seas.

Chapter 7

The Age of Discovery

Understanding Global History

Think about the following statements as you read about explorations from the 1400s to the 1700s.

1. Nations choose what they borrow and adapt from other nations.
2. Events occurring in one part of the world have influenced developments in other parts of the world.
3. People should learn to understand and appreciate cultures different from their own.

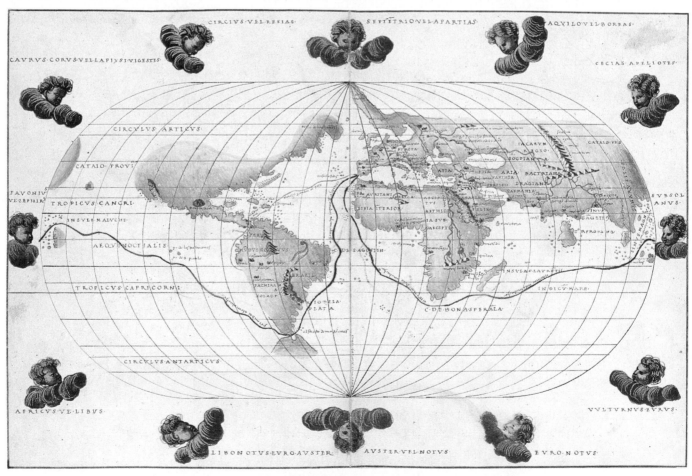

This map was drawn by a Renaissance mapmaker. It shows Magellan's route around the world.

Learning New Words and Terms

compass: an instrument used by sailors to help find their location at sea

colonies: places ruled by another country; colonies are usually found far away from the parent country

Think As You Read

1. Why did Europeans want to go to faraway lands in the 1400s and 1500s?
2. How did the Renaissance help bring about an Age of Discovery?
3. How did the voyages of exploration affect Europe and the world?

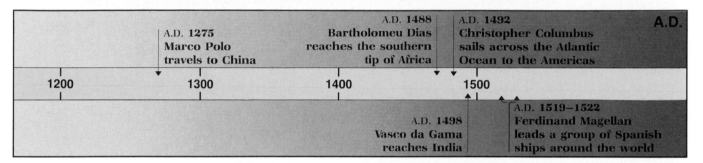

A.D. **1275** Marco Polo travels to China

A.D. **1488** Bartholomeu Dias reaches the southern tip of Africa

A.D. **1492** Christopher Columbus sails across the Atlantic Ocean to the Americas

A.D.

1200 — 1300 — 1400 — 1500

A.D. **1498** Vasco da Gama reaches India

A.D. **1519–1522** Ferdinand Magellan leads a group of Spanish ships around the world

An Interest in Faraway Lands Grows

The Crusaders who traveled to the Holy Land in the 1100s and 1200s returned to Europe with new foods, spices, and fine cloths. These goods made Europeans wonder about Asia and Africa. Some of these goods came from the Muslim lands of the Middle East. Others came from India, China, and the Spice Islands (present-day Indonesia). Islamic merchants had gone to Asia by sea and overland routes. They returned to the Middle East with many new things.

The Renaissance also helped the Europeans to become interested in other lands. As you remember, Europe discovered the Greek and Roman past during the Renaissance. In the late 1400s and early 1500s, Europeans were ready to discover the world outside of their own lands. The more people learned about faraway places the more they wanted to know. The printing press helped spread information. People read books about the travels of traders and adventurers. Europeans wanted to cross lands and oceans to learn more about different countries.

Europeans Seek Riches

Many Europeans wanted to go and see the lands of Asia and Africa. But few Europeans had visited these lands before the 1400s. An Italian merchant, Marco Polo, had gone to China in

Marco Polo before Kublai Khan, the ruler of China.

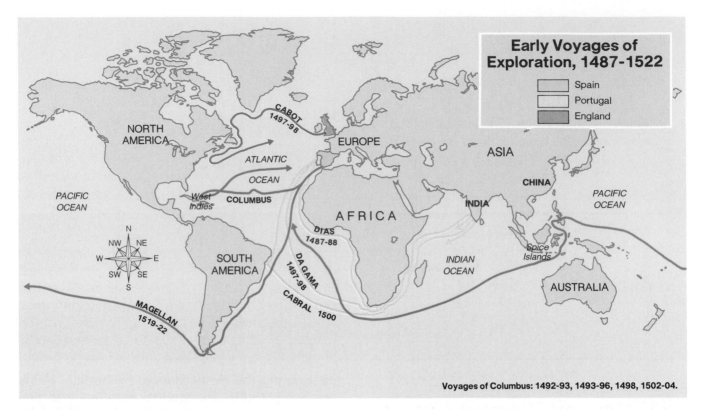

Early Voyages of Exploration, 1487-1522

Spain
Portugal
England

NORTH AMERICA

CABOT 1497-98

EUROPE

ASIA

ATLANTIC OCEAN

OCEAN

PACIFIC OCEAN

CHINA

PACIFIC OCEAN

West Indies

COLUMBUS

INDIA

A F R I C A

N
NW NE
W E
SW SE
S

SOUTH AMERICA

DIAS 1487-88

DA GAMA 1497-98

CABRAL 1500

INDIAN OCEAN

Spice Islands

AUSTRALIA

MAGELLAN 1519-22

Voyages of Columbus: 1492-93, 1493-96, 1498, 1502-04.

1275. He wrote a book about his adventures. This book became very well-known in Europe. It told of the wealth of the Chinese ruler and the ways of life of the country.

The writings of Marco Polo and other travelers interested many in Europe. Merchants hoped to find gold, silver, spices, and fine cloth in the lands outside Europe. Kings and nobles wanted gold and silver to buy silks and spices. These goods were greatly desired in Europe. Kings also wanted gunpowder to use against their enemies. They had learned about gunpowder from the Muslims who brought it to Europe. The Muslims learned about gunpowder from its inventors, the Chinese.

Strong kings were able to carry out their ideas. They paid sea captains to seek and find the new lands of great wealth. They hoped to rule these lands and then build empires. Sea captains and soldiers joined in the search for new lands. They hoped to become rich by finding faster, shorter routes to Asia and Africa.

A Water Route to Asia

People in Europe knew about the faraway land of China from Marco Polo's book. However, the trip to China and eastern Asia was long and dan-gerous. Travelers had to take the land route. Carrying goods over the land was also costly. And there was something else they had to deal with.

The main trade with Asia was carried out by a few Italian cities. If a European country wanted things from Asia, it had to buy from merchants in these cities. The Italian cities were in charge of the land trade routes between Europe and Asia. Because of this fact, the Italian merchants could charge as much as they wanted for Asian goods. If Europeans could find another trade route to Asia they wouldn't have to do business with just a few merchants in one or two cities. They could get the things they wanted at a cheaper price. Perhaps a water route to Asia could be found.

By the mid-1400s, the Europeans were trying to reach India, China, and other Asian lands by sea.

New Skills and Inventions Help Explorers

During the Renaissance, shipbuilders improved the ways in which they built ships. They built ships that could sail across the oceans. The ships were larger, too. They could carry more food and supplies for longer trips. Europeans learned much from other peoples. What they learned helped them become better explorers. For example, they improved the **compass.** This was a Chinese invention that made it easier to set a course for a ship and to follow it. Sea travel was still dangerous, but it was not as frightening as it had been.

Portugal Leads the Way

In the 1400s, Portugal led the way in explorations of other lands. Prince Henry backed the explorations. He was called the Navigator because of his interest in exploration. Prince Henry wanted to build his nation's wealth. One way to do this was to find a way to the Spice Islands of Asia. Over the years Portuguese sea captains sailed along the west coast of Africa. They were looking for a sea route to India. They searched for gold and slaves there. In 1488, Bartholomeu Dias reached the southern tip of Africa. Portugal's way was now open to India and the spices of Asia.

Some Famous Voyages

In the following years, voyages of discovery were made by many countries. Some of these were:
- 1492 Christopher Columbus sailed from Spain across the Atlantic Ocean. He hoped to find a short route to Asia by sailing west. He landed in the Americas instead.
- 1498 Vasco da Gama (VASS-koh duh GAH-muh) of Portugal reached India.
- 1519–1522 Ferdinand Magellan (muh-JELL-un) led a group of five Spanish ships on a voyage around the world. He sailed around South America and across the Pacific Ocean. Magellan was killed during the voyage but one ship reached the Spice Islands of Asia and returned to Spain. Magellan's trip proved it was possible to sail around the world.

The Results of Explorations

During the 1400s and 1500s, the countries of Europe desired new lands for themselves. France, England, and the Netherlands all wanted a part of the rich spice trade to be found in Asia. They wanted to break Portugal's hold on the trade. **Colonies** and trading posts were set up by the Europeans in Asia, Africa, and in the Americas. Spain and Portugal began to build empires in North and South America. As late as the 1700s, Captain Cook searched for and claimed New Zealand and Australia for the British.

The landing of Christopher Columbus in the Americas.

Exercises

A. Finding the Main Ideas:

Put a check next to the sentences that give the main ideas of what you have just read.

_____ **1.** The Renaissance caused the exploration of other lands.

_____ **2.** Marco Polo wrote about the riches to be found in Asia.

_____ **3.** The compass was improved in the 1400s.

_____ **4.** Because shipbuilding and sailing were improved upon, exploration was made possible.

_____ **5.** The Crusaders returned to Europe with silks and spices.

_____ **6.** Explorations were carried out by many countries of Europe.

_____ **7.** Portuguese sea captains took the lead in the search for a shorter route to Asia.

B. What Did You Read?

Choose the answer that best completes each sentence. Write the letter of your answer in the space provided.

_____ **1.** Before the 1400s, few Europeans had visited
    a. Asia.
    b. Africa.
    c. the Spice Islands.
    d. all of the above.

_____ **2.** The invention and improvement of the compass aided
    a. soldiers.
    b. apprentices.
    c. sailors.
    d. merchants.

_____ **3.** An Italian merchant who went to China in the 1200s and wrote about his adventures was
    a. Vasco da Gama.
    b. Marco Polo.
    c. Prince Henry.
    d. a crusader.

_____ **4.** The first voyage around the world was led by
    a. Captain Cook.
    b. Columbus.
    c. Magellan.
    d. none of the above.

C. Map Skills:

Use the letters on the map to identify the following areas. Write the correct letter in the space provided.

_____ **1.** Africa

_____ **2.** Asia

_____ **3.** Australia

_____ **4.** The Indian Ocean

_____ **5.** Europe

_____ **6.** The Pacific Ocean

_____ **7.** North America

_____ **8.** The Atlantic Ocean

_____ **9.** South America

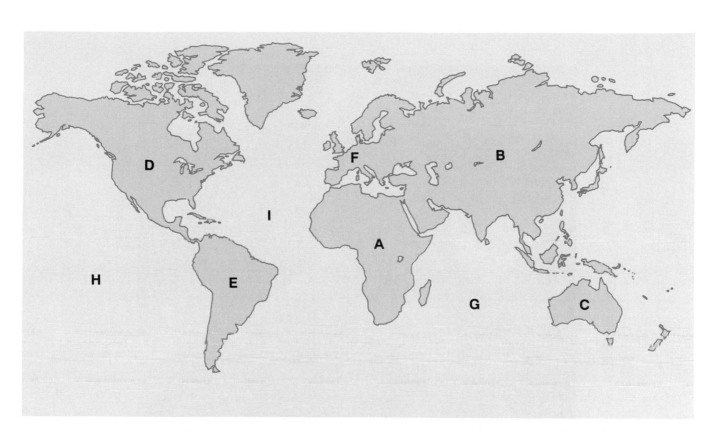

D. Understanding Global History:

On page 180, you read about three factors in global history. Which of these factors applies to each statement listed below? Fill in the number of the correct statement on page 180 in the space provided.

_____ **1.** During the age of exploration, Europeans discovered the world outside their borders. Asians and Africans also discovered Europeans.

_____ **2.** The Crusaders traveled to the Holy Land to free it from Muslim control. The goods they brought back made Europeans want to know all about Asia and Africa.

_____ **3.** Europeans improved upon the inventions of other cultures. They became better explorers through the use of these inventions.

Unit 4
Democracy and Nationalism Grow in Europe

The early rulers of England had unlimited power. In time, they had to share some of their power with the nobles. In 1215, the English nobles forced the king to sign the Magna Carta. This document limited the power of the ruler. The Magna Carta marked an early step in the growth of democracy. You will read about the growth of democracy in Unit 4.

The powers of the English ruler were further limited after the Magna Carta. Rulers were forced to call together the nobles and some commoners to ask for money. These meetings between nobles and common people led to the creation of Parliament. By the early 1700s, the power to make laws had passed from the English rulers to Parliament.

Rule by Parliament did not develop in France. Discontent in that nation led to a revolution. The king was overthrown and a republic was set up. The French people gained their rights. The symbol of liberty is shown in the picture opposite. The republic did not last long, however. Napoleon Bonaparte took control of the government of France. He then led France in an effort to conquer Europe. That effort failed.

The democratic spirit of the French Revolution led to reforms in Europe. In England, voting reforms gave more people a voice in government. Nationalism—the feeling of loyalty to one's nation—also grew in the 1800s. In Europe the spirit of nationalism led to the unification of Italy and Germany. In southeastern Europe and the Middle East, nationalism helped to bring about the downfall of the Ottoman Empire. You will learn about nationalism as you read this unit.

In Unit 4, you will read the following chapters:

1 Early Democracy in England
2 Kings Against Parliament in England
3 Crisis and Revolution in France
4 The Growth of Democracy in Europe
5 Nationalism and the Unification of Italy
6 Nationalism and the Unification of Germany
7 Nationalism and the Ottoman Empire

Chapter 1

Early Democracy in England

Understanding Global History

Think about the following statements as you read about the beginnings of democracy in England.
1 Present culture is shaped by the past.
2 Contact among peoples and nations can lead to cultural changes.

The Bayeux Tapestry tells the story of the Norman conquest of England.
The Norman duke, William, is in the center. Two advisors stand behind him.

Learning New Words and Terms

The following words are used in this chapter. Think about the meaning of each one.

monarch: another name for a king or queen; the ruler of a nation

Magna Carta: the agreement signed by King John of England in 1215; it limited the power of the English monarch

Think As You Read

1. How did England come to be ruled by a monarch with absolute power?
2. How did the Magna Carta limit the powers of the English monarch?
3. In what way did the Magna Carta mark the start of democracy in England?

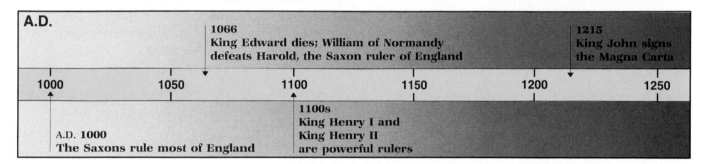

A.D.

1066
King Edward dies; William of Normandy defeats Harold, the Saxon ruler of England

1215
King John signs the Magna Carta

| 1000 | 1050 | 1100 | 1150 | 1200 | 1250 |

A.D. 1000
The Saxons rule most of England

1100s
King Henry I and King Henry II are powerful rulers

Kings and Nobles Share Power

You have been reading about the many changes that came to Europe after the Middle Ages. Europeans wanted to know about the world outside of their borders. The Reformation brought changes in religious life. A revolution in industry and trade began. Art and literature blossomed.

How were these changes shown in government? Who held power in Europe during these years of change? To answer these questions, you must look back to the Middle Ages.

As you may remember, Europeans lived under a system called feudalism during the Middle Ages. In the feudal system, nobles (the upper class) ruled over the common people (the lower class). The common people had few rights and even less power.

During the Middle Ages, Europe was made up of many small kingdoms. And each kingdom was made up of many territories. Each territory was ruled over by a local noble. Some of these nobles were as powerful as the **monarch.** This was the king or queen who was supposed to be their ruler.

Saxon Kings Rule England

This was the situation in England until the early 1000s A.D. Before that time England had been ruled by many different peoples. First it was ruled by the Celts. Then came the Romans, then the Danes, and then the Anglo-Saxons. As you read on pages 22–23, each of these peoples added to the language and the way of life in England. Each left their mark on the government as well.

By about A.D. 1000, the Saxons ruled most of England. Saxon kings had to share power with their nobles. Because of this, no ruler of England had absolute power. This situation changed in A.D. 1066.

The Normans Conquer England

In 1066, King Edward, the Saxon ruler of England died. At that time his cousin, Duke William, was ruling Normandy. This is now part of France. William claimed that King Edward had chosen him to be the next king of England. But Harold, the Saxon King (after Edward's death) and the Saxon nobles did not agree. So William put together an army and crossed the English Channel.

William fought Harold at the Battle of Hastings and defeated him. This was in 1066. Because of this victory, William, the Duke of Normandy became known as William the Conqueror. His conquest of England became known as the Norman Conquest.

As king of England, William wanted to have absolute power. He took over the lands of the Saxon nobles. William made himself the owner of all the land in England. He then gave large sections of land to nobles who backed him. He also made the nobles promise loyalty to him.

English Kings Gain More Power

The kings who followed William the Conqueror tried to rule the same way he did. They tried to be absolute monarchs. They came to believe that they ruled with the consent, or approval, of God. They did not believe they needed the consent of the people or even the nobles.

King Henry I and King Henry II were the most powerful rulers of England. Both kings wanted the nobles to have less power. They did a number of things to make this happen. First, they made new laws. According to the new laws, most court cases would be tried by the king's court. Before, cases were tried by the courts of local nobles. The king's army was also made stronger. Now all men had to serve in the king's army. If they didn't serve, they had to pay money.

The Magna Carta—A Step Towards "Government by the People"

Many English nobles were upset by the actions of Henry I and Henry II. They believed the kings held too much power. Matters grew worse during the rule of King John. The people did not like King John. He forced the English nobles to pay taxes that they felt were not fair. These taxes were often used to pay for useless wars.

GROWTH OF ROYAL POWER IN EARLY ENGLAND

Date	Event	Form of Government
A.D. 407	Romans leave	No organized government
400	Anglo-Saxons invade. They set up 7 separate kingdoms	Each of the 7 kingdoms controlled its own government, courts, army, and taxation. At times, all 7 united under a single king to drive out Danes and other invaders
1066	Normans conquer England. William I claims the throne	An absolute monarchy is established
1100	King Henry I inherits the throne	King William I and his successors claim ever-increasing royal powers until
1134	King Henry II inherits the throne	
1199	King John inherits the throne	*Magna Carta*
1215	Nobles force King John to sign the Magna Carta	Sets limits on the powers of kings and queens

King John signing the Magna Carta. John was a son of King Henry II. He was called "Lackland" because he was poor and landless.

Many nobles in England thought it was now time for the king to have less power. In addition, the English nobles wanted to have their rights spelled out.

In A.D. 1215, the nobles wanted King John to give up some of his powers. He refused. The nobles decided to act. A group of them met with King John. They told him that he must give them certain rights. If he did not, they would turn against him.

The king was frightened. On June 15, 1215, he met with the nobles in a meadow known as Runnymeade. There he signed an agreement with the nobles. This was called the **Magna Carta,** or Great Charter.

How the Magna Carta Limited the Power of Rulers

The Magna Carta was a big step toward limiting the power of English monarchs. It stated the following:

- Nobles could be tried for a crime only before a jury of their equals.
- The king or queen could not make the people pay new taxes unless the Great Council of nobles agreed.
- The king or queen could not delay or deny a trial to any noble.

The Magna Carta meant that the king was not above the law. He had to obey the law, just as everyone else did.

The Magna Carta was meant mainly for the nobles. It did little for the common people. As the years went by, however, the ideas put forward in the Magna Carta came to apply to all the people. The Magna Carta helped to further the idea of democracy, or government by the people. It prepared the way for rights that later became known as "the Rights of Englishmen." After many years, these rights came to apply to women as well as to men.

There had been no democracy in Europe since the time of the early Greeks. The Magna Carta was a small step back toward government by the people.

191

Exercises

A. Finding the Main Ideas:

Put a check next to the sentences that give the main ideas of what you have just read.

_____ **1.** The nobles of England lived well.

_____ **2.** The Magna Carta furthered democracy in England.

_____ **3.** The Magna Carta limited the powers of English kings and queens.

_____ **4.** Many disputes arose between kings and nobles in England.

_____ **5.** For a time, the kings of England tried to be absolute rulers.

B. What Did You Read?

Choose the answer that best completes each sentence. Write the letter of your answer in the space provided.

_____ **1.** Unlimited power of kings was brought to England by
   a. the Romans.
   b. William the Conqueror.
   c. the Saxons.
   d. the Celts.

_____ **2.** The Saxon kings of England
   a. were absolute rulers.
   b. defeated the Romans.
   c. shared power with the nobles.
   d. defeated the Norman invaders.

_____ **3.** William the Conqueror made the English nobles
   a. lend him money.
   b. accept the Magna Carta.
   c. accept Saxon rule.
   d. give him their lands.

_____ **4.** All of the following are true about the Middle Ages *except*
   a. the power of some nobles was almost as great as that of their kings or queens.
   b. the common people had almost no power.
   c. there was a great deal of democracy under feudalism.
   d. the kingdoms of Europe were divided into small territories.

C. Checking for Details:
Read each statement. Put an F in the space next to each statement if it is a fact. Put an O in that space if it is an opinion. Remember that facts can be proved, but opinions cannot.

_____ **1.** An absolute ruler makes all decisions.

_____ **2.** The Saxons were once the strongest group in England.

_____ **3.** William the Conqueror was a better ruler than the Saxon king.

_____ **4.** The English nobles should have forced King John to give up the throne.

_____ **5.** The Magna Carta helped further the ideas of democracy.

_____ **6.** King Henry I tried to increase his power as England's monarch.

_____ **7.** William deserved to become king of England.

_____ **8.** The king's courts were more fair than the local nobles' courts.

_____ **9.** Many kings felt they ruled with the consent of God.

_____ **10.** The Magna Carta was meant mainly for the nobles.

D. Thinking It Over:
Answer each of the following questions in two or three sentences. Use a separate piece of paper.

1. How did unlimited rule by kings come to England?

2. How did King Henry I, King Henry II, and King John try to limit the power of the nobles in England?

3. How did the kings of England lose power because of the Magna Carta?

E. Understanding Global History:
On page 188, you read about two factors in global history. Which of these factors applies to each statement listed below? Fill in the number of the correct statement on page 188 in the space provided.

_____ **1.** The Saxon language and system of government brought changes to English culture.

_____ **2.** After many years, the ideas in the Magna Carta applied to women as well as to men.

_____ **3.** The rights suggested in the Magna Carta came to apply to the common people as well as to the upper class.

Chapter 2

Kings Against Parliament in England

Understanding Global History

Think about the following statements as you read about the growth of democracy in England.

1 Events occurring in one part of the world have influenced developments in other parts of the world.

2 Present culture is shaped by the past.

3 Nations borrow and adapt ideas and institutions from other nations.

After the overthrow of King Charles I, England became a republic. Oliver Cromwell was chosen to head the new government. In 1653, Cromwell, shown standing in the center, put an end to Parliament.

Learning New Words and Terms

The following words are used in this chapter. Think about the meaning of each one.

divine right: a monarch's belief that he or she has been given the right to rule by God

depose: to remove someone from office by force

warrant: a written order issued by a court allowing a search or other action

bail: money left with a court so that an accused person may be let out of jail until the time of his or her trial

Think As You Read

1. How did England's Parliament grow out of the Great Council?
2. What were the rights of the English people that developed in the 1600s and 1700s?
3. Why was membership in Parliament expanded?
4. How did the civil war in England, in 1648, affect relations between the monarchy and the Parliament?
5. How has the growth of democracy in England affected the rest of the world?

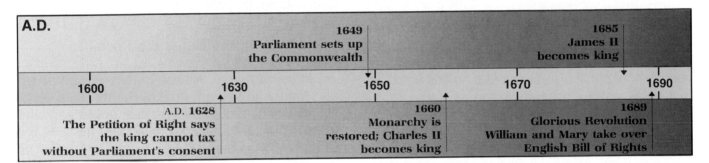

A.D.

1649 Parliament sets up the Commonwealth

1685 James II becomes king

1600 1630 1650 1670 1690

A.D. **1628** The Petition of Right says the king cannot tax without Parliament's consent

1660 Monarchy is restored; Charles II becomes king

1689 Glorious Revolution William and Mary take over English Bill of Rights

The Origins of England's Parliament

When King John signed the Magna Carta, in 1215, he agreed to put limits on his power. One such limit had to do with taxes. In the past, when an English monarch needed money, he would call together the main nobles at a Great Council meeting. The monarch would then order the nobles to give a certain amount of money to the treasurer. The Magna Carta took away some of this taxing power. The king or queen now needed the consent of the Great Council before placing new taxes on the nobles.

As time went on, the monarchs needed more and more money. Because of this, the Great Council was called into session more often.

In 1272, Edward I became king of England. King Edward needed money to fight a war. He called the Great Council into session. He also invited a number of knights, business leaders, and wealthy farmers from each region. The king hoped his invitation would make these people feel important. Then they would help him raise the money he needed for the war. His idea worked. Edward got the help he needed.

From then on, nobles, knights, business people, and wealthy farmers all met in the Great Council. After many years, the council came to be known as Parliament. The name comes from the French world *parler,* which means "to speak." The members of Parliament did a great deal of speaking. They discussed important issues of the day. They questioned the king's policies.

The Power of Parliament Grows

At first all members of Parliament met together. However, after 1295, Parliament had two separate houses. The nobles met in the House of Lords. The merchants, business people, and rich farmers met in the House of Commons.

During the next 300 years, the powers of Parliament grew. For example,

- Parliament gained the right to set all taxes. The House of Commons could propose all new taxes.
- Parliament could tell the king how to spend the money raised through taxes.
- Parliament gained the power to approve changes in laws.

King Versus Parliament

The growing power of the Parliament led to fights with the kings. King Charles I, who ruled from 1625 to 1649, had serious problems with Parliament. King Charles believed that he ruled by **divine right.** He believed God gave him the right to rule the country. Therefore, the people had no right to question anything he decided.

King Charles needed money to fight several wars. Parliament would not back him. So, he tried to make people loan him money. When they would not, Charles had them thrown in jail.

Charles's actions angered the members of Parliament. After all, he was taking away their power to set taxes. Parliament decided to act.

The Petition of Right

In 1628, Parliament presented the Petition of Right to King Charles I. The Petition of Right stated that the king could not tax without Parliament's consent. It also stated that no one could be put in jail without a good reason.

King Charles agreed to the terms of the Petition of Right. He did not follow them, however. He continued to raise taxes. When Parliament objected, he dissolved, or ended, the meeting of Parliament.

Eleven years later, Charles called a meeting of Parliament. He needed money to fight a war against Scotland. When Parliament took steps to limit the king's power, Charles led troops into Parliament and arrested its leaders.

Civil War in England Results in the Overthrow of the King

A civil war, or war within England, followed Charles's actions. The war lasted from 1642 to 1649. Charles I and those who backed him fought against Parliament. The House of Commons led those who backed Parliament. Parliament won and King Charles I was put to death.

In 1649, Parliament set up a republic. A republic is a government run by those elected by the people. The republic was known as the Commonwealth. It lasted until 1660. During this time there was no monarch and no House of Lords. The House of Commons and its leader, Oliver Cromwell, held all the power. Soon Cromwell fought with the House of Commons. Cromwell then put an end to Parliament. He ruled England alone during most of the Commonwealth period.

Kings Are Restored in England

In 1658 Cromwell died. In 1660 Charles II became king. He was able to get along well with Parliament. When Charles died, his brother, James, became king. James II did not get along with Parliament. James angered Parliament by trying to take too much power into his own hands. Parliament decided to **depose** him, or remove him from the throne by force.

Parliament invited James's daughter Mary and her husband, William of Orange, to take over the English throne. William was the leader of the Netherlands. In 1689, William and Mary became rulers of England. What happened during the bloodless overthrow of James came to be known as the Glorious Revolution.

The Bill of Rights Limits the Power of Monarchs

Before they were allowed to take office William and Mary had to sign a Bill of Rights. This Bill of Rights placed many limits on their powers and the powers of future rulers of England. From 1689 on, English monarchs had to accept Parliament as the main force in the English government. The ideas in the English Bill of Rights were used by the Americans in 1787, when they wrote their Constitution.

Since the late 1600s, the House of Lords in Parliament has held less and less power. The House of Commons came to have more power. Members of the House of Lords inherit their position. Members of the House of Commons are elected by the people. Thus, the power of the Commons grew as more people in England were granted the right to vote. Today, the House of Commons has most of the governing power in Parliament.

In England, People Gain More Rights

The English people came to have more power through their elected representatives. They also came to have more rights. By 1700, English people had a number of rights.

These rights included more freedom of speech and freedom to publish one's opinions. They also included the right to be protected from unreasonable searches. Searches of a person's property could only be done when a judge issued a search **warrant.** A judge may do so only when there is

William and Mary being offered the crown of England. The overthrow of James II and the events that followed are known as the Glorious Revolution.

reason to believe that the search will turn up something illegal.

The rights of the English were also given to people who were thought to have broken the law. These people had the right to be freed on **bail** until their trial. This meant that a person could get out of jail by leaving money with the court and promising to return for the trial. An accused person also had the right to have a lawyer and a quick trial by a jury.

The rights of the English people grew over hundreds of years. Once they were formed, they were also important to other nations. For instance, many of the same rights are spelled out in the Bill of Rights of the United States.

Parliamentary Government and Limited Monarchies Spread to Other Countries

England's system of government has also spread to other lands. Many nations of the world today have a parliamentary government. For example, Canada has a Parliament. Canada was once ruled by England and now has a parliamentary system.

Other nations have also followed England's way of limiting the powers of rulers. Many of Europe's present-day kings and queens rule as constitutional monarchs. They have no real power in running the government. The move toward democracy in Europe owes much to the events in England in the 1600s and 1700s.

Exercises

A. Finding the Main Ideas:
Put a check next to the sentences that give the main ideas of what you have just read.

_____ **1.** The Magna Carta was an important document.

_____ **2.** The House of Commons became the most powerful part of the English government.

_____ **3.** The members of the House of Lords inherit their jobs.

_____ **4.** During the 1600s and 1700s, English rights and the power of Parliament grew.

_____ **5.** Beginning with the Magna Carta, various limits have been placed on the powers of the English monarchy.

B. What Did You Read?
Choose the answer that best completes each sentence. Write the letter of your answer in the space provided.

_____ **1.** A search warrant may be issued by a judge only
  a. to protect the officers on duty.
  b. if there is reason to believe a search will turn up something illegal.
  c. to guarantee the rights of the accused.
  d. for all the above reasons.

_____ **2.** The rights of English people do _not_ include the right
  a. of free speech.
  b. to have a lawyer.
  c. to work.
  d. to have a quick trial.

_____ **3.** Since the late 1600s, the House of Lords in England has
  a. gained power.
  b. kept most of its power.
  c. lost much of its power.
  d. been done away with.

_____ **4.** The rise of Parliament
  a. gave more power to the English ruler.
  b. gave all power to the middle class.
  c. helped nobles to get more money.
  d. helped to limit the power of the English ruler.

C. Checking for Details:

Read each statement. Put a T in the space next to each statement if it is true. Put an F in that space if it is false. Put an N if you cannot tell from the reading if it is true or false.

_____ **1.** Taxes in England were very high during the 1200s.

_____ **2.** Search warrants are issued by judges.

_____ **3.** Merchants have always wanted to be members of Parliament.

_____ **4.** William and Mary were invited by Parliament to rule England.

_____ **5.** Farmers, merchants, and business people sat in the House of Commons.

_____ **6.** The Magna Carta protected the English king.

_____ **7.** The English civil war came about from a fight for power between Parliament and the king.

_____ **8.** Parliament set up a republic in England in the 1200s.

_____ **9.** Bail helps some people escape punishment.

_____ **10.** Charles II ruled England after the Commonwealth came to an end.

D. Complete the Sentence:

Fill in the word or term that best completes each statement below. Choose your answer from the follow ing list of words.

elected	accused	throne	deposed
money	lawyer	monarch	merchants
republic	democracy	elected	taxes

1. The Magna Carta made the _____ ask the Great Council for its consent for any new

_____.

2. The Bill of Rights gave _____ people the right to have a _____.

3. After many years, _____ were allowed to sit as members of the House of Commons.

4. Differences with the king led Parliament to set up a _____ in 1649.

5. James II was _____ as king and had to leave the _____.

6. Powers in a democracy are mostly given to _____ officials.

E. Behind the Headlines:

Each headline has a story behind it. Write two or three sentences that support or tell about each of the following headlines. Use a separate piece of paper.

BILL OF RIGHTS SIGNED BY WILLIAM AND MARY

PARLIAMENT MEETS IN TWO HOUSES

ENGLISH PEOPLE PROUD OF THEIR RIGHTS

F. Word Matching:

Match each word in Column A with the correct meaning in Column B. Write the letter of each answer in the space provided.

Column A

_____ **1.** bail
_____ **2.** warrant
_____ **3.** dissolve
_____ **4.** depose
_____ **5.** republic
_____ **6.** divine right

Column B

a. to end the meeting of a lawmaking body
b. God-given right to rule
c. money left with the court so an accused person may be free until a trial is held
d. government run by elected representatives of the people
e. written order issued by a court allowing a search or other action
f. to remove from office
g. a long distance away

G. Understanding Global History:

On page 194 you read about three factors in global history. Which of these factors applies to each statement listed below? Fill in the number of the correct statement on page 194 in the space provided.

_____ **1.** The rights of the Magna Carta first applied to nobles. In time those rights were given to all people in England.

_____ **2.** The English parliamentary form of government spread to and exists in many parts of the world today.

_____ **3.** Parliament deposed James II. It then invited William and Mary to come from the Netherlands to rule England.

_____ **4.** The American Bill of Rights contains the same ideas as stated in the English Bill of Rights.

Enrichment:
John Locke Challenges Absolute Rule by Monarchs

What gave the English Parliament the right to force out King James II? Many people at the time wondered. But a philosopher named John Locke thought he had the answer. His ideas were new in the 1600s.

Locke believed that people had first lived with no government and no laws. However, life became so violent that people chose a leader to rule them. People gave up some of their freedoms so that the leader could rule, said Locke. However, the people kept their natural rights. These were the rights of life, liberty, and property.

What if a ruler tried to take away the people's natural rights? Then, said Locke, the people should throw out the ruler. They should replace him or her with someone who would promise to protect the people's rights.

Many people in the English Parliament accepted Locke's ideas. So they felt that it was all right to depose James II and invite William and Mary to replace him.

Locke's ideas had important effects in other nations. For example, in America Thomas Jefferson had read about Locke's ideas. Jefferson included ideas similar to Locke's when he wrote the American Declaration of Independence in 1776.

John Locke

Chapter 3

Crisis and Revolution in France

Understanding Global History

Think about the following statements as you read about the French Revolution.
1 Events occurring in one part of the world have influenced developments in other parts of the world.
2 Present culture is shaped by the past.
3 Nations borrow and adapt ideas and institutions from other nations.

The storming of the Bastille marked the start of a revolution in France. It took place on July 14. Today, the people of France celebrate July 14 as a national holiday.

Learning New Words and Terms

The following words are used in this chapter. Think about the meaning of each one.

laissez-faire: "let alone"; the idea that government should not regulate or interfere with business

the Enlightenment: the name given to the revolution in thinking that took place in the 1700s; enlightenment means an ability to see and understand things

estates: the name given to the three groups in the French representative assembly

fraternity: feeling of unity among people

Think As You Read

1. Why did the French middle class favor the idea of less government regulation?
2. How was France affected by the American Revolution?
3. Why did Louis XVI call together the Estates-General?
4. What were the important laws passed by the National Assembly?
5. What were some results of the Reign of Terror?
6. What were some of the contributions of Napoleon Bonaparte to France?

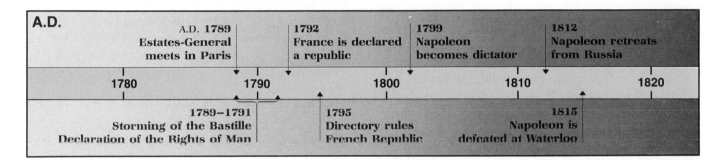

A.D.

| A.D. **1789** Estates-General meets in Paris | **1792** France is declared a republic | **1799** Napoleon becomes dictator | **1812** Napoleon retreats from Russia |

| 1780 | 1790 | 1800 | 1810 | 1820 |

| **1789–1791** Storming of the Bastille Declaration of the Rights of Man | **1795** Directory rules French Republic | **1815** Napoleon is defeated at Waterloo |

Absolute Rulers in France

The beginnings of democracy had come to England by the early 1300s. Yet they came to other countries much later. Democratic ideas did not take hold in France until the late 1700s.

France had been united in the mid-1400s after a number of wars. The French monarchs took steps to gain absolute, or complete, power in the united French nation. They held absolute power for over 300 years. French monarchs believed they ruled by divine right. They believed God gave them the right to rule.

France had an assembly that represented the people during the Middle Ages. It did not become powerful like the English Parliament, however. By the 1700s, the French people had few rights. Also, they had little experience with a parliamentary form of government.

The French Are Unhappy with Their Government

During the 1700s, many French people were unhappy with the government. There were a num-

King Louis XIV ruled France during the 1600s. He built the palace of Versailles. Here, Louis and his court lived in luxury.

ber of reasons for this. The government was run by officials who took bribes. They sometimes even stole money from the treasury. Also, the tax system was terrible. The rich people who owned land paid almost no taxes. Peasants and those who lived in the city were made to pay most of the taxes.

The Middle Class Opposes Government Regulations

The rising middle class in France was angry at the government. They believed that government regulations, or rules, were ruining them. The government made rules about prices and what people could earn. It was also in charge of trade with foreign countries.

Many middle-class French people believed in the ideas of a Scotsman named Adam Smith. Smith had written a book in the late 1700s. It was called *The Wealth of Nations.* Smith believed that if business people were allowed to make profits freely, then everyone in the society would benefit. The profits made in a business would pay the salaries of the workers. Then the nation would gain wealth. Therefore, governments should not regulate or interfere with business. Smith and others supported a **laissez-faire** (LEHS-ay FAIR) economic system.

The French middle class wanted the government to follow the ideas of Adam Smith. The French middle class wanted to be left alone.

A Revolution in Thinking

Smith's idea of laissez-faire was one of many new ideas that were becoming well known in France in the 1700s. John Locke's views were also well liked (see page 201). Other thinkers of this period were the Baron de Montesquieu (mahn-tus-KYOO), Jean Jacques Rousseau (roo-SOH), and Voltaire. The revolution in thinking that was started by these people has been called **the Enlightenment**. Another name for the time of the Enlightenment is the Age of Reason. "Enlightenment" means the ability to see and understand things.

The Ideas of the American Revolution Spread to France

The American Revolution broke out in 1775. Nearly all of France favored the American colonists. Toward the end of the war, France openly joined the Americans in their fight against the Brit-ish. The ideas of the American Revolution and the Declaration of Independence became known to many French people.

The French nobles favored the colonists. They hoped to see Great Britain defeated. They hoped Great Britain would lose its colonies in North America. French peasants, business people, and merchants favored the American colonists because they were fighting for freedom. During the American Revolution, belief in liberty and freedom spread from America to France.

The French King Calls Together the Estates-General

By 1788, the French government was in serious trouble. The treasury was empty. Earlier kings had spent money on wars. The French kings had also spent money on themselves. They lived in grand style. In the late 1700s, King Louis XVI had to find new sources of income. He decided to seek help from the French Estates-General. In 1789, the Estates-General met in Paris for the first time in almost 200 years.

In France, the representatives of the people belonged to the Estates-General. It got this name because the people of France were divided into three groups. These groups were called **estates.** The First Estate was made up of church officials. The Second Estate was composed of nobles. The Third Estate was made up of peasants, city workers, and the middle class.

The National Assembly Is Formed

When the Estates-General met in 1789, the king declared that each estate would have only one vote. The Third Estate represented over 96 percent of the population and had 600 representatives. However, it was given no more votes than any other estate.

The Third Estate was against this. They wanted more votes. The king did not do anything about it, however. So, the Third Estate took matters into its own hands. Members of the Third Estate and others who wanted reform met at a tennis court. There, they promised not to separate as a group until they wrote a constitution for France. The king gave in at this point. He allowed the estates to meet together in one body. This was the National Assembly. In the Assembly, votes would be divided more fairly among the estates.

This cartoon shows the burdens of the Third Estate. The First and Second Estates (the clergy and the nobility), are riding on the back of the Third Estate (the common people).

The Start of a Revolution in France

The king finally accepted the National Assembly. However, when he began gathering troops near the meeting of the Assembly, the people of Paris became angry. They feared he would try to stop the National Assembly by force. On July 14, 1789, an angry group of people attacked the Bastille. This was a prison in Paris. There were only seven prisoners in the Bastille. This action, however, served as a warning to the king. It was the first time the French people took up arms against the government.

Changes Brought About by the National Assembly

In the next two years (1789–1791) the National Assembly met and wrote a new constitution. It also passed a series of reform laws. These laws gave less power to the monarch. They also provided for a one-house parliament. The laws also put an end to the old system of taxes. Business people gained greater freedom.

The National Assembly also issued the Declaration of the Rights of Man. This document was partly based on the English Bill of Rights and the American Declaration of Independence. It called for equality for all French citizens. It also stated that private property should be protected.

Fear of Revolution Spreads

What was happening in France frightened the rulers of Europe. They feared revolution might spread to their kingdoms. Austria and Prussia sent armies into France to try to end the Revolution. The leaders of the Revolution in France believed King Louis XVI was helping Prussia and Austria. They removed the king from office and held elections for a new parliament.

France Becomes a Republic

The new French parliament was called the National Convention. In 1792, the Convention declared France a republic. It adopted the slogan, "Liberty, Equality, **Fraternity**." A new army was formed. A Committee of Public Safety was set up. Its main goal was to remove the enemies of the Revolution.

Fear of its enemies led the republic to move away from democratic ideas. Louis XVI and his queen, Marie Antoinette, were ordered killed in 1793. A period of bloodshed followed.

The Reign of Terror

The new French army was able to defeat the Prussians and Austrians. However, the new leaders of France were still afraid the Revolution might fail. From 1793 to 1794, they arrested and killed those who were against the Revolution. This time became known as the Reign of Terror. Thousands of people were beheaded during the Reign of Terror. Anyone who was against the Revolution was killed.

The Reign of Terror crushed the French nobles and the supporters of monarchy. But, at the same time, it harmed the Revolution. Before long, the leaders of the Revolution were accusing each other of working to overthrow the new government. Many were killed.

The leadership of the Revolution now passed out of the hands of the National Convention. In 1795, a committee called the Directory took over rule of the French republic. The leaders of the Revolution could not control the nation. In 1799, a young army general, Napoleon Bonaparte, took over the government. Napoleon became dictator of France.

Napoleon Bonaparte Leads France

The French Revolution had at first been saved by the new army it created. The new army was much better than the old army. Nobles had led the old army. When Austrian and Prussian troops invaded France, the new army was able to defeat them.

In the new army hundreds of young officers had been promoted. They had been given important command posts. One young officer of the new army was Napoleon Bonaparte. He was 24 years old when France was invaded by those who were against the Revolution. Napoleon was promoted quickly. He became a general at the age of 26. He won victories against the Austrians in Italy. Next, he led his armies against the English forces in Egypt. Napoleon was less successful in Egypt. However, his fame still grew.

While Napoleon gained fame in battle, the Reign of Terror was spreading through France. In 1795, the power of government was given to the Directory. By this time the democratic ideas of the Revolution were in danger.

By 1799, the Revolution had gotten out of control. Given the weakened state of the government, a strong leader could step in and take command. Napoleon Bonaparte proved to be that leader. He returned to France in 1799 as a war hero. Napoleon then took control of the government.

Napoleon Declares Himself Emperor of France

Napoleon did not believe in democracy. However, he pretended to believe in the republic and the Revolution. Napoleon's real goal was to rule all of Europe.

In 1804, Napoleon made himself Emperor of France. He took personal command of the army. France was soon at war with most of Europe and Great Britain. Napoleon was a great general and won many battles. However, he could not defeat Great Britain. The British navy would not let him invade the island nation. Napoleon had to remain in Europe.

The British government feared Napoleon's goals. They also feared that he might spread the

Napoleon as Emperor of France. Napoleon first gained fame as a young general during the French Revolution.

ideas of the French Revolution. For these reasons they kept leading wars against Napoleon.

Napoleon Is Defeated

In 1812, Napoleon made his greatest mistake. He sent a half million of his best soldiers to take over Russia. After some early victories, the French became trapped deep inside Russia. They had little food or shelter. The weather was deathly cold. Small groups of Russian soldiers made surprise attacks against the French. At the same time, the Russian government would not talk about peace terms. Napoleon had to order a retreat. Most of his army was lost in the Russian war. Because of this, Napoleon's power was badly weakened.

In 1814, Napoleon was back at war in Europe. He was defeated by the united forces of Great Britain, Austria, Russia, and Prussia. Napoleon was taken prisoner and sent to live outside of France.

Napoleon escaped in 1815. He got together a new French army in a comeback effort. However, his efforts failed. Napoleon's army was defeated

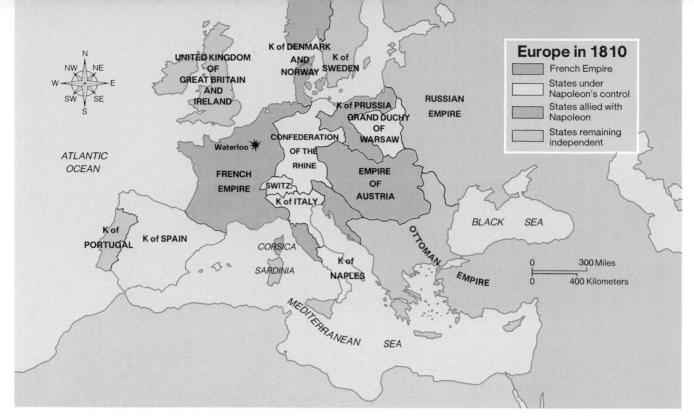

Europe in 1810

- French Empire
- States under Napoleon's control
- States allied with Napoleon
- States remaining independent

at the battle of Waterloo (in present-day Belgium). This time Napoleon was sent to live on the island of St. Helena, in the South Atlantic Ocean. He died there in 1821.

Factors That Influenced the French Revolution

The years 1789–1815 brought great changes to France, Europe, and many parts of the world. These were the years of the French Revolution and the rule of Napoleon Bonaparte.

The leaders of the French Revolution owed much to others. They were influenced by the writers and thinkers of the Enlightenment. The economic ideas of Adam Smith also influenced many leaders of the French Revolution. The French were also strongly influenced by the American Revolution (1775–1783).

The Results of the French Revolution and the Age of Napoleon

These many influences did not stop the leaders of the French Revolution from making errors. However, they did help the French leaders to make important changes in French life and government. For example,

- During the Revolution the government ended the feudal rights of nobles. It gave greater freedom to merchants and business people.
- The government started a new and fairer system of taxes. These new taxes made the burden on peasants and business people lighter.
- The National Assembly changed the system of local government. It set up local assemblies to rule the people in each part of the country.
- The government of the Revolution issued the Declaration of the Rights of Man. This declaration gave more rights to all the people.
- The large amount of land that was owned by the Church was broken up and sold to peasants. For the first time, many French farmers could own their own land.
- The powers of Church and government were separated. The Roman Catholic church was strongly against this. However, the Church remains a part of French life to this day.
- Slavery was abolished, or outlawed, in France and its possessions. This action set free tens of thousands of black people.
- Napoleon also introduced many reforms.
- He helped make public education better.
- He introduced changes to France's financial system.
- He also set up the Code Napoléon in 1804. This code gave a single set of laws for France and the territories it ruled. The Code Napoléon influenced codes in other countries.

The leaders of the French Revolution owed much to the ideas of other lands. In turn, the ideas of the French Revolution have greatly influenced many people in many parts of the world since the 1800s.

Exercises

A. Finding the Main Ideas:

Put a check next to the sentences that give the main ideas of what you have just read.

_____ **1.** The American Revolution influenced the French Revolution.

_____ **2.** The National Assembly passed a number of reform laws.

_____ **3.** The French people attacked the Bastille on July 14, 1789.

_____ **4.** The French government faced a crisis in the 1700s.

_____ **5.** Adam Smith developed the idea of laissez-faire.

_____ **6.** The French Revolution became less democratic as time went on.

_____ **7.** Napoleon Bonaparte took advantage of France's weakened government to gain power.

B. What Did You Read?

Choose the answer that best completes each sentence. Write the letter of your answer in the space provided.

_____ **1.** The Estates-General was
   a. a representative assembly.
   b. made up of three groups.
   c. less powerful than England's Parliament.
   d. all of the above.

_____ **2.** Most French people belonged to the
   a. First Estate.
   b. Second Estate.
   c. Third Estate.
   d. Directory.

_____ **3.** The National Assembly provided for
   a. a new system of taxes.
   b. a limited monarchy.
   c. a constitution for France.
   d. all of the above.

_____ **4.** The Committee of Public Safety sought to
   a. protect the king.
   b. end the Reign of Terror.
   c. remove enemies of the Revolution.
   d. select a new king.

_____ **5.** Napoleon's ambition was to rule all of
   a. France.
   b. Great Britain.
   c. North America.
   d. Europe.

C. Checking for Details:

Read each statement. Put a T in the space next to each statement if it is true. Put an F in that space if it is false. Put an N if you cannot tell from the reading if it is true or false.

_____ **1.** Wealthy landowners paid most of the taxes in France.

_____ **2.** The French middle class favored the ideas of Adam Smith.

_____ **3.** Most French people were poor farmers.

_____ **4.** Foreign armies tried to crush the French Revolution.

_____ **5.** The Bastille was not used as a prison after 1789.

_____ **6.** Napoleon overthrew the Directory.

_____ **7.** The American Revolution took place before the French Revolution.

_____ **8.** The Reign of Terror was used by the nobles against the leaders of the Revolution.

D. Time Line Skills

In which period of time did each of the following events occur? You may look at the time line on page 203 and the text for help.

_____ **a.** Estates-General meets in Paris

_____ **b.** French people attack the Bastille

_____ **c.** National Convention declares France a republic

_____ **d.** The Directory takes over rule of France

_____ **e.** Napoleon takes over the government of France

f. Napoleon defeated at Waterloo

E. Understanding Global History:

On page 202 you read about three factors in global history. Which of these factors applies to each of the statements listed below? Fill in the number of the correct statement on page 202 in the space provided. If no factor applies, fill in the word NONE.

_____ **1.** The French treasury was bankrupt in 1788.

_____ **2.** The French middle class believed in the ideas of Adam Smith, a Scot.

_____ **3.** During the American Revolution, belief in liberty and freedom spread from America to France.

_____ **4.** French people celebrate the attack on the Bastille every year on July 14.

_____ **5.** The Code Napoléon influenced codes of law in many countries.

Chapter 4

The Growth of Democracy in Europe

LE CONGRÈS.

There were so many parties at the Congress of Vienna that someone said "The Congress dances, but accomplishes nothing." The delegates to the Congress of Vienna did much, however. They redrew the borders of Europe after the defeat of Napoleon.

Learning New Words and Terms

The following words are used in this chapter. Think about the meaning of each one.

liberal: forward-looking; favoring gradual change

feminist: having to do with women's rights

Think As You Read

1. What nations made up the Quadruple Alliance? What were the aims of the alliance?
2. What democratic reforms did the British government bring about?

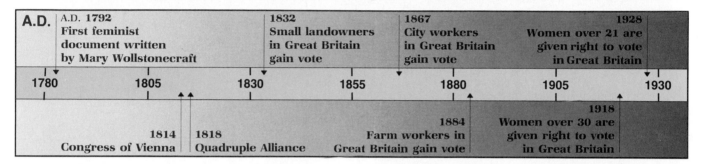

A.D.

| A.D. **1792** First feminist document written by Mary Wollstonecraft | **1832** Small landowners in Great Britain gain vote | **1867** City workers in Great Britain gain vote | **1928** Women over 21 are given right to vote in Great Britain |

1780   1805   1830   1855   1880   1905   1930

1814 Congress of Vienna **1818** Quadruple Alliance **1884** Farm workers in Great Britain gain vote **1918** Women over 30 are given right to vote in Great Britain

The Congress of Vienna

The French Revolution and the rule of Napoleon effected life throughout Europe. The ideas of liberty, equality, and fraternity stirred people all over the continent. The rulers of other countries feared unrest would spread to their lands. So when Napoleon was first defeated, in 1814, these nations met at Vienna. (Vienna is the capital city of Austria.) Great Britain, Austria, Russia, and Prussia led the meeting. One of its goals was to undo the changes made by the French Revolution and Napoleon. The name given to the meeting of these nations was the Congress of Vienna. A congress is a kind of gathering.

The Quadruple Alliance

The Congress of Vienna led to the organization of the Quadruple Alliance. It was called this because quadruple means "involving four things." The Quadruple Alliance was made up of four nations—Great Britain, Austria, Russia, and Prussia. These countries formed the alliance to prevent democratic revolutions in Europe. They hoped to stamp out the influence of the French Revolution. Prince Metternich of Austria was very important in influencing events. Metternich believed that absolute monarchies were the only good governments.

France was now led by King Louis XVIII. (He was the brother of Louis XVI, who was killed.) A

Prince Metternich was an important delegate to the Congress of Vienna.

211

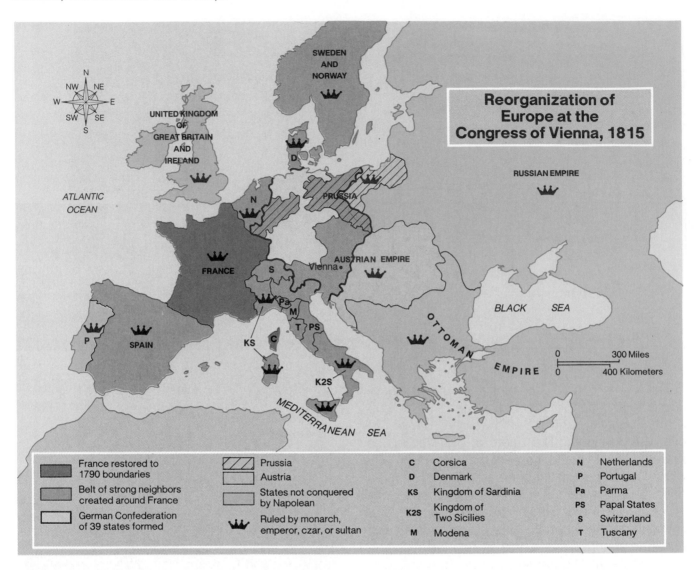

Reorganization of Europe at the Congress of Vienna, 1815

	France restored to 1790 boundaries		Prussia	C	Corsica	N	Netherlands
	Belt of strong neighbors created around France		Austria	D	Denmark	P	Portugal
	German Confederation of 39 states formed		States not conquered by Napolean	KS	Kingdom of Sardinia	Pa	Parma
			Ruled by monarch, emperor, czar, or sultan	K2S	Kingdom of Two Sicilies	PS	Papal States
				M	Modena	S	Switzerland
						T	Tuscany

limited monarchy had been restored in France after the fall of Napoleon. France joined the alliance in 1818. Great Britain left in 1820. Armed forces from the Quadruple Alliance helped crush revolutions in Spain and in two Italian kingdoms.

People in Europe Demand Reforms

The members of the Quadruple Alliance hoped to "turn back the clock." They wanted to return to the days of absolute monarchs. However, progress toward democracy continued. The desire for reform could not be crushed. Workers and peasants in Europe were unhappy with their lives. People living in cities complained of poor housing and bad health conditions. The poorer classes, and many in the middle class, felt they had no voice in government. Women began to ask for more rights. The effort to spread democracy was felt in

all of Europe. It is most clearly seen, however, in events in Great Britain.

Room for Change in Great Britain

In many ways the British had the most **liberal** government in Europe. Britain's government was forward-looking. It was more willing than others to accept gradual change. There was room for more change in Britain, however. For example, there were limits on the right to vote. Voting was generally limited to men who owned land. Catholics and Jews were not allowed to vote or hold office. Women could not vote or hold office. As you can see, only a small group of people could vote in Great Britain.

In addition, the way of electing members of Parliament was often done outside of the law. Votes

Mary Wollstonecraft, shown on the right, was an English feminist. She lived from 1759 to 1797. Women in Europe took part in reform movements. Women's groups, such as the one shown on the left, raised money for the cause of reform.

could be bought. Bribes were a common part of British political life.

Leaders in Great Britain Bring About Reform

In the 1800s, leaders in Great Britain brought about reforms. These reforms brought a greater amount of democracy to Britain. Catholics and Jews were allowed to vote and hold office. The system of choosing members of Parliament was slowly changed.

More people in Great Britain gained the right to vote. This came about as a result of several reform bills. These were
- *The Reform Bill of 1832*—gave the right to vote to the middle class. Before 1832, only large landowners were allowed to vote. Now, small landowners and tenants could vote.
- *The Reform Bill of 1867*—gave the right to vote to city workers. Most of these workers did not own land. They did not own their own homes, either. They paid rents.
- *The Reform Bill of 1884*—gave the right to vote to agricultural workers.

Women in Great Britain Demand Equal Rights

Women wanted equal rights, too. During the 1800s, a small but determined group of women in England began the **feminist** movement. An English writer and feminist, Mary Wollstonecraft supported equal education for men and women. She wrote the first great feminist document in 1792.

Feminists demanded
- the right of women to vote.
- the right to hold office.
- the right to receive a full education.
- the right to control their own property.

Most men were not in favor of equal rights for women in the 1800s. However, there were some men who did agree with the feminist movement.

By the end of the 1800s, feminists in Great Britain had won some victories. A growing number of women were able to go to colleges. A few women became doctors and lawyers. In 1918, women in Great Britain over the age of 30 were given the right to vote. Finally, in 1928, all women over the age of 21 were given voting rights.

Exercises

A. Finding the Main Ideas:

Put a check next to the sentences that give the main ideas of what you have just read.

_____ **1.** Several European nations met at the Congress of Vienna.

_____ **2.** Great Britain brought about a number of democratic reforms in the 1800s.

_____ **3.** The government of England is made up of a monarch and Parliament.

_____ **4.** Some nations tried to crush nationalism and democracy after 1815.

_____ **5.** Women could go to schools and colleges more easily after 1900.

_____ **6.** Feminists worked to gain the same rights as men throughout the 1800s.

B. What Did You Read?

Choose the answer that best completes each sentence. Write the letter of your answer in the space provided.

_____ **1.** In many ways, the English government in the early 1800s was
  a. less liberal than other governments.
  b. a nearly perfect government.
  c. the most liberal government in Europe.
  d. the least liberal government in Europe.

_____ **2.** The demands for reform in England and Europe in the 1800s included
  a. better health conditions.
  b. better housing.
  c. more rights for women.
  d. all of the above.

_____ **3.** Members of the quadruple Alliance did *not* include
  a. Spain.
  b. England.
  c. Austria.
  d. Russia.

_____ **4.** The Reform Bill of 1867 gave the right to vote to
  a. all men.
  b. women.
  c. city workers.
  d. all of the above.

214

C. Checking for Details:

Read each statement. Put a T in the space next to each statement if it is true. Put an F in that space if it is false. Put an N if you cannot tell from the reading if it is true or false.

_____ **1.** The Congress of Vienna met off and on until 1820.

_____ **2.** Women first gained the right to vote in England in 1928.

_____ **3.** By 1870, important steps toward democracy had been made in Prussia.

_____ **4.** Political reform did not affect democracy.

_____ **5.** The Quadruple Alliance was against democracy.

_____ **6.** In 1800, England had the most liberal government in Europe.

_____ **7.** Education became more widespread for women by the end of the 1800s.

_____ **8.** The feminist movement wanted the right to vote for women.

D. Thinking It Over:

Answer the following question in an essay of at least 50 words. Use a separate piece of paper.

How did reforms in the 1800s affect women and workers?

E. Word Meanings:

Look up the following words in the glossary. Write the meaning next to each word.

liberal: _____

feminist: _____

F. Understanding Global History:

On page 210, you read about three factors in global history. Which of these factors applies to each statement listed below? Fill in the number of the correct statement on page 210 in the space provided.

_____ **1.** British women gained full voting rights in 1928.

_____ **2.** Napoleon's army carried the spirit of the French Revolution to the rest of Europe.

_____ **3.** The French Revolution finally led to the forming of the Quadruple Alliance.

215

Chapter 5

Nationalism and the Unification of Italy

Understanding Global History

Think about the following statements as you read about the unification of Italy.

1 Events occurring in one part of the world have influenced developments in other parts of the world.

2 Present culture is shaped by the past.

Giuseppe Garibaldi led Italian troops in the fight to unify Italy. In this picture he is holding the Italian flag.

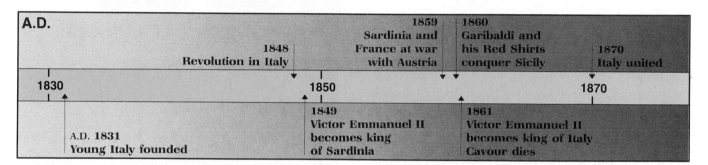

A.D.

| | | 1848 Revolution in Italy | 1859 Sardinia and France at war with Austria | 1860 Garibaldi and his Red Shirts conquer Sicily | 1870 Italy united |

1830 — 1850 — 1870

A.D. 1831 Young Italy founded

1849 Victor Emmanuel II becomes king of Sardinia

1861 Victor Emmanuel II becomes king of Italy Cavour dies

A Feeling of Nationalism Grows In Italy

Italy is in southern Europe. Located on the Mediterranean Sea, it had been the center of the Roman Empire. Italy had been joined together in one country all during early Roman times. When Rome fell, in the late 400s A.D., Italy broke into a number of small kingdoms. Over the next 1,000 years, Italy stayed separated.

In the early 1800s, Napoleon Bonaparte conquered Italy. He grouped together some of the kingdoms so he could rule more easily.

Napoleon's action had another result, however. It helped Italian **nationalism**. By joining kingdoms, Napoleon had made new chances for Italians to get to know each other. This made Italians feel as if they belonged to one nation.

Obstacles to Unification

In 1815, after the Congress of Vienna, Italy was still made up of a number of kingdoms and states. Many people in Italy were in favor of **unification**. There were several reasons, however, why Italy could not easily be joined together.

- First, Austria was against a united Italy. Austria was then a powerful nation to the north of Italy

(see map, page 219). The Austrians wanted Italy to remain divided and weak.
- Second, many of the rulers of small Italian kingdoms were against a united Italy. They feared it might mean the loss of their own powers.
- Third, the pope was against a united Italy. He feared that unity might cause the Roman Catholic church to lose land it held in Italy. At that time most of central Italy was ruled by the Church and its officials.

Mazzini Works for a United Italy

Several groups in Italy favored unity. One such group was called Young Italy. It was founded in 1831. The leader of Young Italy was Giuseppe Mazzini (joo-ZEH-pay mah-ZEE-nee). Mazzini spent his life trying to bring about a united Italian republic. He was sent to jail. He also was forced to leave Italy for a time. As a result of his leadership, Mazzini became known as "the soul" of Italy.

A Revolt in Italy Fails

In 1848, revolts broke out in parts of Europe. They were led by people who favored more democracy and individual rights. The revolutionaries in Italy wanted freedom and democracy. Italy's

1848 revolution, like those in the rest of Europe, failed.

Austrian and French troops helped to crush the Italian revolution. During the revolt, the king of Sardinia tried to help the uprising. (The kingdom of Sardinia was made up of Piedmont, Nice and Savoy, and the island of Sardinia.) He declared war on Austria. He hoped this would force Austria to divide its army. Then the Italian revolution would have a better chance. Instead, this brave act led to the defeat of Sardinia. Even though it was defeated, Sardinia won the respect of all Italy.

Cavour and Sardinia Lead the Drive Towards Unity

The Austrians made the king of Sardinia leave office. His son, Victor Emmanuel II, became king in 1849. He made Camillo di Cavour his **prime minister**. Cavour introduced reforms that made Sardinia stronger. It became the leader of the effort for Italian unity. His wise actions won Cavour the nickname of "the brain" of Italy.

Cavour knew Italy could not be united as long as Austria ran its affairs. So, in 1859, Sardinia joined France in a war against Austria. Together they hoped to end Austrian rule of some parts of northern Italy. These parts would then be divided between France and Sardinia.

The fighting was going well when France suddenly ended the war. The French were afraid that a united Italy would be a threat to them. Because of the French pullout, Sardinia did not get all the territory it had hoped to get. However, Sardinia did **annex** the neighboring region of Lombardy (see map, page 219). This nearly doubled the size of Sardinia.

The success of Sardinia made it the center of nationalist feeling in Italy. In 1860, the people of the regions of Modena, Parma, and Tuscany turned against Austria and joined with Sardinia.

Garibaldi Brings Together Southern and Northern Italy

A new leader arose in Italy. His name was Giuseppe Garibaldi (GAIR-uh-BAL-dee). He was a soldier. Garibaldi's skill as a soldier led him to be called "the sword" of Italian unity. In 1860, Garibaldi set out to conquer the Kingdom of the Two Sicilies (see map, page 219). He wanted the Two Sicilies to join together with the rest of Italy.

Count Cavour used diplomatic means to win Italian unity.

Garibaldi's army was made up of 1,000 volunteers. They were called "Red Shirts" because of the red woolen shirts they wore.

Garibaldi's goal was to unite Italy. He set out to do this with a small army. He believed that thousands of Italians would come to join him. Garibaldi was right. He invaded Sicily. Then many Sicilian soldiers joined with the Red Shirts. Together they freed Sicily.

Garibaldi then sailed with his army to the Italian mainland. He moved north to the area of Naples.

Unification Is Won

While Garibaldi was moving north to Naples, Cavour sent an army south from Sardinia. By the end of 1860, the two armies had freed most of Italy. Garibaldi met Victor Emmanuel in October 1860. The soldier greeted the monarch as king of Italy and then retired. King Victor Emmanuel II of Sardinia became the ruler of a nearly united Italy in March 1861. Three months later, Cavour died.

In 1860, the people of the Kingdom of the Two Sicilies voted to join Sardinia. This was one of the steps that led to the unification of Italy.

Only two parts of Italy were not yet free of foreign control. Rome remained in the hands of the pope. Venetia (vuh-NEE-sha), a kingdom in the north, was ruled by Austria. Soon, both Rome and Venetia would also become part of the now united Italy.

In 1866, the Italians joined Prussia in a war against Austria. Austria was badly beaten. A treaty gave Italy the territory of Venetia. The new government of Italy still had much to do, however. The problem of Rome had to be solved. In 1870, France fought a war against Prussia. France had kept some troops in Rome to back the pope. Now it had to take out these troops to fight Prussia. Italy took the opportunity to take over Rome. The pope's army put up a small fight. It was no match for the Italian troops, though. After adding Rome, Italy was finally one united nation.

Nationalism played a big role in bringing Italy together. Skilled leaders and a bit of luck also led to the unification of Italy. The new nation owed much to the spirit of nationalism and to its heroes, Mazzini, Cavour, and Garibaldi.

Unification of Italy

- Kingdom of Sardinia created in 1815
- Added to Sardinia, 1859-60
- Lost by Sardinia, 1860
- Added to Italy, 1866-70

P Parma
M Modena
T Tuscany

Exercises

A. Finding the Main Ideas:
Put a check next to the sentences that give the main ideas of what you have just read.

_____ **1.** Napoleon defeated Italy.

_____ **2.** Many factors held back Italian unity.

_____ **3.** The goal of "Young Italy" was to unite the nation.

_____ **4.** Sardinia led the efforts to unite Italy.

_____ **5.** The efforts of Mazzini, Cavour, and Garibaldi were important to the unification of Italy.

_____ **6.** Victor Emmanuel II became king of a united Italy.

B. What Did You Read?
Choose the answer that best completes each sentence. Write the letter of your answer in the space provided.

_____ **1.** The appointment of Cavour as prime minister of Sardinia
    a. pleased Austria.
    b. strengthened Sardinia.
    c. weakened Sardinia.
    d. had little effect on Italy.

_____ **2.** Sardinia joined France against Austria in 1859 and
    a. was able to found a united Italian state.
    b. won the war but gained no new territory.
    c. gained the territory of Lombardy.
    d. gained Rome.

_____ **3.** When Napoleon took over Italy, he
    a. set up a republic.
    b. made himself king of Italy.
    c. joined together a number of kingdoms.
    d. increased the number of kingdoms.

_____ **4.** An important result of the 1848 revolt in Italy was that
    a. Sardinia defeated Austria.
    b. Mazzini became the leader of Sardinia.
    c. all Italy was united.
    d. Sardinia won the respect of all Italy.

C. Checking for Details:

Read each statement. Put a T in the space next to each statement if it is true. Put an F in that space if it is false. Put an N if you cannot tell from the reading if it is true or false.

_____ **1.** After the Congress of Vienna, Italy was made up of many states.

_____ **2.** Napoleon ruled Italy wisely.

_____ **3.** Mazzini was a rich man.

_____ **4.** Austria favored a united Italy.

_____ **5.** The pope did not want a united Italy.

_____ **6.** Cavour was a better leader than Mazzini.

_____ **7.** Sardinia won the respect of Italy after the 1848 revolt.

_____ **8.** Garibaldi led a small group to take over Sicily.

_____ **9.** Italy fought Prussia in 1866.

_____ **10.** Italy was completely united in 1870.

D. Who Were They?

Name the person or groups of people described in each sentence. Write the answer in the space provided.

_____ **1.** He was the prime minister of Sardinia. He knew that Austria's control of Italy must end.

_____ **2.** His army freed Sicily and southern Italy from foreign rule.

_____ **3.** He conquered Italy in the early 1800s and his actions helped Italian nationalism.

_____ **4.** He led the "Young Italy" movement and was sent to jail for his efforts to unite the nation.

_____ **5.** He became the first king of a united Italy.

_____ **6.** He ruled over most of the land in central Italy.

_____ **7.** He tried to help the Italian revolt of 1848 by declaring war on Austria.

E. What Does It Mean?

Read the passage below and write the essay as directed. Use a separate piece of paper for your essay.

In 1858, the king of Sardinia spoke to his parliament. Hundreds of men and women were in the audience. Many had been made to leave other parts of Italy because they favored a united Italy.

During his speech the king said, "We are not deaf to the cry of anguish [suffering] that comes to us from other parts of Italy." These words were greeted with wild cheers. A member of the audience later said, "When the king spoke of 'the cry of anguish' everyone cheered. We cheered that king who remembered us and promised us a country. He was king in our hearts."

In at least 100 words, write an essay telling:

a. what the king meant by a "cry of anguish."
b. why the audience cheered the king's remarks.
c. why people felt the king was the king in their hearts.

F. Understanding Global History:

On page 216, you read about two factors in understanding history. Which of these factors applies to each statement listed below? Fill in the number of the correct statement on page 216 in the space provided. If no factor applies, fill in the word NONE.

_____ **1.** In 1870 Italy became a united country.

_____ **2.** The French leader, Napoleon Bonaparte, played an important role in Italian history. His actions lead to a spirit of nationalism in Italy.

_____ **3.** Giuseppe Garibaldi is a great hero of the Italian people.

Enrichment:
The Spirit of Nationalism

Nationalism is an important force in the world today. You can think of nationalism as the sense of loyalty that people feel toward their country or area. This feeling of nationalism did not begin until the late 1700s. Since that time it has been felt in all parts of the world.

Usually the spirit of nationalism grows because people have things in common with other people in their nation or region. They often have a *common language.* That is, as a rule the people of a nation speak the same language. Also, people in a country usually have a *common territory.* They live in the same general place.

The people of a nation share a common history and a common government. Also, they often share a *common culture* and *common beliefs.* They have the same customs, literature, music, and way of life.

Some countries, such as Great Britain, had a feeling of nationalism before the 1800s. In general, however, people gave their loyalty to the local rulers of their small kingdoms or regions.

Feelings of nationalism grew in the late 1700s. They began first in France. There the French people drew together to fight the nations that were against their Revolution. French pride in their nation and its army became an example to other peoples. Other examples of nationalism are pride in one's flag and national anthem.

Nationalism often went hand in hand with efforts by colonies to gain freedom from their parent countries. This was true in Latin America. In 1804, the people of Haiti won freedom from France. Mexico gained its freedom from Spain in 1821. Nearly all of the nations of South America won their freedom from Spain or Portugal before 1822.

As you have read, the spirit of nationalism spread from place to place and from continent to continent. The ideas and words of people in one part of the world were used by people elsewhere. Nationalism became the path that lead to freedom. Sometimes it also led to more democracy and personal freedom.

Toussaint L'Ouverture led a slave revolt in Haiti in the 1790s. The slaves rose up when they heard of the revolution in France. Haiti was then a colony of France.

Nationalism and the Unification of Germany

Understanding Global History

Think about the following statements as you read about the unification of Germany:

1. Events occurring in one part of the world have influenced developments in other parts of the world.
2. The culture in which we live influences our view of other people.
3. Present culture is shaped by the past.

Prussian troops hail William I as the first kaiser of the united Germany.

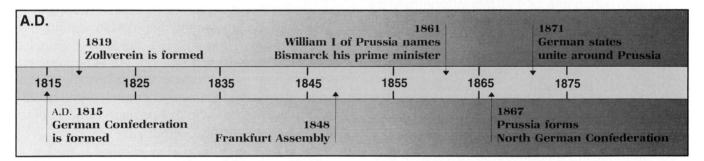

A.D.

1815	1825	1835	1845	1855	1865	1875	

1819 Zollverein is formed

1861 William I of Prussia names Bismarck his prime minister

1871 German states unite around Prussia

A.D. 1815 German Confederation is formed

1848 Frankfurt Assembly

1867 Prussia forms North German Confederation

The Beginning of Nationalism in Germany

The feeling of nationalism was growing all through Europe in the early 1800s. As you have read, it began in France during the French Revolution. It also helped unite Italy. Nationalism played an important part in the history of Germany as well.

In 1800, the people of Germany were divided into many kingdoms. At that time, most Germans felt loyal only to their local king or lord. However, a feeling of nationalism started to grow among some Germans. They dreamed of a united nation. They wanted a single country under one ruler. They wanted a single set of laws for all Germans.

Germany's First Step Toward Unity

In 1806, Napoleon took over the German kingdoms. He found it hard to run German affairs for many reasons. Each kingdom had its own laws. Each kingdom had its own money. Each had its own local rulers.

Napoleon took care of this problem by joining together many of the small kingdoms. He gave his relatives and friends the job of ruling these kingdoms. He then grouped the kingdoms into a loose **confederation**. It was called the Confederation of the Rhine (see map, page 207). The Rhine is a river in western Germany.

The Confederation of the Rhine was Germany's first step toward unity. It helped a feeling of nationalism grow among Germans. So, without meaning to, Napoleon had helped the German kingdoms move toward unity as a nation.

Germans Look to Prussia for Leadership

The Germans helped defeat Napoleon at Waterloo in 1815. His defeat led to the end of the Confederation of the Rhine. However, there was still an idea of German unity. After the Congress of Vienna, in 1815, a new German Confederation was formed. The German Confederation was made up of 39 German states including Austria and Prussia (see map, page 212).

Austria led the German Confederation. It was soon clear, however, that the confederation's real strength lay in the state of Prussia. More and more Germans looked to Prussia for leadership. There were important reasons for this. Prussia had the strongest army of the German kingdoms. It had played a key part in defeating Napoleon. Prussia also had the most well organized government of the German kingdoms.

225

A Customs Union Helps Economic Unity

The idea of joining all German areas into a single country came slowly. In 1819, the German states and kingdoms took the first step toward forming a single nation. Prussia organized a **customs union**. This union was called the Zollverein (TSAWL-fer-ine).

The customs union was set up to solve an important trade problem. The German states had been taxing each other's goods. This caused higher prices. It also led to less trade among the states. The customs union tried to take away these taxes. It helped to further economic unity.

The customs union did much to bring the many states and kingdoms of Germany together. By 1842, most of the German states belonged to the customs union. Austria was the only large state that did not join.

Obstacles to Unification

The movement toward German unity did not come easily. There were Germans who did not get along well because of religious differences. Most Germans in the north were Protestants. Germans in the south were mainly Roman Catholic. There were regions with long-standing disagreements and jealousies. The German states wanted to keep their own customs and traditions.

Also, Austria was against German unity. The Austrians did not join with the German states in the customs union, as you know. The Austrian government wanted Germany to stay weak and divided. As long as the German states were divided, the Austrians could rule them.

The Frankfurt Parliament Attempts to Unite Germany but Fails

The democratic revolutions that swept most of Europe in 1848 also came to German lands. Many Germans began asking for greater democracy. They were nationalists and liberals. The people even elected representatives to an assembly, or meeting, in the city of Frankfurt (see map, page 227). The 1848 meeting came to be known as the Frankfurt Assembly.

The members of the Frankfurt Assembly proposed that Germans unite under a democratic constitution. The assembly was later broken up by the Prussian king. But leaders soon met again in Frankfurt. This time they came together as a parliament. In 1849, the parliament issued a constitution for the German states. It also asked the king of Prussia to become king of a united Germany.

The king of Prussia refused the crown. The parliament stopped meeting soon afterward. Many leaders were forced to leave the country. The German states stayed separated. Their governments were still in the hands of people who were against national unity and democracy.

Some of the people who were against unification were **conservative**. That is, they were against most changes in government and society. Others were **reactionary**. These people wanted to return to the ideas and the ways of the past.

Bismarck Plans to Make Prussia Powerful

German unity seemed impossible during the next 12 years. Then, in 1861, the king of Prussia died. His brother became king. He was crowned King William I of Prussia. William made a rich landowner named Otto von Bismarck prime minister. Putting Bismarck in this position turned out to be the key to uniting Germany.

Otto von Bismarck was prime minister of Prussia. He was responsible for the unification of the German states.

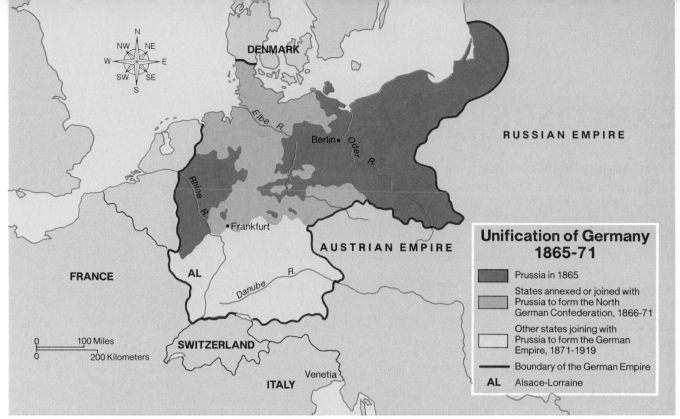

Bismarck saw that it was possible to unite all Germans under Prussian leadership. He wanted to set up an absolute monarchy. He proposed to unite Germany under the monarchy by a policy he called "blood and iron." By this, Bismarck meant a policy of war.

Bismarck began by raising money to make the Prussian army stronger. Then he set about using the army to make Prussia a world power.

How Bismarck Reached His Goal

Bismarck's goal was to take power away from Austria. This nation was Prussia's main rival. Bismarck reached his goal through the following actions:

- First, in 1864, Prussia joined Austria to fight a war against Denmark. The Prussians and Austrians won. Bismarck then started a fight with Austria over the land the Austrians had taken from Denmark.
- The fight between Prussia and Austria led to war in 1866. The war lasted only seven weeks. In that time the Prussians and their Italian allies crushed Austria.
- In 1867 Prussia formed the North German Confederation. Most of the other German states joined Prussia in this confederation. Prussia was its most powerful state.
- Bismarck still hoped to bring all the German states together. He believed that if there was an outside danger, the German states would join together to fight it. So in 1870, Bismarck started a war with France. He suggested to some German states that the French meant to dominate them or maybe even take them over. When the German states learned this, they helped Prussia defeat the French.
- After the defeat of France in 1871, the other German states joined with Prussia in a united Germany. They called themselves the German Empire. The German Empire came into being in 1871. The German states named King William I of Prussia to be the kaiser (KY-zur), or emperor, of Germany.

Long-Range Effects of Bismarck's Methods

Bismarck's methods of uniting Germany had long-range effects. These long-range effects shaped the way Germans thought about themselves and their nation. Prussia was a warlike state. It became the main force in the new, united Germany. Bismarck's policy of "blood and iron" became a part of the German way of thinking. German nationalism included pride in the nation's military strength.

Also, Germany was united by force and war. It was not united by democratic means. Germany did not develop a tradition of democracy. As a result, the Germans became used to the idea of rule by a single person. As you can see, Otto von Bismarck had a lasting effect on Germany and its people.

Exercises

A. Finding the Main Ideas:

Put a check next to the sentences that give the main ideas of what you have just read.

_____ **1.** Bismarck helped bring about German unity.

_____ **2.** Germany fought a war with France in 1870–1871.

_____ **3.** Napoleon's actions helped further German nationalism.

_____ **4.** The customs union was formed to improve trade among the German states.

_____ **5.** Prussia was the leader among the German states.

B. What Did You Read?

Choose the answer that best completes each sentence. Write the letter of your answer in the space provided.

_____ **1.** Austria was against German unity
   a. but did nothing to stop it.
   b. for religious reasons.
   c. because Austria wanted a democratic Germany.
   d. because Austria wanted to rule the German states.

_____ **2.** Napoleon helped to further German unity by
   a. giving the Germans a common language.
   b. defeating all of Germany.
   c. joining together many of the small kingdoms in Germany.
   d. making Prussians the rulers of Germany.

_____ **3.** Prussia's wars with Denmark, Austria, and France
   a. led to the ruin of the German states.
   b. led to the forming of the German Empire.
   c. left the German states disunited.
   d. made the German states strong but not united.

_____ **4.** Bismarck's policy for joining the German states together included
   a. uniting Germans by democratic means.
   b. improving industries in the German states.
   c. using war and rule by an absolute monarch.
   d. none of the above.

_____ **5.** The Zollverein was
   a. a customs union.
   b. organized by Prussia.
   c. an attempt to further economic unity among the German states.
   d. all of the above.

C. Understanding What You Read:

Tell whether each of the following involves (M) military, (G) governmental, or (E) economic aspects of German history. Place the correct answer in the space provided.

_____ **1.** Confederation of the Rhine is organized

_____ **2.** Customs union established

_____ **3.** Frankfurt Assembly held

_____ **4.** Bismarck named prime minister of Prussia

_____ **5.** Prussia defeats Denmark

_____ **6.** William I named kaiser of united Germany

_____ **7.** Prussia defeats France

_____ **8.** Prussian king turns down offer of crown from Frankfurt Assembly

D. Word Meanings:

Match each word in Column A with the correct meaning in Column B. Write the letter of each answer in the space provided.

Column A

_____ **1.** confederation
_____ **2.** customs union
_____ **3.** conservative
_____ **4.** reactionary

Column B

a. leader of the government
b. to bring about some action
c. favoring a return to the ideas and ways of the past
d. a loose organization
e. against great change in society
f. organized to handle tax and trade matters

E. Understanding Global History:

On page 224, you read about three factors in global history. Which of these factors applies to each statement listed below? Fill in the number of the correct statement on page 224 in the space provided.

_____ **1.** Germany was united by a policy of war and absolute rule. This affected Germany's government in later years.

_____ **2.** The defeat of Napoleon at Waterloo led to the end of the Confederation of the Rhine.

_____ **3.** The Prussian people's pride in their army led them to believe that Prussia should rule its neighbors.

Nationalism and the Ottoman Empire

Constantinople was the capital of the Ottoman Empire.

Learning New Words and Terms

The following words are used in this chapter. Think about the meaning of each one.

sultan: ruler of the Ottoman Empire
allied: joined together with a country, person, or group for a common purpose
secular: worldly or ordinary, rather than religious in nature.

Think As You Read

1. How did the Seljuk Turks affect the Christian world?
2. How large was the Ottoman Empire? How well was it run?
3. How was the Ottoman Empire affected by the spirit of nationalism?

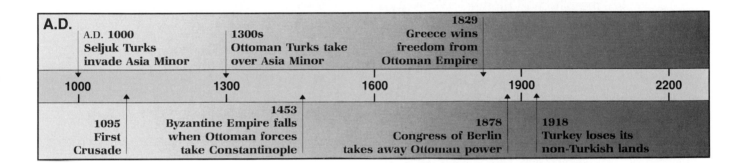

A.D.

A.D. 1000 Seljuk Turks invade Asia Minor	1300s Ottoman Turks take over Asia Minor	1829 Greece wins freedom from Ottoman Empire	

| 1000 | 1300 | 1600 | 1900 | 2200 |

| 1095 First Crusade | 1453 Byzantine Empire falls when Ottoman forces take Constantinople | 1878 Congress of Berlin takes away Ottoman power | 1918 Turkey loses its non-Turkish lands |

The spirit of nationalism was not limited to any one continent, people, or religion. It swept across most of Europe and the Americas in the 1700s and 1800s. Nationalism also affected lands in the Middle East and North Africa during those years.

Seljuk Turks Invade Asia Minor

The Middle East is found at the eastern end of the Mediterranean Sea. It had been ruled by Muslims since the mid-600s A.D. Asia Minor was nearby. It was part of the Byzantine Empire (see pages 147 and 156). The Byzantine rulers were Christians.

Soon after A.D. 1000, the Seljuks invaded Asia Minor. The Seljuks first came from central Asia. They were a Turkic tribe. The Seljuk Turks, as they became known, were Islamic. They also were fierce warriors. They swept into Asia Minor and soon threatened the city of Constantinople.

The Christians answered the Seljuk threat by starting the First Crusade in 1095 (see page 168). The crusaders kept the Seljuks from taking Constantinople.

Their defeat in Constantinople weakened the Seljuks. They were finally defeated by Mongol armies pushing west from Asia in the mid-1200s.

Suleiman I was one of the most famous sultans of the Ottoman Empire. The Ottoman Empire reached the height of its power during his rule.

231

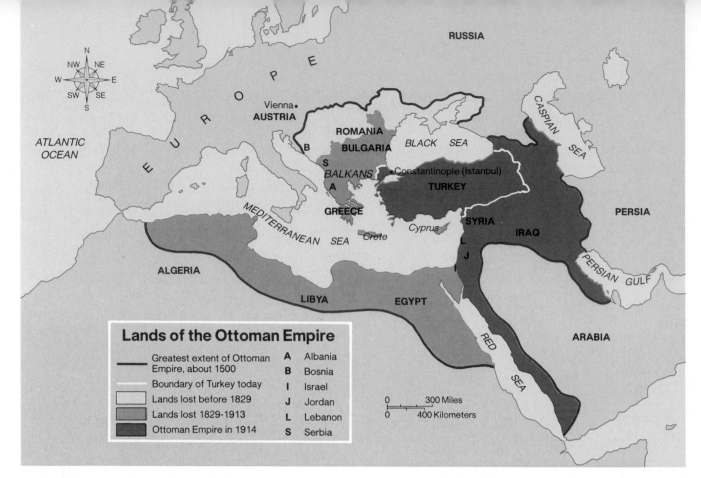

Lands of the Ottoman Empire

Greatest extent of Ottoman Empire, about 1500
Boundary of Turkey today
Lands lost before 1829
Lands lost 1829-1913
Ottoman Empire in 1914

A Albania
B Bosnia
I Israel
J Jordan
L Lebanon
S Serbia

0   300 Miles
0   400 Kilometers

The Ottoman Turks Take Control of Asia Minor

In the 1300s, the Ottoman Turks took control of Asia Minor. Like the Seljuks, they were also Muslims. They slowly spread their control and crossed into the Balkan area of Europe (see map above). During the 1400s, the Ottoman Turks held large parts of the Balkans.

In 1453, the Ottoman forces took Constantinople. Their victory helped bring an end to the Byzantine Empire. By the 1500s, the Ottoman Empire was at its height. That empire included parts of Asia, North Africa, and the Middle East.

The Ottoman rulers tried to push further into Europe. They failed, though they nearly captured the city of Vienna several times. After that, the Ottoman Empire began to decline.

Decline of the Ottoman Empire

Though the Ottoman Empire stayed large, it lost much of its power as time went on. There were several reasons for this.

- In the early 1800s, the Ottoman Empire was very large. It included such Balkan areas as Greece, Albania, Serbia, Bosnia, Bulgaria, and Romania. It also included Egypt, Libya, parts of Arabia, and the areas that are today Syria, Lebanon, and Israel (see map above). The empire was so large that it was hard to manage.

- The government was poorly run and corrupt. The Ottoman **sultan** often showed little thought for his subjects. Government officials took bribes. Also, they often kept for themselves the taxes taken from the people.

- The Ottoman rulers were not well liked by their subjects.

Greece Wins Its Freedom

It is not surprising, then, that a spirit of nationalism grew among the people in the Ottoman Empire. For example, nationalism brought on a revolt in Greece. Almost all Europeans were in favor of this revolt. In 1829, Greece won its freedom from the Ottoman Empire. This loss of land made the empire weaker.

Other Nations Take Advantage of Ottoman Weakness

The Ottoman Empire was made even weaker by its dealings with other countries. The countries of Europe used the Ottoman Empire to gain the advantage in their rivalries with each other. One example of this situation involved the Balkan states.

During the 1820s, the people of Serbia revolted against the Turks. With the help of other countries, the Serbs gained some self-rule. The Romanians and Bulgarians also desired self-rule.

The Russians decided to take advantage of the trouble in the Balkans. The Russians were trying to spread out toward the Mediterranean Sea. They hoped to gain control of a warm-water port. Such a port could be used all year round. However, the Ottoman Empire blocked Russia's route to the Mediterranean. The Russians thought that if they seemed to be in favor of the Balkan revolts, the Ottoman Empire would fall. Then the Russians could take over a warm-water port.

Great Britain, France, Prussia, and Austria were against Russia's efforts. They acted against Russia by siding with the Ottoman Empire. However, the Ottoman Empire still lost two wars with Russia. In each case, they were weakened by more loss of territory.

The Congress of Berlin, in 1878, Changes the Map of Europe

As the Ottoman Empire lost land, Russia gained. Other European countries were against Russia's getting more land. So, in 1878, the major European countries held a meeting in Berlin. Berlin was the capital of Germany. The meeting became known as the Congress of Berlin. It would not accept Russian expansion.

The Congress of Berlin also made several changes in the map of Europe. For example,

- Austria-Hungary now ruled Bosnia and the other lands in the Balkans.
- Serbia and Romania were given freedom from the Ottoman Empire.
- Bulgaria got self-rule but stayed within the Ottoman Empire.
- Great Britain got Cyprus and took over the rule of Egypt.

Most of the changes brought about by the Congress of Berlin took away the power of the Ottoman Empire.

The Fall of the Ottoman Empire

The Ottoman Empire finally fell in the early 1900s. The Ottoman ruler fought a war with Italy from 1911 to 1912. The Italians won and took over Libya in North Africa. In 1912 and 1913, the Ottoman ruler fought the Balkan states. The Ottoman Empire was defeated. The Ottoman Empire (now known as Turkey) **allied** itself with Germany in World War I (1914–1918). When the Germans were defeated, in 1918, Turkey lost its remaining non-Turkish lands.

The Republic of Turkey Is Born

After World War I, Turkish nationalists took over the government. Their leader was Mustafa Kemal (moos-tah-FAH keh-MAL). He was an army officer. The nationalists set up the Republic of Turkey. They had a parliamentary government. Kemal became its first president.

As the president of Turkey, Kemal was in favor of a new spirit of nationalism. The name of the Ottoman capital city was changed from Constantinople to the Turkish name Istanbul.

Kemal also tried to make Turkey more modern. The old Islamic traditions, customs, and ways of dress were changed to suit modern times. He even had the people take on new, modern names. He changed his name to Kemal Atatürk. Atatürk means "father of the Turks." The main religion of Turkey remained Muslim, however. The government was **secular**.

Atatürk was a strong leader who wanted to improve Turkey. He hoped that the people's spirit of nationalism would help them build a great Turkish nation.

Atatürk led the movement to modernize Turkey.

Exercises

A. Finding the Main Ideas:
Put a check next to the sentences that give the main ideas of what you have just read.

_____ **1.** The spirit of nationalism greatly affected the people of the Ottoman Empire.

_____ **2.** The Congress of Berlin was called by the major European powers.

_____ **3.** The Islamic rule of the Ottoman Turks helped spark nationalism in the Balkans.

_____ **4.** European power politics helped speed the decline of the Ottoman Empire.

_____ **5.** Constantinople fell to the Ottoman Turks in 1453.

_____ **6.** The Seljuks influenced Asia Minor.

B. What Did You Read?
Choose the answer that best completes each sentence. Write the letter of your answer in the space provided.

_____ **1.** The Seljuks were replaced by the
　a. Europeans.
　b. Christians.
　c. Ottoman Turks.
　d. none of the above.

_____ **2.** The Ottoman Empire was
　a. a secular state.
　b. an Islamic state.
　c. a Christian state.
　d. a military dictatorship.

_____ **3.** The Ottoman Empire did *not* include
　a. Greece.
　b. Libya.
　c. Syria.
　d. Vienna.

_____ **4.** In 1878, the Congress of Berlin
　a. gave Bosnia to Austria-Hungary.
　b. let Britain rule Egypt.
　c. opposed Russia's expansion.
　d. did all of the above.

C. Checking for Details:
Read each statement. Put a T in the space next to each statement if it is true. Put an F in that space if it is false. Put an N if you cannot tell from the reading if it is true or false.

_____ **1.** Greece won its freedom from the Ottoman Empire.

_____ **2.** The rulers of the Byzantine Empire were Muslims.

_____ **3.** The Ottoman Empire was run in an efficient manner.

234

_____ **4.** Britain and France backed Russia against the Ottoman Empire.

_____ **5.** The other European powers forced Russia to accept the decisions of the Congress of Berlin.

_____ **6.** The Seljuk threat to Constantinople led to the First Crusade.

_____ **7.** Russia wanted to spread its influence to the Mediterranean.

_____ **8.** The Ottoman Turks ruled the Balkans, a part of southeastern Europe.

_____ **9.** Turkey fought against Germany in World War I.

D. Time Line:

When did each of the following events take place? Write the date in the space provided.

_____ **1.** First Crusade   _____ **3.** Greeks win freedom from Ottoman Empire

_____ **2.** Fall of Byzantine Empire   _____ **4.** Turkey takes part in World War I

E. Word Meanings:

Match each word in Column A with the correct meaning in Column B. Write the letter of each answer in the space provided.

Column A   Column B

_____ **1.** allied   **a.** changed
_____ **2.** sultan   **b.** joined with
_____ **3.** secular   **c.** the Ottoman ruler
                            d. to use someone or something to advance one's own interests
                            e. worldly; not religious in nature

F. Understanding Global History:

On page 230, you read about five factors in global history. Which of these factors applies to each statement listed below? Fill in the number of the correct statement on page 230 in the space provided. If no factor applies, fill in the word NONE.

_____ **1.** Turkey set up a parliamentary government modeled after the ones in Europe.

_____ **2.** Though its customs have been changed, Turkey is still an Islamic nation.

_____ **3.** The defeat of Germany in World War I caused Turkey to lose its non-Turkish lands.

_____ **4.** The Christians felt they had to stop the Seljuks, with their different religion, from ruling Constantinople.

Unit 5
The Industrial Revolution Has Global Impact

Ways of making and trading goods have changed greatly over the years. In Unit 5, you will read about how trade has changed from ancient times to the present day. Large-scale trade was helped by new methods of doing business. These methods included bookkeeping, insurance, and joint-stock companies.

The invention and improvement of the steam engine in the 1700s led to the first Industrial Revolution. In this unit, you will learn how the invention of steam-driven machines led to greater production of goods.

The first Industrial Revolution of the 1700s was followed by a second Industrial Revolution. This took place in the mid-1800s. Electricity became the energy used to run machines. Larger and better steam engines, such as the one shown opposite, came into being. You will learn how all aspects of life were affected by the second Industrial Revolution.

Still another revolution was brought about. This time the change was in agriculture. The Industrial Revolution had led millions of people to leave the farms for the cities. New inventions made farm work easier. Farmers were thus able to produce more crops for growing city populations.

The Industrial Revolutions have affected all nations to some degree. In Unit 5, you will learn how the economies of nations are joined together by ties of interdependence.

In Unit 5, you will read the following chapters:

1 The Pre-Industrial World
2 The First Industrial Revolution
3 The Second Industrial Revolution
4 The Agricultural Revolution
5 The Industrial Revolution Has Worldwide Effects

Chapter 1

The Pre-Industrial World

Understanding Global History

Think about the following statements as you read about business and commerce before the 1700s.

1. Nations borrow and adapt ideas and institutions from other nations.
2. Contact among peoples and nations can lead to cultural changes.
3. Location, topography, and resources affect interaction among people.

The Portuguese arrived in China in the 1500s. They set up a trading post in the Chinese city of Macao, shown here.

Learning New Words and Terms

The following words are used in this chapter. Think about the meaning of each one.

bazaars: marketplaces found in the Middle East and Asia

caravans: groups of travelers moving together over the land with their goods

bookkeeping: the organized recording of what a business takes in and what it spends

investors: people who buy shares of stock in a company

Think As You Read

1. How were most goods made before 1700?
2. How did trade change in the time between 1450 and 1650?
3. How was business affected by such things as bookkeeping, insurance, and joint-stock companies?

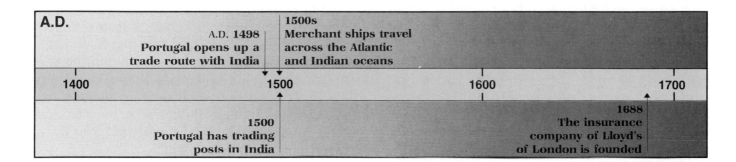

A.D.

A.D. **1498**
Portugal opens up a trade route with India

1500s
Merchant ships travel across the Atlantic and Indian oceans

| 1400 | 1500 | 1600 | 1700 |

1500
Portugal has trading posts in India

1688
The insurance company of Lloyd's of London is founded

Trade Exists Since Early Times

Trade has existed since early times. People in all parts of the world have made and exchanged, or traded, goods. Tools, weapons, cloth, and jewelry were among these goods.

Through trade, people learned about how things were made in other parts of the world. For example, Europeans learned how to make many new things after trading with Chinese merchants.

Europeans learned to make silk from the Chinese. They also learned to make porcelain dishes. We still call these dishes "china." A form of gunpowder was first made in China and then spread to Europe. The compass, paper, and block printing also began in China.

Handmade Goods

Before the 1700s A.D., most goods were made by hand. People in the Middle East made carpets by hand. They also made textiles, or cloth, by hand. In southern Africa people made iron tools and weapons by hand. Woolen cloth was made by hand in northern Europe. Wine, beer, and the barrels in which they were kept were made by hand all through Europe.

A Chinese crafts worker painting a lantern.

239

In most cases, goods were made by highly skilled crafts workers. They used skills that had been developed over many years. Goods made by hand took time to make. A skilled bootmaker might take weeks to make a pair of fine boots.

There was a great demand for skilled crafts workers. Many of them were paid to travel to faraway places to work. For example, Peter the Great, the ruler of Russia from 1689 to 1725, hired skilled boatbuilders from Holland. They built a navy for Russia. They also trained Russians to be boatbuilders.

A Network of Trade

One of the earliest trading networks was the one among the peoples of the Middle East and Europe, Asia, and Africa. Goods made in one part of the world were sold in other parts of the world. For example, the people of the Middle East made silk goods by hand. They also made linens, gold and silver jewelry, and fine swords. These and many other things were sold in local **bazaars.** In addition, Middle Eastern goods were sold in India, China, Europe, and Africa.

Middle Eastern merchants used ships to carry some goods from the Middle East. They also formed **caravans** to carry their goods over the land. In a caravan, a merchant would use camels to carry the goods. Merchants often hired soldiers to protect the caravan from robbers.

Trade Brings Change

Trade between different lands led to many changes. People in one place might use some of the foods from another place. They might adapt other styles of clothing to suit their own environment. People also became more open to the ways of life of other peoples.

Trade brought other changes as well. Goods that had once been unknown became widely used. Silks and spices from Asia had been luxuries in Europe. They were products that people enjoyed having, but did not really need in order to live. These luxuries now became necessities—at least to rich Europeans. After a time, the silks and spices and other goods came into use by a greater number of Europeans.

A bazaar in a Middle Eastern city around the 1700s.

Stocks being bought and sold in a London street. The time is the early 1700s.

Europe's Trade Shifts to New Areas

Before the 1400s, most of Europe's trade had been with other parts of Europe, and across the Mediterranean Sea with Africa and the Middle East. In the 1500s, Europe's trade spread into new areas.

Portugal opened an all-water route to India. This was made possible by Vasco da Gama. He reached India in 1498. The opening of an all-water route made it easier and cheaper for Portugal to trade with India. In 1500, Pedro Cabral set up trading posts for Portugal in India.

Spain opened the Americas to outside contacts in the 1500s. This was done through the conquests of Mexico and Peru (see pages 120 and 129). In the 1500s, hundreds of merchant ships regularly crossed the Atlantic and Indian oceans. They carried goods from one part of the world to be sold in another part of the world.

Bookkeeping and Insurance

The increase in trade in the 1500s meant European merchants had to keep better records. This led to a better system of **bookkeeping.** The new system made it possible for merchants to know how much money their businesses spent. It also became possible for merchants to know how much profit, if any, their businesses made.

Merchants and other business people also began to use more insurance. Business people faced risks every day. Goods might be lost because of theft, fires, or the sinking of ships. Insurance companies took over the risks involved in shipping goods. They charged a set amount for this service. The greater the risk, the higher the amount. Merchants were willing to pay for the insurance. If something went wrong with a shipment of goods, merchants knew that the insurance company would pay for the loss.

Joint-stock Companies

Another change was the way businesses raised money to improve and grow. They came to depend more and more on joint-stock companies.

Joint-stock companies raised money by selling shares of stock in the company. The people who bought shares were called **investors.** Together all of the investors owned the company. The profits were divided among the investors depending on the number of shares each one had bought.

Joint-stock companies made it possible to raise large sums of money. Many investors together could put more money into a company than a single business owner could. These large amounts of money made it possible for businesses to grow and for new businesses to start.

241

Exercises

A. Finding the Main Ideas:

Put a check next to the sentences that give the main ideas of what you have just read.

_____ **1.** Insurance helped reduce the risk of doing business.

_____ **2.** Goods made by hand took a long time to make.

_____ **3.** Goods were made by hand before 1700.

_____ **4.** Europeans began to change their way of doing business in the 1500s.

_____ **5.** Joint-stock companies raised money.

B. What Did You Read?

Choose the answer that best completes each sentence. Write the letter of your answer in the space provided.

_____ **1.** The people of the Middle East made
    a. linens.
    b. silk goods.
    c. gold jewelry.
    d. all of the above.

_____ **2.** During the 1500s, trade opened up for the first time between Europe and
    a. Africa.
    b. the Middle East.
    c. India and the Americas.
    d. Australia.

_____ **3.** Joint-stock companies were mainly organized to
    a. offer insurance against theft.
    b. raise money by offering shares of ownership.
    c. reduce investments.
    d. do all of the above.

_____ **4.** The art of making porcelain dishes came to Europe from
    a. the Americans.
    b. Africa.
    c. China.
    d. Australia

C. Checking for Details:

Read each statement. Put a T in the space next to each statement if it is true. Put an F in that space if it is false. Put an N if you cannot tell from the reading if it is true or false.

_____ **1.** Europeans learned how to make silk from the Chinese.

_____ **2.** Caravans carried goods over the land.

_____ **3.** Before 1700, most goods were made by machines.

_____ **4.** Peter the Great paid his Dutch boatbuilders well.

_____ **5.** The finest goods in the world came from the Middle East.

_____ **6.** Portugal opened an all-water route to India.

_____ **7.** Bookkeeping is hard to learn.

_____ **8.** Joint-stock companies were used for investment purposes.

_____ **9.** Insurance companies did not charge a set amount.

_____ **10.** Goods can be made as quickly by hand as by machine.

D. Thinking It Over:

Answer each of the following questions in two or three sentences. Use a separate piece of paper.

1. How did trade with other lands affect people's clothing, eating habits, and way of life?

2. How was business aided by joint-stock companies?

E. Complete the Sentence:

Use the following words or terms to complete each sentence below.

silks	theft	necessities	spices	Africa
insurance	Holland	fire	bazaars	

1. People in _____ made iron tools by hand.

2. Skilled boatbuilders from _____ were hired by Peter the Great to build Russia's navy.

3. Handmade goods were sold in _____ in the Middle East.

4. _____ and _____ are some luxuries that became _____ to some people in Europe.

5. _____ and _____ are two examples of risks to business people. Such

risks are reduced by the use of _____.

F. Word Meanings:

Match each word in Column A with the correct meaning in Column B. Write the letter of each answer in the space provided.

Column A

_____ **1.** textiles
_____ **2.** investors
_____ **3.** caravans
_____ **4.** luxuries
_____ **5.** bookkeeping

Column B

a. items that people enjoy having but that are not necessary
b. goods made by knitting and weaving; cloth
c. systems of payments to gain protection against possible losses
d. groups of travelers moving together over the land with their goods
e. keeping organized records of what a business takes in and what it spends
f. people who buy shares of stock in businesses

G. Understanding Global History:

On page 238 you read about three factors in global history. Which of these factors applies to each statement listed below? Fill in the number of the correct statement on page 238 in the space provided. If no factor applies, fill in NONE.

_____ **1.** Trade with other lands and cultures led to changes in clothing, food, and attitudes toward others.

_____ **2.** Overland caravans and ships were used in the trade between the Middle East and Asia, Africa, and Europe.

_____ **3.** Europeans learned how to make silk and porcelain dishes from the Chinese.

An early textile factory.

Enrichment:
The Factory System

As trade and business grew, it became necessary to change the way goods were made. In order to see how goods were made in the 1600s and 1700s, let us look at the wool industry in England.

The first step in making wool cloth was to clip the wool from the sheep. Then the wool was sold to the *factor,* or middle man. The factor brought the wool to a group of people who would card, or comb, it. Next, the factor took the wool to other people who would dye it.

The factor then brought the wool to a farmer's house. The farmer's wife or daughter would spin the wool into thread on the family spinning machine. Spinning was thought to be woman's work because the hands of the spinner had to be smooth. There were few smooth hands in farm families, but women's hands were thought to be the best for the job. Also, unmarried women in a household were given the job of spinning. Hence, the development of the word "spinster" to describe an unmarried woman.

When the wool had been spun into thread, the factor returned. He then took the thread to another farm family that owned a small weaving machine. In their spare time, this family would weave the thread into cloth. Finally, the factor picked up the finished cloth and brought it into town. There he sold it to a *clothier* who used it to make clothing.

All this carrying between farmers, carders, spinners, weavers, and clothiers was a big bother. It was also an expensive way to make cloth. This system of production was called the *domestic* system. The word "domestic" means having to do with things in the home. The domestic system got its name because much of the work was done in people's homes.

A woman spinning wool.

By the 1700s, this way of making cloth began to change. Now factors rented or built large buildings near fast-running streams. In the buildings were machines that could card, dye, spin, and weave cloth. The nearby streams provided waterpower for the machines. The factors then hired workers who would be paid to run the machines.

With this new arrangement all production was brought under a single roof. These new buildings, called *factories,* became the center of England's wool industry.

Chapter 2

The First Industrial Revolution

Understanding Global History

Think about the following statements as you read about the first Industrial Revolution.

1. Basic human needs—food, clothing, and shelter—are influenced by our environment and our culture.
2. People use the environment to achieve economic goals.
3. Nations are linked by a network of economic interdependence.

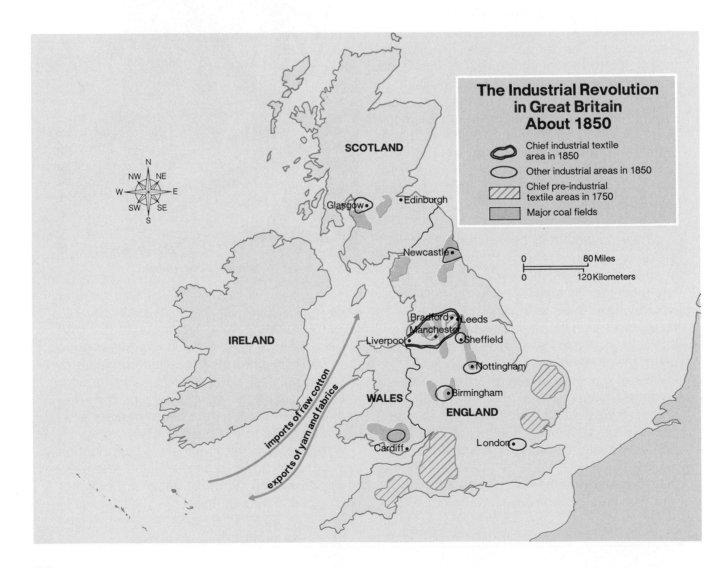

The Industrial Revolution in Great Britain About 1850

Chief industrial textile area in 1850

Other industrial areas in 1850

Chief pre-industrial textile areas in 1750

Major coal fields

SCOTLAND

Glasgow • • Edinburgh

Newcastle •

IRELAND

Bradford • • Leeds
Manchester
Liverpool • • Sheffield

• Nottingham

WALES

• Birmingham

ENGLAND

Cardiff •

London •

imports of raw cotton

exports of yarn and fabrics

0   80 Miles
0   120 Kilometers

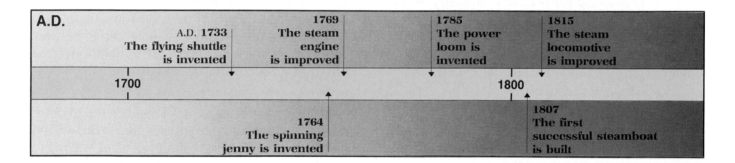

A.D.

| 1700 | A.D. **1733** The flying shuttle is invented | **1769** The steam engine is improved | **1785** The power loom is invented | 1800 | **1815** The steam locomotive is improved |

1764 The spinning jenny is invented

1807 The first successful steamboat is built

Goods Are Made at Home

Almost all goods were made by hand from early times until the 1700s. Those machines that were used were small and simple. They were not able to make large amounts of goods at one time. Most of the machines belonged to those who ran them. These people made the goods in their own homes. Most machines ran on human power and waterpower. Making goods in the home is called the **domestic system.**

The Start of the Factory System

The domestic system gave way to the factory system in the 1700s. Under the factory system all parts of production are carried out under one roof. The machines are housed in buildings called **factories.** The buildings belong to the factory owners, not to the people who run the machines. The people who run the machines are hired by the factory owners. The workers are paid wages to run the machines.

The factory system made it possible to make more goods and to lower costs. It also encouraged the invention of better machinery and the discovery of a new kind of energy. The movement away from work done by human hands to work done by machines is called **industrialization.** Industrialization changed every aspect of society. The change in society was so great it came to be called a **revolution.**

The Industrial Revolution Begins in Great Britain

The first Industrial Revolution started in Great Britain in the 1700s. The reasons why it started in Great Britain are listed below.

In the 1700s, Britain had

- the workers needed in the new industries.
- the inventions and know-how to start up new industries.
- iron and coal. These were important to industry.
- a way of moving goods from factories to market.
- people who had money to invest in the new businesses.
- colonies to supply raw materials and buy finished products.
- a government that supported growing industry
- peace at home. The British were able to put all their efforts into building industry.

The Industrial Revolution in Great Britain Began in the Cotton Industry

British merchants had been buying cotton cloth overseas since the Middle Ages. It was quite costly. Then, in the 1600s, English merchants began buying raw cotton overseas. They then hired people in England to make it into cloth. At that time, cotton cloth was made by the domestic system. In this system farm families did the spinning and weaving of cotton in their homes. They worked on their own machines in their spare time. Under this system, however, there was never enough cotton cloth for all the people who wanted to buy it.

In the 1700s, the British cotton industry moved to factories. One important reason for this was the invention of new machines. These machines sped up the spinning and weaving of cotton. This led to a sharp increase in the production of cotton cloth.

New Machines

The first important invention was the flying shuttle. It was invented by John Kay in 1733. The flying shuttle made it possible for one worker to do the work of two and to make a wider piece of cloth. Soon cotton could be woven so fast that there was a shortage of cotton thread.

To get more cotton thread, James Hargreaves invented the spinning jenny in 1764. The spinning jenny (named after Hargreaves's wife) used the idea of the spinning wheel. But the spinning jenny was much faster. It could spin as many as 80 threads at one time.

In 1769 Richard Arkwright invented the water frame. It further increased the amount of cotton thread that could be spun. Finally, Samuel Crompton invented the spinning mule in 1779. This machine could spin thread even faster than the spinning jenny or water frame could.

The spinning mule caused a problem, however. Now the weaving machines could not keep up with the spinning machines. This problem, too, was soon taken care of by a new invention.

In 1785 Edmund Cartwright invented the power loom. The power loom made it possible to weave thread at a much greater speed.

Inventions Change Cloth Making

As you can see, each new invention led to other inventions. Inventions in weaving led to inventions in spinning. This, in turn, led to new inventions in weaving. As a result, the method of cloth making was dramatically changed in only a little over 50 years.

Textile workers at home. Women spun cotton into thread. Men did the job of weaving the threads into cloth.

Steam Power

By the mid-1700s, the factory owners had new machines for making cotton cloth. Now they needed newer and better ways to run the machines. Until that time they had used waterpower. Waterpower, however, did not have the force needed to run heavy machines. Also, to use waterpower, a factory had to be near fast-running water. The factory owners now turned to steam.

The first steam engines had been made in France. However, the idea of using steam power soon spread to other parts of Europe. In 1705, Thomas Newcomen, an English engineer, developed an improved steam engine. It was used to pump water out of coal mines.

James Watt, a Scottish engineer, improved upon Newcomen's idea. Watt found a way to control the supply of steam in the steam engine. This was in 1769. Watt's steam engine was highly adaptable. It was soon designed to run many of the new machines in factories. With steam power as an energy source, the Industrial Revolution moved ahead quickly. Factories no longer needed to locate near fast-running rivers. Through the use of the steam engine, heavy machines could be run anywhere.

Sources of Money

Machines played a large part in the Industrial Revolution. Other factors also played an important part in the change. These factors were money, workers, raw materials, and markets.

Business people got money by use of joint-stock companies. Business people also set up corporations. Like joint-stock companies, corporations got money to expand by selling shares of stock to investors.

Sources of Workers

Workers to run the machines in the factories came from several sources. Many workers in the early days of the Industrial Revolution were women and children. They could work the machines and were paid lower wages than men.

Workers also came from farm villages. Life in the English countryside was changing. People were leaving the farms. They went to look for work in the factories. The most important changes in the countryside were the laws passed by Parliament. These were called the Enclosure Acts.

George Stephenson's locomotive.

These acts closed off the common lands in English villages. Before this, villagers had shared the use of common lands. Many grazed their animals on the common land at no cost. The lands were now divided among individual landowners. This forced poor villagers off the common lands. Many of them moved to the cities to work in factories.

Raw Materials and Markets

Raw materials such as coal, iron, tin, and cotton were needed if industry was to grow. Some countries have more raw materials than others. But many raw materials had to be obtained from foreign lands. A country could trade with other countries for raw materials. It could also make use of its colonies in foreign areas. For example, in the early 1700s, Great Britain bought lumber, tar, and cotton from its colonies in North America.

Colonies were also helpful in another way. They could serve as markets for the manufactured goods of the home country. Other markets could be found at home and in foreign lands.

Of course, markets were important so that an industry could grow. Also important was a good way of getting goods to those markets. The steam engine played an important part in this.

Steam Helps Transportation

In 1807, an American, Robert Fulton, built the first successful steamboat. In 1815, George Stephenson, an Englishman, improved upon the steam locomotive. In the next 50 years, railroad lines were built in Great Britain, the United States, and many parts of Europe. These railroads helped get raw materials to factories and finished goods to market.

Exercises

A. Finding the Main Ideas:
Put a check next to the sentences that give the main ideas of what you have just read.

_____ **1.** The English climate helped bring about the first Industrial Revolution.

_____ **2.** The Industrial Revolution in Great Britain began in the cotton industry.

_____ **3.** The domestic system ended at the beginning of the first Industrial Revolution.

_____ **4.** Several important inventions helped bring about the first Industrial Revolution.

_____ **5.** Great Britain found the money, workers, raw materials, and markets it needed for the first Industrial Revolution.

B. What Did You Read?
Choose the answer that best completes each sentence. Write the letter of your answer in the space provided.

_____ **1.** The way of making cotton cloth was
   a. the same in the 1800s as it had been in earlier times.
   b. helped by the domestic system.
   c. changed dramatically in a little over 50 years.
   d. made expensive by machine production.

_____ **2.** The spinning jenny, water frame, and spinning mule all
   a. improved the weaving process.
   b. increased the amount of thread being spun.
   c. decreased the cost of machines.
   d. increased the cost of cotton cloth.

_____ **3.** The Enclosure Acts helped to provide factories with
   a. money.
   b. workers.
   c. cotton.
   d. steam engines.

_____ **4.** Foreign lands served as a source of
   a. money and raw materials.
   b. machines and money.
   c. raw materials and markets.
   d. machines and markets.

C. Checking for Details:

Read each statement. Put an F in the space next to each statement if it is a fact. Put an O in that space if it is an opinion. Remember that facts can be proved, but opinions cannot.

_____ **1.** The domestic system gave way to the factory system in the early 1700s.

_____ **2.** Waterpower was a good form of energy.

_____ **3.** The Enclosure Acts forced many farmers to leave the countryside.

_____ **4.** Farm families did not like the factory system.

_____ **5.** The spinning jenny was hard to run.

_____ **6.** The power loom improved the process of weaving.

_____ **7.** The best steam engines were made in England.

_____ **8.** Women and children were a source of factory labor during the Industrial Revolution.

_____ **9.** Raw materials were too costly.

D. Matching:

Match the names of the inventors in Column A with their inventions in Column B. Put the letter of each answer in the space provided.

Column A

_____ **1.** John Kay
_____ **2.** James Watt
_____ **3.** Robert Fulton
_____ **4.** Edmund Cartwright
_____ **5.** George Stephenson

Column B

a. steamboat
b. power loom
c. spinning jenny
d. steam locomotive
g. steam engine
f. flying shuttle

E. Understanding Global History:

On page 246 you read about three factors in global history. Which of these factors applies to each statement listed below? Fill in the number of the correct statement on page 246 in the space provided.

_____ **1.** Waterpower was used in early factories to run the machines.

_____ **2.** Some raw materials had to be obtained from foreign lands.

_____ **3.** After the Enclosure Acts, poor farmers in England could not use the common lands to meet their basic needs. Many had to go to work in factories.

Chapter 3

The Second Industrial Revolution

Understanding Global History

Think about the following statements as you read about the second Industrial Revolution.

1. Nations borrow and adapt ideas and institutions from other nations.
2. Events occurring in one part of the world have influenced developments in other parts of the world.
3. Basic human needs—food, clothing, and shelter—are influenced by our environment and our culture.

A steel mill in Europe in the late 1800s. The workers are pouring the liquid metal into forms.

Learning New Words and Terms

The following words are used in this chapter. Think about the meaning of each one.

principle of interchangeable parts: the idea of making items with identical parts so that parts in any one item could be replaced by the parts from another item

assembly line: a moving belt in a factory on which an item travels as it is being assembled

mass production: the making of large numbers of goods that are all the same

division of labor: a way of making goods in which each worker makes only one part of the product

strike: the action of a group of workers who protest by refusing to work

labor unions: workers' organizations formed to give workers a united voice in dealing with their employers

collective bargaining: the process by which workers and employers try to reach agreements about such things as wages and working conditions

Think As You Read

1. What was the main source of power in the second Industrial Revolution?
2. What factors made the mass production of goods possible?
3. What inventions were part of the second Industrial Revolution?
4. How did workers' lives change as a result of the Industrial Revolution? How did workers react to those changes?

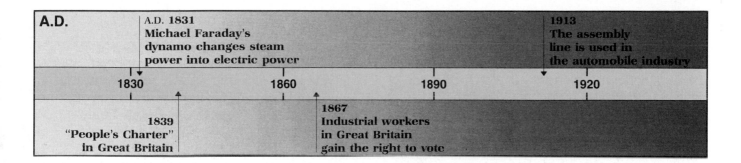

A.D.	A.D. **1831** Michael Faraday's dynamo changes steam power into electric power		**1913** The assembly line is used in the automobile industry
1830	1860	1890	1920
1839 "People's Charter" in Great Britain	**1867** Industrial workers in Great Britain gain the right to vote		

The Way Is Set for the Second Industrial Revolution

The 1700s and early 1800s brought great changes in the way people lived. Many of these changes came from the revolutions in the way goods were made. The 1700s saw the end of the domestic system of production. It was replaced by the factory system of production. The new factories were in cities. Many people from the country moved into the cities looking for work.

Steam power was the kind of energy used in the first Industrial Revolution. Then, in 1831, Michael Faraday invented the dynamo. The dynamo changed steam power into electric power. This pointed the way to the second Industrial Revolution. Electricity would now be the main energy source.

Also, the number of people in Europe grew quickly after 1750. There were many more people to buy goods. It was up to industry to supply those goods.

Iron, Coal, and Steel

Many of the machines developed during the first Industrial Revolution were made of iron. Because of this, the need for iron grew rapidly. Iron is made by heating the raw material called iron ore. At first, this heat was provided by burning wood or charcoal. Then, in the 1800s, it was found that coal worked better than wood or charcoal. Countries with large amounts of coal had a better chance of developing their industries. Some of these countries were Great Britain, the United States, and Germany.

The telegraph was one of the many inventions of the Industrial Revolution. This picture shows the arrival of the Atlantic telegraph cable in Newfoundland, Canada in 1866. The Atlantic cable made it possible to send messages between Europe and North America.

Iron was used for many of the new machines of the Industrial Revolution. Steam engines, railroad tracks, spinning machines—all were first made of iron. Iron had one serious problem, however. It was not very strong. Iron railroad tracks could not support the weight of fast-moving railroad cars. Iron steam engines often blew up because they could not stand the high pressure of the steam.

Inventors knew about a stronger metal. This metal was steel, which is made from iron. Steel was very costly to make, however. Then, in the 1850s, an American and a British inventor worked out a cheaper steel-making process. It was called the Bessemer process.

Cheap steel brought many changes. Railroad cars could now travel faster on strong steel rails. Steel bridges could now span wide rivers and deep mountain gorges. City buildings with steel girders could rise high in the air. The Bessemer process was a very important discovery of the second Industrial Revolution.

Petroleum Becomes Important

In the 1850s there was another important development. A group of Americans learned that petroleum, or crude oil, could be used for machin-ery and also for lighting and heating. There was a large supply of crude oil in the United States. However, no one had known what to do with it. Now kerosene, made from crude oil, could be used in lamps, stoves, and room heaters. Oil could be used to make machines in factories run smoothly.

Later, petroleum became even more important. In the early 1900s, two new inventions greatly increased the demand for petroleum. These were the internal combustion, or gasoline, engine and the diesel engine. These are the kinds of engines used today in cars, trucks, and buses. Petroleum could be made into gasoline and diesel fuel to power these engines.

Other Inventions and Improvements

Several other inventions were important in the second Industrial Revolution. These include the telegraph, telephone, and electric light bulb. The telegraph and telephone greatly sped up communication. The electric light bulb brought clean, dependable light to homes and factories.

The improvement of machine tools was also important to the Industrial Revolution. Lathes and other machines made production more accurate.

Interchangeable Parts

In the early 1800s, Eli Whitney made valuable use of lathes. These new machines shaped metal by turning it at high speed. Whitney used lathes to make gun parts. These gun parts were the same and interchangeable. A barrel in one gun, for example, would fit exactly into any other gun of the same type. When the different gun parts were made they could be fitted together to make guns. Whitney's method of production uses the **principle of interchangeable parts.**

The idea of interchangeable parts was very important. Before that time, every gun had been made by hand. Two guns might have seemed to be the same, but there were always slight differences. When part of a gun broke, a new part had to be made specially to fit that gun. With the use of interchangeable parts, repairs could be made easily with factory-made parts that were the same.

Better Machines

Of course, the principle of interchangeable parts could be used to make many other things besides guns. However, the making of interchangeable parts depended upon accuracy. During the last half of the 1800s, high-speed, accurate machines were invented. The machine-tool industry made it possible to make parts with speed and accuracy. Die-casting machines were also invented. These machines could stamp out formed metal parts in one operation.

The Assembly Line Leads the Way to Mass Production

The **assembly line** was developed in the automobile industry in 1913. On the assembly line, the automobile traveled along a moving belt past a number of workers. As it came to each worker, that worker added one part to the car, such as a door or the engine. By the time it reached the end of the line, the car was finished. It could now be driven off under its own power.

The assembly line led to **mass production.** Mass production is the making of large numbers of products, all the same. Mass production soon became an accepted part of industry in all parts of the world.

Many of the workers in the early textile factories were women. They saw factory work as a chance to earn their own wages and be independent.

The Life of Factory Workers

You have been reading about the inventions and discoveries that dramatically changed factory production. But what about the people who worked in those factories? How did workers' lives change because of the Industrial Revolution? Their lives were very different from what their lives would have been in the days of the domestic system of production. The immediate effects of the Industrial Revolution are described here. You will read about the long-term positive effects of the Industrial Revolution on pages 267–268.

Before, most workers worked for themselves. In the past a worker could decide when to work. Now workers had to follow the clock. They had to arrive at a certain time. They could stop for lunch only at a certain time. They had to work all day until a certain time.

There were other changes as well. Under the domestic system a worker made a whole product from beginning to end. Now each worker made only one part of the product. This method of making only parts of goods is called **division of labor.** Using this method, workers could produce goods more quickly. However, the workers felt less pride in their product than they had before.

Working and Living Conditions

In early factories, workers worked 14 hours a day, 6 days a week. The working conditions were terrible. Factories often were dark, dirty, and poorly ventilated. Machines had no safety devices, so people often got hurt. There was no accident insurance. Men, women, and children as young as five years old worked in these factories.

Living conditions for workers were not much better. Many lived in overcrowded slum apartments, called tenements. They had little furniture. Several children might share a single bed. Food was poor. They had little, if any, fresh meat, milk, and vegetables. Sickness was common.

Workers React

How did workers feel about these working and living conditions? At first some British crafts workers were against the use of machines altogether. They entered factories late at night and broke the machines.

Other workers tried to protest their long hours and poor working conditions. One way was to refuse to work. When workers, as a group, refuse to work, their action is called a **strike.**

Workers also tried to form organizations called **labor unions.** A labor union would represent all of the workers in a factory. It would try to make the factory owner raise wages and improve working conditions. When the union leaders and factory owner met to discuss these issues, it was called **collective bargaining.**

Factory owners were against the workers forming unions. When workers went on strike, police and strikebreakers were used against them. Until 1825, unions in Great Britain were not legal. After 1825, more and more people joined unions.

Workers Demand Voting Rights

Some workers in England felt that the best way to improve working conditions was to gain the right to vote. Then workers could have a real say in the decisions that affected their lives. So, they

London in the 1800s. What does this picture tell about life for workers in the cities?

Boy miners. Children were an important part of the work force in the mines and factories of the 1800s and early 1900s.

began to present their demands to Parliament. They asked for such reforms as the right of all men to vote and the use of the secret ballot. In 1839, the workers listed their reforms in "A People's Charter." Supporters of the People's Charter became known as Chartists.

The Chartists did not achieve their goals. During the 1840s the Chartist movement declined. However, workers still wanted voting rights.

Voting rights in Great Britain had already spread somewhat. The Reform Bill of 1832 had reduced property requirements for voting. It had brought greater representation to people in the growing industrial cities. Then, in 1867, a second reform bill gave the vote to most industrial workers.

Workers Join Unions and Form Political Parties

Meantime, membership in labor unions was still growing. By the late 1800s workers' unions had become strong. Millions of workers joined unions in Great Britain, France, Germany, Italy, and other countries.

Workers also formed new political parties. These labor parties elected members to parliaments in most of the European countries. No labor parties of any size were organized in the United States, however. Labor unions in the United States were fairly small in the late 1800s.

Workers Gain Reforms

Pressure from workers and other reformers in Great Britain led to a number of laws dealing with working conditions. These laws limited the work day to ten hours. They also placed greater limits on child labor. Other laws tried to improve health and safety conditions in factories. These improvements of labor conditions were not, however, always enforced. In addition, wages for women workers stayed below wages paid to men.

The Industrial Revolution Spreads

The Industrial Revolution brought changes to many parts of life. It had affected where people lived. It had influenced how they worked. It had even changed how they traveled and the ways they communicated.

These changes first started in England. Between 1850 and the early 1900s, the United States and the countries of Western Europe had started their own industries on a large scale. The Industrial Revolution was brought to Asia by Europeans. In the late 1800s and early 1900s, industries started up in India, China, and Japan. The Japanese built an industrial economy in a very short span of time—from the late 1800s to 1914. Japan's government supported the drive to industrialize. It hired many experts from other countries to teach the Japanese new skills.

Exercises

A. Finding the Main Ideas:

Put a check next to the sentences that give the main ideas of what you have just read.

_____ **1.** Workers tried to change some of the conditions caused by the Industrial Revolution.

_____ **2.** Eli Whitney developed the idea of interchangeable parts.

_____ **3.** Electrical power was the main energy source of the second Industrial Revolution.

_____ **4.** Coal, steel, petroleum, and machine tools were important to the second Industrial Revolution.

_____ **5.** The 1700s saw the end of the domestic system of production.

_____ **6.** The cotton gin was important to the Industrial Revolution.

B. What Did You Read?

Choose the answer that best completes each sentence. Write the letter of your answer in the space provided.

_____ **1.** Eli Whitney made an important contribution to industrialization when he developed
    a. steel for guns.
    b. the assembly line.
    c. machine tools.
    d. interchangeable parts for guns.

_____ **2.** The second Industrial Revolution is linked to the
    a. steel industry.
    b. mass production of goods.
    c. machine-tool industry.
    d. all of the above.

_____ **3.** The internal-combustion engine brought great changes to
    a. machine tools.
    b. transportation.
    c. steelmaking.
    d. all of the above.

_____ **4.** The Chartists favored
    a. voting rights for all men and women.
    b. new business charters.
    c. voting rights for all men.
    d. none of the above.

C. Checking for Details:

Read each statement. Put a T in the space next to each statement if it is true. Put an F in that space if it is false. Put an N if you cannot tell from the reading if it is true or false.

_____ **1.** The factory system replaced the domestic system.

_____ **2.** Steam-driven machines did not increase production.

_____ **3.** Michael Faraday's dynamo produced steam power.

_____ **4.** Henry Bessemer improved the way of weaving cloth.

_____ **5.** In early factories workers often worked 14 hours a day, 6 days a week.

_____ **6.** Eli Whitney invented the cotton gin.

_____ **7.** The assembly line was used in the domestic system.

_____ **8.** Machine tools made it possible to reproduce parts accurately.

_____ **9.** The Reform Bill of 1832 gave voting rights to more British men.

_____ **10.** The English found a way of making steel in 1740.

D. Word Meanings:

Look up the following words in the glossary. Write the meaning next to each word.

1. mass production _____

_____

2. division of labor _____

_____

3. assembly line _____

_____

E. Understanding Global History:

On page 252 you read about three factors in global history. Which of these factors applies to each statement listed below? Fill in the number of the correct statement on page 252 in the space provided. If no factor applies, fill in the word NONE.

_____ **1.** Eli Whitney, an American, developed the principle of interchangeable parts. This principle became the basis for mass production in all parts of the world.

_____ **2.** The machine-tool industry made the mass production of goods possible.

_____ **3.** Nations with large coal resources had an advantage in developing their industries.

259

Chapter 4

The Agricultural Revolution

Understanding Global History

Think about the following statements as you read about the revolution in farming.
1 Nations borrow and adapt ideas and institutions from other nations.
2 Basic human needs—food, clothing, and shelter—are influenced by our environment and our culture.

Cyrus McCormick walking behind his new invention, the mechanical reaper.

Learning New Words and Terms

The following words are used in this chapter. Think about the meaning of each one.

scientific farming: the use of experiments and scientific information to improve farm production

cash crops: crops raised to be sold instead of to be eaten or used on the farm

Think As You Read

1. How did the Agricultural Revolution help the Industrial Revolution?
2. How were farmers helped by science and inventions?
3. How has the Agricultural Revolution affected farm population and the production of food?

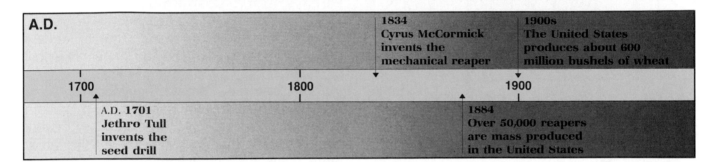

A.D.

1834 Cyrus McCormick invents the mechanical reaper

1900s The United States produces about 600 million bushels of wheat

1700　　1800　　1900

A.D. 1701 Jethro Tull invents the seed drill

1884 Over 50,000 reapers are mass produced in the United States

The Agricultural Revolution Starts with the Enclosure Acts

As you have read, the Industrial Revolution brought a great many changes to society. However, the Industrial Revolution would not have been possible without a revolution in agriculture, or farming. Like the Industrial Revolution, the Agricultural Revolution began in Great Britain.

The Agricultural Revolution started with the Enclosure Acts of the 1700s. Under the enclosure movement, farms were joined to make larger farms. Many small landowners could no longer hold out against the larger ones. Some became tenant farmers. They farmed land that was owned by others. Some moved to the cities.

Landowners Try New Farming Methods

The landowners who stayed in the country began trying new ways of farming. Their efforts are examples of **scientific farming.** In the early 1700s, Lord Townshend, an English farmer, introduced crop rotation. Before then, farmers had left one part of land unplanted each year. This stopped the soil from losing its fertility. With crop rotation, the farmer could alternate different crops in each part of the field. This helped to save the soil. It also led to more production.

Robert Bakewell, another Englishman, developed a system of stock breeding. His methods increased the amount of milk, beef, and wool that cows and sheep produced.

Another example of scientific farming was introduced by an English farmer, Jethro Tull. He found that crops grew better when there were fewer weeds. He also found that loosening the soil between rows made output better. Tull invented a horse-drawn machine to break up the soil.

Later, the Agricultural Revolution spread to the United States and Europe. A German, Baron von Liebig (LEE-bick) developed the idea of chemical fertilizers. These made it possible to grow more crops on the same land.

New Farm Machines

The invention of new farm machines also aided the Agricultural Revolution. In 1701 Jethro Tull invented a seed drill. This made it possible to plant more seeds and to space them properly. In 1819, Jethro Wood invented a cast-iron plow. This was much better than the wooden ones that had been used since early times. In 1833, John Lane invented an even better plow. This one was made of steel. The new steel plows made plowing much easier.

261

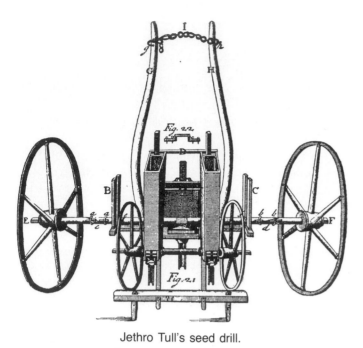

Jethro Tull's seed drill.

All of these inventions, as well as scientific farming, made it possible to produce larger crops. The new machines also reduced the number of people needed to produce those crops. Many of these people who would have been farmers moved to the cities instead. They tried to find work in the factories of the Industrial Revolution.

Further Changes in Agriculture Are Helped by the Industrial Revolution

Cyrus McCormick, an American, invented the mechanical reaper in 1834 when he was only 25 years old. This machine was used to harvest grain. By 1840 McCormick set up a factory to mass produce his farm machine. By 1884, his company was selling over 50,000 machines a year.

The mechanical reaper was sold to farmers in the United States and many other places in the world. Thus, the methods developed by the Industrial Revolution helped further the advances made during the Agricultural Revolution.

During the 1800s, the thresher, harvester, and combine were also invented. These inventions greatly increased farm production. In 1890 one farmer could do as much with one machine as 20 farmers had done by hand in 1770.

Shifts in Population

The second Industrial Revolution sped up the shift of people from the country to the cities. Factories grew up in many parts of the world, especially in the United States and Europe. The factories made the machines needed by farmers. With the machines, farms could make the raw materials and food needed by factories and those people living in cities.

During the late 1800s and early 1900s, the farm population continued to grow. However, it grew at a slower rate than the general population.

Farmers Turn to Cash Crops

During the period of the Agricultural Revolution, farmers turned to **cash crops.** That is, farmers raised crops to be sold. They no longer grew only crops needed by the farm family itself.

Farms also grew larger. They were run more and more by large companies. Using modern equipment, fewer people were needed to work one large farm than to run many smaller family farms. Thus, the increase in the size of farms reduced the percentage of people in farming.

The Rise in Food Production

As the number of people in farming went down, people feared that there would not be enough food. They thought that this shortage of food would be made worse by the steady rise in the world's population.

While many countries in Asia and Africa cannot raise enough food for their people, food production in the United States has risen steadily. For example, the United States produced about 600 million bushels (21,120 million liters) of wheat in 1900. It produced 2.3 billion bushels (almost 50 billion liters) of wheat in 1980. The United States produced about 2.6 billion bushels (91.5 billion liters) of corn for grain in 1900. It produced 6.6 billion bushels (about 170 billion liters) of corn for grain in 1980. Today, the United States, Canada, and some other countries raise so much wheat and corn, they have become major suppliers of these crops to other countries.

The revolution in farming began in Great Britain. From there it spread to the United States and Europe. In time, countries all over the world were benefiting from the science, inventions, and larger crops of the revolution in farming.

Exercises

A. Finding the Main Ideas:

Put a check next to the sentences that give the main ideas of what you have just read.

_____ **1.** During the Agricultural Revolution, farm population fell but farm production rose.

_____ **2.** The United States produced about 600 million bushels (21,120 million liters) of wheat in 1900.

_____ **3.** The Agricultural Revolution helped bring about the Industrial Revolution.

_____ **4.** Science and inventions helped bring about the Agricultural Revolution.

_____ **5.** Farm machines were mass-produced during the late 1800s.

B. What Did You Read?

Choose the answer that best completes each sentence. Write the letter of your answer in the space provided.

_____ **1.** The invention of farm machinery resulted in
  a. more farmers producing fewer crops.
  b. fewer farmers producing the same amount of crops.
  c. more farmers moving to farms.
  d. fewer farmers producing greater amounts of crops.

_____ **2.** The movement of many people to the cities led to fear of
  a. war.
  b. food shortages.
  c. democracy.
  d. dictatorship.

_____ **3.** Scientific agriculture did *not* play a part in
  a. breeding animals.
  b. the use of fertilizers.
  c. the use of crop rotation.
  d. control of the weather.

_____ **4.** The Industrial Revolution had
  a. no effect on agriculture.
  b. some effect on agriculture.
  c. a great effect on agriculture.
  d. the effect of increasing family farming.

C. Graph Skills:

Draw a line graph showing the changes in European population between 1850 and 1990. The figures below have been rounded off.

1850—270 million people   1970—460 million people
1900—420 million people   1990—499 million people

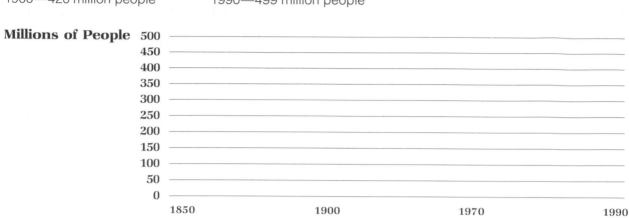

Draw a bar graph showing the changes in the United States population between 1850 and 1990. The figures below have been rounded off.

1850—25 million people   1970—200 million people
1900—75 million people   1990—249 million people

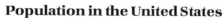

D. On Your Own:

Write an essay of two or three sentences on the following question. Use a separate sheet of paper. What do the pie charts below suggest about how life in the United States has changed since 1800?

Population in the United States

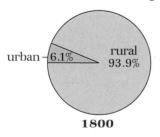
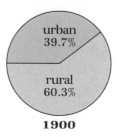
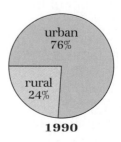

E. Checking for Details:

Read each statement. Put a T in the space next to each statement if it is true. Put an F in that space if it is false. Put an N if you cannot tell from the reading if it is true or false.

_____ 1. Cash crops lessened American interest in agriculture.

_____ 2. The Agricultural Revolution began first but continued during the Industrial Revolution.

_____ 3. Cast-iron plows cost more than wooden plows.

_____ 4. McCormick mass-produced farm machines.

_____ 5. Steel plows made it easier for farmers to plow their fields.

_____ 6. The Agricultural Revolution did not spread around the world.

_____ 7. The Industrial Revolutions slowed the movement of people to the cities.

_____ 8. The size of farms grew larger during the Agricultural Revolution.

_____ 9. The Enclosure Acts in England helped bring about the first Industrial Revolution.

_____ 10. Wheat brings a higher price to farmers than corn.

F. Understanding Global History:

On page 260 you read about two factors in global history. Which of these factors applies to each statement listed below? Fill in the number of the correct statement on page 260 in the space provided. If no factor applies, fill in the word NONE.

_____ 1. The decline in the number of people in farming did not lead to food shortages. Instead, new farm machines helped the farmers produce even more food.

_____ 2. The Agricultural Revolution began in Great Britain but soon spread to other parts of the world.

_____ 3. As farmers produced more food, many people from the country moved to the cities to work in the factories.

Chapter 5

The Industrial Revolution Has Worldwide Effects

Understanding Global History

Think about the following statements as you read about the worldwide effects of the Industrial Revolution.

1 Basic human needs—food, clothing, and shelter—are influenced by our environment and our culture.

2 Events occurring in one part of the world have influenced developments in other parts of the world.

3 Nations are linked by a network of economic interdependence.

4 Contact among people and nations can lead to cultural changes.

Hong Kong harbor. Products made in Hong Kong's factories are shipped all over the world.

Think As You Read

1. How did the Industrial Revolution change trade relations among nations?
2. What have been some of the good and bad effects of the Industrial Revolution?
3. What were Adam Smith's ideas about business?
4. How did industrialization shape the ideas of Adam Smith and Karl Marx?

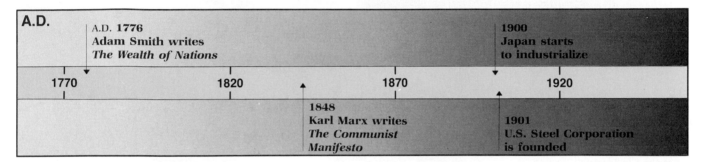

A.D.

A.D. **1776**
Adam Smith writes
The Wealth of Nations

1900
Japan starts
to industrialize

1770   1820   1870   1920

1848
Karl Marx writes
The Communist
Manifesto

1901
U.S. Steel Corporation
is founded

Industrialization Is Part of Our Lives

The Industrial Revolution began in the early 1700s. It lasted into the 1800s. The Industrial Revolution is still very much a part of our lives today. The impact of industrialization has been felt all over the world.

One of the good results of industrialization has been the mass production of goods. Mass production has made goods available to greater numbers of people.

In general, industrialization has made life better for most people. For example, people don't need to spend as much time getting food, clothing, or shelter. These things are readily available in most industrialized countries. As a result, people have more time to themselves—to relax or learn new things. Poverty and hunger still affect many millions of people. However, fewer people have probably been affected in the past 200 years.

Corporations Grow

Another result of industrialization has been the growth of large corporations. While countries were building up their industries, it took a great deal of money to start a new business. A factory needed many costly machines. It needed large numbers of workers. These workers had to be paid. To raise all this money, business people often formed corporations. As you have read, corporations raise money by selling shares of stock to investors. These investors then share in the corporation's profits.

In 1901, the United States Steel Corporation was founded. It was the first privately held corporation worth 1 billion dollars. Since that time, a great many billion-dollar corporations have been formed. Today, there are giant corporations in the United States, Great Britain, Japan, France, Hong Kong, and Italy.

Multinational Corporations

Not too long ago a new kind of corporation began. It is called a **multinational** corporation. The investors are from different countries. Factories of the corporation are found all over the world. Multinational corporations do business in several countries at the same time.

The Effects of Industrialization Are Felt Around the World

Industrialization has reached countries all over the world. It spread from Great Britain and the United States to Europe. Later it reached such countries as Japan and the Soviet Union.

In 1900, Japan was just starting to industrialize.

Developing countries are trying to build their industries. These Indian workers are using advanced instruments to find out more about water power.

Today, it is a world leader in producing ships, steel, automobiles, and computers.

The Soviet Union is another country that industrialized not too long ago. The development of its industry, too, has been very quick. In 1917, for example, Russia produced less than 5 million tons (4.5 million metric tons) of steel. Today, the Soviet Union produces over 149 million tons (135 million metric tons) of steel.

Nations Are Interdependent

Industrialization has made the nations of the world interdependent. Europe, Japan, and the United States depend on nations in South America, Asia, and Africa for many raw materials. They also depend on these countries as markets for finished manufactured goods.

Europe, Japan, and the United States depend on such countries as Saudi Arabia, Indonesia, Mexico, and Nigeria for their crude oil. They buy tin from Malaysia, Bolivia, and Indonesia. They need copper from Chile, Peru, Zaire, and South Africa. They need uranium from South Africa, Niger, and Zaire. These countries buy finished goods from the more industrialized countries.

Industrialization—Good and Bad

Industrialization has had both good and bad effects. The standard of living has gone up in many less industrialized countries. More hospitals and schools have now been built. These countries have built new roads. They have also improved telephone, radio, and television.

Industrialization has also had some bad effects. The less industrialized countries have given up many of their natural resources to the industrialized nations. Often they have been paid only a small amount for these resources. Also, as a rule, these countries have not been able to build their own industries. So, they cannot compete with the more industrialized countries.

Some countries have had another problem because of industrialization. Their traditional customs, beliefs, and ways of living were often not suited to the industrial life of cities, factories, and mass-produced goods. Sometimes the traditional culture has broken down when it came in contact with the industrial way of life.

In many traditional cultures, for example, the family was the center of people's lives. Parents, children, grandparents, and cousins all lived together or nearby. The young people learned skills and customs from the older people.

When the Industrial Revolution came, this often changed. Children went to school. Some adults went to work in factories. The family was no longer the center of people's lives. Children now learned new things at school or from the radio or television. They began to question the old ways of their parents and grandparents. Conflicts often arose within families. Some people blamed industrialization for the breakdown of the old ways.

Adam Smith's Ideas

The Industrial Revolution caused people to think about many important issues. Were the changes caused by industrialization good or bad? Should workers have to fight to get by, while some owners were very rich? How much should governments be involved in economic affairs? Many writers wrote their answers to these important questions. Two were especially well known. They were Adam Smith and Karl Marx.

As you read on page 204, Adam Smith wrote the book *The Wealth of Nations,* in 1776. He was considered the founder of modern economics. Adam Smith believed that business people should be left alone to run their businesses. He said that people would buy the goods that were worth the most for the money. Companies whose goods were not the best or were too costly would not be able to sell their goods. They would go out of business. This competition among businesses was good, said Smith.

Smith Favors Laissez-Faire

Smith believed that no one should interfere with businesses. He favored the idea of laissez-faire. That is, government should let businesses alone to run their own affairs. In this way everyone would come out better, Smith said. **Consumers,** or people who buy goods, would get the best goods for the lowest price. Businesses that could last through this competition would grow. Countries would benefit from a healthy economy.

Many people agreed with Smith's idea. Some business owners used his ideas to argue against labor unions. They said that unions interfered with business. So, unions should be against the law, they said.

Karl Marx wrote his ideas in a book called *The Communist Manifesto* in 1848. His book became the basis of the communist revolutions in Russia and China.

The Views of Karl Marx

Another writer whose views are very well-known was Karl Marx. He was born in Germany in 1818 and became a philosopher, social scientist, and revolutionary. Karl Marx developed the idea of communism.

Marx believed that all of history could be seen as the history of class struggle. That is, people with money and power have been in conflict with people with no money or power. At first it was owners against slaves. Later it was lords against serfs. Now, said Marx, it was the struggle between factory workers and employers. Workers do all the work. Employers get all the money.

Marx believed that this struggle would soon lead to a revolution. The workers would rise up. They would take control of the government. After the revolution the government would own all property. There would be no more class struggle between workers and employers. There would be a classless society where everyone was the same.

The Impact of Industrialization

The Industrial Revolution had a great impact around the world. It changed how people work. New mass-produced goods were made for people to use. Trade relations among nations underwent change, too.

Industrialization is still going on in many countries of the world today. It has brought both benefits and problems to those countries. Almost all of these countries have decided to continue to develop their industries. They feel that the good outweighs the bad.

Exercises

A. Finding the Main Idea:

Put a check next to the sentence that gives the main idea of what you have just read.

_____ **1.** The Industrial Revolution had high costs.

_____ **2.** Japan became an industrial country not too long ago.

_____ **3.** The Industrial Revolution has had lasting effects on countries of the world.

_____ **4.** Raw materials are very important for industrialization.

B. What Did You Read?

Choose the answer that best completes each sentence. Write the letter of your answer in the space provided.

_____ **1.** Most of the less developed countries are in
   a. Asia, Africa, and South America.
   b. North America.
   c. Europe
   d. none of the above.

_____ **2.** Giant corporations of the world can be found in
   a. the United States and Great Britain.
   b. Japan and Hong Kong.
   c. France and Italy.
   d. all of the above.

_____ **3.** One result of the Industrial Revolution was
   a. the growth of large corporations.
   b. the end of large corporations.
   c. the end of mass-produced goods.
   d. the smooth change from traditional ways of life to industrial ways of life.

_____ **4.** Adam Smith believed that
   a. history is the history of class struggles.
   b. government should not interfere with businesses.
   c. multinational corporations are good for the world economy.
   d. the Industrial Revolution was bad for the people of the world.

C. Checking for Details:

Read each statement. Put an F in the space next to each statement if it is a fact. Put an O in that space if it is an opinion. Remember that facts can be proved, but opinions cannot.

_____ **1.** The Soviet Union is a newly developed industrial nation.

_____ **2.** Multinational corporations are good for the world economy.

_____ **3.** Japan produces the best automobiles in the world.

_____ **4.** The Industrial Revolution has affected trade among nations.

_____ **5.** The Industrial Revolution has done more harm than good.

_____ **6.** Karl Marx believed that one day workers would run the governments of the world.

_____ **7.** There are too many large corporations.

_____ **8.** The United States Steel Corporation was the first billion-dollar corporation.

_____ **9.** Japan is a world leader in the production of computers.

_____ **10.** The United States depends too much on other nations for raw materials.

D. Behind the Headlines:

Explain in two or three sentences what each headline might tell about the good or bad features of the Industrial Revolution. Use a separate piece of paper.

1. FIVE NEW COPPER MINES OPENED IN SOUTH AMERICA BY U.S. AND FRENCH COMPANIES

2. FAMILIES LEAVE FARMS IN SOUTHEAST ASIAN VILLAGES—LOOK FOR WORK IN FACTORIES IN CITIES

E. Understanding Global History:

On page 266 you read about four factors in global history. Which of these factors applies to each statement listed below? Fill in the number of the statement on page 266 in the space provided. If no factor applies, fill in the word NONE.

_____ **1.** The Industrial Revolution has led to improvements in health and education in less developed nations. However, it has also led to the breakdown of past ways of life.

_____ **2.** The Industrial Revolution has made the United States, Japan and Europe dependent on countries in Asia, Africa, and South America for raw materials.

_____ **3.** In general, the Industrial Revolution has made life better for most people.

_____ **4.** The Industrial Revolution began in Great Britain and soon spread to the United States and Europe.

271

GLOSSARY

adapt (uh-DAPT) to change something to fit your own needs **(32)**
allied (uh-LIED) joined together with a country, person, or group for a common purpose **(233)**
alms (AHMZ) money or goods given to the poor **(161)**
Anglo-Saxon (ANG-gloh SACK-sun) a white person of English nationality or descent **(21)**
annex (uh-NEKS) to add on to a state's or nation's territory **(218)**
apprentice (uh-PREN-tiss) a person learning a craft or trade with the help of a master teacher **(176)**
arch (ARCH) curved structure made to bear weight from above **(49)**
artifacts (ART-ih-fakts) objects made by human work, such as tools or weapons **(15)**
artisan (ART-ih-zun) a person skilled in a craft **(56)**
assembly line (uh-SEM-blee LINE) a moving belt in a factory on which an item travels as it is being assembled **(255)**

bail (BAYL) money left with a court so that an accused person may be let out of jail until the time of his or her trial **(197)**
barter (BAR-tur) the exchange of goods and services **(154)**
bazaars (buh-ZAHRZ) marketplaces found in the Middle East and Asia **(240)**
bookkeeping (BOOK-keep-ing) the organized recording of what a business takes in and what it spends **(241)**

capital (KAP-ih-tul) money used to start a business **(177)**
caravans (KA-ruh-vanz) groups of travelers moving together over the land with their goods **(240)**
caribou (KA-rih-boo) North American reindeer **(102)**
cash crops (KASH KROPS) crops raised to be sold instead of to be eaten or used on the farm **(262)**
caste (KAST) a social group into which a person is born **(70)**
central authority (SEN-trul aw-THAH-rih-tee) government or ruling group **(84)**
civil wars (SIV-ul WORZ) wars between groups of people of the same nation **(56)**
clans (KLANZ) groups of related families **(84)**
climate (KLY-mut) the kind of weather in a place over a long period of time **(63)**
clue (KLOO) a guide to solving a problem or mystery **(95)**
collective bargaining (kuh-LEK-tiv BAR-guh-ning) the process by which workers and employers try to reach agreements about such things as wages and working conditions **(256)**
colonies (KOL-uh-neez) places ruled by another country; colonies are usually found far away from the parent country **(183)**
commercial cities (kuh-MURSH-ul SIT-eez) cities whose main business is trade and banking **(176)**
compass (KUM-puss) an instrument used by sailors to help find their location at sea **(182)**
confederation (kun-fed-uh-RAY-shun) a league or loose organization of independent states who join together for a purpose **(225)**
conservative (kun-SURV-uh-tiv) against great changes in society or government **(226)**
consumers (kun-SOO-murz) people who buy and use goods **(269)**
crescent (KRESS-unt) shaped like a quarter moon **(48)**
Crusades (kroo-SAYDZ) the wars carried out to free the Holy Land from Muslim control **(168)**
cultural diffusion (KUL-chur-ul dif-YOO-zhun) the spreading of ideas and customs from one culture to other cultures **(31)**
cuneiform (kew-NEE-a-form) wedge-shaped writing used in ancient Sumer **(48)**
customs union (KUS-tumz YOON-yun) an organization of several states that handles tax and trade matters **(226)**

deciphered (dih-SYF-urd) made understandable **(16)**
delta (DEL-tuh) deposit of earth and sand at the mouth of a river **(55)**
democracy (duh-MOCK-ruh-see) a form of government in which the people rule themselves either directly or through elected officials **(137)**
dependent (duh-PEN-dunt) needing something or someone **(3)**
depose (dih-POZE) to remove someone from office by force **(196)**
descendants (duh-SEND-unts) people who are born of a certain group or family; offspring **(96)**
desert (DEZ-urt) very dry land **(63)**
disciplines (DISS-uh-plinz) areas of knowledge or learning **(15)**

divine right (dih-VYN RYT) a monarch's belief that he or she has been given the right to rule by God **(196)**

division of labor (dih-VIZH-un uv LAY-bur) a way of making goods in which each worker makes only one part of the product **(255)**

domesticated animal (duh-MESS-tih-kay-tid AN-ih-mul) an animal tamed by humans **(42)**

domestic system (duh-MESS-tik SIS-tum) a system of making goods in which most of the work is done in people's homes **(247)**

dynasties (DY-nus-teez) ruling families in China **(77)**

economic system (eck-uh-NOM-ik SIS-tum) the economy; the nation's system of producing, distributing, and consuming goods **(4)**

economy (ih-KON-uh-mee) the nation's system of producing, distributing, and consuming goods **(4)**

the Enlightenment (in-LYT-un-munt) the name given to the revolution in thinking that took place in the 1700s; enlightenment means an ability to see and understand things **(204)**

erosion (ih-ROE-zhun) gradual wearing away of the soil **(108)**

estates (uh-STAYTS) the name given to the three groups in the French representative assembly **(204)**

ethnic (ETH-nik) usually having to do with the various races within a country **(21)**

extinct (ek-STINGKT) no longer existing **(107)**

factories (FACK-tuh-reez) places where goods are made **(177)**
buildings where machines do all parts of production under one roof **(247)**

famine (FAM-in) a time when people do not have enough to eat **(3)**

feminist (FEM-in-ist) having to do with women's rights **(213)**

fertile (FUR-til) able to produce much plant growth **(48)**

feudalism (FYOO-duh-liz-um) a system of rule that came into being from the arrangement between lords and vassals **(154)**

flourish (FLUR-ish) to grow and prosper **(64)**

fraternity (fruh-TURN-ih-tee) feeling of unity among people **(205)**

frontiers (frun-TEERZ) areas that form the edge of settled territory; borders **(78)**

glaciers (GLAY-shurz) slow-moving sheets of ice **(41)**

guilds (GILDZ) groups of merchants and crafts workers **(176)**

heathens (HEE-thunz) people who do not believe in God **(121)**

hegira (huh-JY-ruh) Muhammad's flight from Mecca to Medina **(161)**

Hispanic (hih-SPAN-ik) a person of Spanish-speaking origin **(21)**

humanists (HYOO-muh-nists) the name given to the scholars of the Renaissance; they were interested in all aspects of human life **(169)**

igloos (IG-looz) Inuit homes built with ice and snow **(102)**

immigrants (IM-ih-grunts) people who come to a nation to settle as permanent residents **(83)**

industrialization (in-dust-ree-uh-lih-ZAY-shun) the change from handwork to work done by machines **(247)**

institutions (in-stih-TOO-shunz) organizations with a special purpose such as schools **(15)**

interdependent (in-tur-dih-PEN-dunt) in global terms, the idea that nations are bound to one another **(3)**

intermarriage (in-tur-MA-rij) marriage between people from different groups **(70)**

investors (in-VEST-urz) people who buy shares of stock in a company **(241)**

iron ore (EYE-urn OR) raw material from which iron can be produced **(64)**

irrigation (ir-ih-GAY-shun) system of supplying land with water from ditches or pipes **(48)**

Islam (is-LAHM) an Arabic word meaning "submitting to the will of God"; the religion founded by Muhammad **(161)**

isthmus (ISS-muss) a narrow strip of land bordered on both sides by water; an isthmus connects two larger bodies of land **(55)**

kayak (KY-ack) Inuit canoe made of a frame covered with animal skins **(102)**

Koran (koh-RAN) the holy book of Islam **(162)**

labor unions (LAY-bur YOON-yunz) workers' organizations formed to give workers a united voice in dealing with their employers **(256)**

laissez-faire (LEHS-ay FAIR) "let alone"; the idea that government should not regulate or interfere with business **(204)**

landforms (LAND-formz) features on the surface of the earth, such as mountains, hills, and plains **(10)**

legend (LEJ-und) a story handed down over the years **(120)**

liberal (LIB-uh-rul) forward-looking; favoring gradual change **(212)**

Magna Carta (MAG-nuh KAR-tuh) the agreement signed by King John of England in 1215; it limited the power of the English monarch **(191)**

majority (muh-JOR-ih-tee) more than half of any number **(32)**

manor (MAN-ur) the lands, including a village and the surrounding lands, held by a noble **(155)**

manufacturing (man-yuh-FACK-chur-ing) the making of goods by hand or machine **(168)**

mass production (MASS pruh-DUCK-shun) the making of large numbers of goods that are all the same **(255)**

medieval (mee-dee-EEV-ul) the period of the Middle Ages **(153)**

migrations (my-GRAY-shunz) movements of people from one place to another **(89)**

mint (MINT) to make coins and paper money **(176)**

monarch (MON-urk) another name for a king or queen; the ruler of a nation **(189)**

mosque (MOSK) the Islamic place of worship **(163)**

multinational (mul-tih-NASH-uh-nel) dealing with many nations **(267)**

nationalism (NASH-un-uh-liz-um) a feeling of pride in and devotion to one's country **(217)**

natural resources (NACH-ur-ul RE-sor-sez) useful materials supplied by nature **(9)**

nomadic (no-MAD-ik) moving from place to place in search of food and water **(9)**

Norse (NORSS) people from Norway **(101)**

origins (OR-ih-jinz) places where things are started **(89)**

parish (PA-rish) the town or village looked after by a priest **(155)**

Parliament (PAR-luh-ment) a political body that makes laws for the nation **(32)**

patriarchs (PAY-tree-arks) heads of churches in the Eastern Orthodox church **(156)**

patricians (puh-TRIHSH-uhnz) rich landowners who ran the government of Rome **(144)**

patrons (PAY-trunz) people who back the arts **(171)**

peninsula (puh-NIN-suh-luh) a piece of land nearly surrounded by water **(113)**

philosophy (fih-LAH-suh-fee) the study of ideas **(138)**

physical environment (FIZ-ih-kul in-VY-run-munt) our surroundings, such as rivers, lakes, trees, air, and soil **(4)**

plebeians (pluh-BEE-uhnz) the common people of Rome **(144)**

pope (POHP) the head of the Roman Catholic church **(155)**

populated (POP-yuh-lay-tid) filled with people **(89)**

primary source (PRY-mer-ee SORS) original documents, articles, and eyewitness accounts of an event written by people who took part in the event **(15)**

prime minister (PRYM MIN-ih-stur) the head of government in Parliament **(32)**; chief government official in a parliamentary system **(218)**

principle of interchangeable parts (PRIN-sih-pul uv in-tur-CHAIN-juh-bul parts) the idea of making items with identical parts so that parts in any one item could be replaced by the parts from another item **(255)**

profit (PROF-it) the money made by business owners from running their businesses **(177)**

prophet (PROF-it) someone who presents religious beliefs as given by God **(161)**

rajah (RAH-juh) Indian tribal chief or ruler **(70)**

reactionary (ree-AK-shuh-ner-ee) favoring a return to ideas and ways of the past **(226)**

reform (rih-FORM) to bring about a change for the better **(170)**

Renaissance (ren-uh-SAHNS) the period from around the 1300s to the 1600s; a term meaning "rebirth" of civilization **(169)**

republic (rih-PUB-lik) a system of government in which citizens who have the right to vote choose their leaders **(144)**

revolution (rev-uh-LOO-shun) a complete or dramatic change **(247)**

ruthless (RUTH-lis) without pity; cruel **(120)**

scientific farming	(sy-un-TIF-ik FAR-ming) the use of experiments and scientific information to improve farm production **(261)**
scribes	(SKRYBZ) people who keep records and do other kinds of writing **(56)**
secondary source	(SECK-un-der-ee SORS) anything written by people who did not take part in the event they are writing about **(15)**
secular	(SEK-yuh-lur) worldly or ordinary, rather than religious in nature **(233)**
self-sufficient	(self-suh-FISH-unt) able to meet all of one's needs by oneself **(155)**
Senate	(SEN-it) the group of patrician Romans who passed the laws in the Roman Republic **(144)**
serfs	(SURFS) peasants tied to the manor **(155)**
social structure	(SOH-shul STRUCK-chur) basis of personal and family relations in society **(114)**
strike	(STRYK) the action of a group of workers who protest by refusing to work **(256)**
sultan	(SUL-tun) ruler of the Ottoman Empire **(232)**
supreme	(suh-PREEM) highest in importance or rank **(119)**

tariff	(TA-rif) a tax placed on imported goods **(176)**
terraced farming	(TEH-rust FARM-ing) farming on a flat, raised piece of land **(128)**
topography	(tuh-POG-ruh-fee) the word used by geographers when they talk about features on the surface of the earth **(23)**
totalitarianism	(toh-tal-uh-TAIR-ee-un-iz-um) a system in which the government has total power over the lives of the people **(128)**
traditions	(truh-DISH-unz) beliefs and customs handed down from earlier times **(9)**
tribute	(TRIB-yoot) forced payment by one nation to another **(119)**

unification	(yoo-nih-fih-KAY-shun) bringing together several parts of a geographical region into one nation **(217)**

vassal	(VAS-ul) a person who receives land from a lord and gives loyalty and service in return **(154)**

warrant	(WOR-unt) a written order issued by a court allowing a search or other action **(196)**

PRONUNCIATION GUIDE TO CHINESE NAMES

The following is a list of Chinese proper names mentioned in this textbook. The first spelling is in *pinyin*. This is a way of spelling Chinese names in English. *Pinyin* was introduced by the Chinese in the 1950s. The spelling in *pinyin* is followed by its pronunciation. The second spelling is in Wade-Giles. This is the older way of spelling Chinese names.

Page where used	*Pinyin* spelling	Pronunciation	Wade-Giles spelling
23	Xizang	SEE TSANG	Tibet
30, 45, 77, 78,	Huang Ho	HWANG HUH	Hwang Ho, Yellow R.
30, 45, 77, 78,	Chang Jiang	CHANG JYANG	Yangtze R.
30	Si	SHEE	Hsi River
77, 78,	Xia	SHYAH	Hsia
77, 78, 84,	Zhou	JOH	Chou
78	Qin	CHIN	Ch'in

Index

1300

1580   1810

5500 BC   10 AD   1100   1450   1700

WORLD HISTORY
FOR A
GLOBAL AGE

ANCIENT HISTORY to the INDUSTRIAL REVOLUTION

300 AD   1600

1350   1827

1500   1780

1828

1785

900 AD   1829

3600 BC   1790

1200

1550   1830

1400   1795

600 AD   1680   1831

JACK ABRAMOWITZ

1000 BC   1800

GLOBE BOOK COMPANY   1832